Listening with All Our Senses

Establishing communication with people on the autistic spectrum or those with profound learning disabilities and sometimes distressed behaviour

Phoebe Caldwell

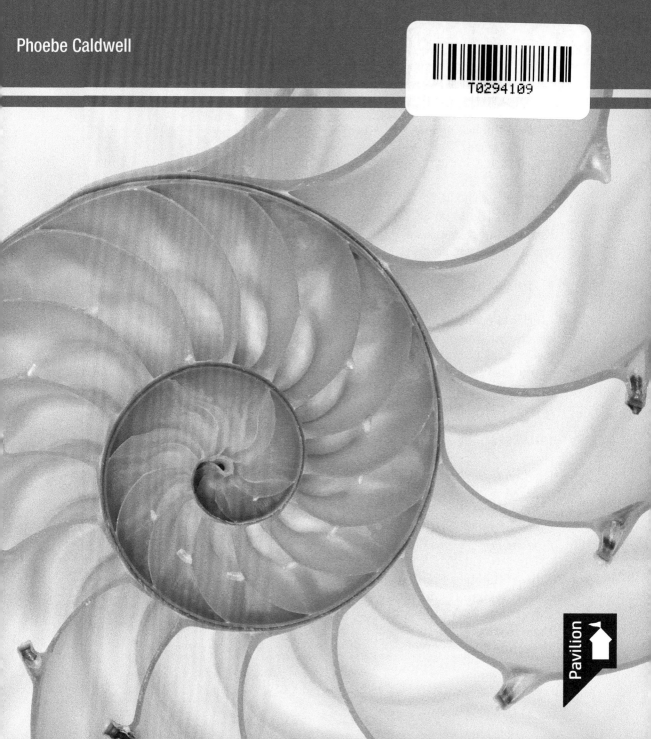

Pavilion

Listening with All Our Senses

Establishing communication with people on the autistic spectrum or those with profound learning disabilities and sometimes distressed behaviour

The authors have asserted their rights in accordance with the Copyright, Designs and Patents Act (1988) to be identified as the authors of this work.

Published by:
Pavilion Publishing and Media Ltd
Rayford House
School Road
Hove, BN3 5HX
Tel: 01273 43 49 43
Fax: 01273 62 55 26
Email: info@pavpub.com
Web: www.pavpub.com

Published 2012

A catalogue record for this book is available from the British Library.

ISBN: 978-1-908993-00-7

Pavilion is the leading publisher and provider of professional development products and services for workers in the health, social care, education and community safety sectors. We believe that everyone has the right to fulfil their potential and we strive to supply products and services that help raise standards, promote best practices and support continuing professional development.

Editor: Kathleen Steeden
Cover design: Pavilion Publishing and Media
Cover artwork: Thinkstock
Page layout: Katherine Paine
Printing: CMP

*The greatest obstacle to conversation
is not knowing the heart of the person
one speaks to...only when people learn
to speak to each other will they
begin to be equal.*

*Han Fei Tzu
3rd century BC*

Acknowledgements

I am indebted to all the people who have contributed to this book and also all the people who have taught me how to listen to them.

Contents

About the authors

Phoebe Caldwell started her career as a biologist. She is now an Intensive Interaction practitioner working mainly with children and adults on the autistic spectrum, many of whom have behavioural distress. Phoebe's methods combine using a person's body language to communicate, with paying attention to those aspects of an individual's environment that are triggering sensory distress. For four years Phoebe was a Rowntree Research Fellow looking at best practice. She teaches management, therapists, parents, teachers, advocates and carers, nationally and internationally, and she has been one of the principal speakers at a BILD annual conference. She is also employed by NHS, social services and community and education services to work with individuals they are finding it difficult to provide a service for. She has published seven books and four training films and a number of academic papers. In 2010, she was awarded the Times/Sternberg Active Life Award for work on autism and contribution to the community, and in July 2011 Bristol University awarded her an Honorary Doctorate of Science for communication with people with autism.

Pene Stevens started working with people with learning disabilities as a healthcare assistant at a small local institution in Bristol. There she met Phoebe Caldwell and started to use Intensive Interaction techniques as a means of instinctively communicating with people who are non-verbal and have difficulty in building relationships.

Pene qualified as a learning disability nurse in 1986 and has worked in both residential and community settings. She has also managed re-provision programmes for people with learning disabilities who are departing institutions and finally leaving NHS provision. In 2004 she was awarded an MSc in learning disabilities/mental health from Kings College London. Pene is now head of profession for learning disability nursing for East Kent; her focus is on improving access to health services for people with learning disabilities.

Pene maintains an interest in understanding the many ways in which people attempt to communicate and the links with behaviour. She continues to collaborate with Phoebe on an informal basis to share information and ideas.

Dr Matt Hoghton is a GP in North Somerset and the Royal College of General Practitioners' Learning Disability Champion at the RCGP Clinical Innovation and Research Centre. He also works part-time as the lead investigator in Confidential Inquiry into the deaths of people with learning disabilities (CIPOLD) at the Norah Fry Research Centre, Bristol University. He has been involved in the care of people with learning disabilities since 1990, developing new clinical pathways, conducting research and introducing annual health checks. He is actively engaged in promoting the development of improved health care for all people with learning disabilities, to meet their unmet needs and reduce health inequalities. He has contributed to several publications including *Care of the Adult with Intellectual Disability in Primary care* (published by Radcliffe Press, 2011). He has been privileged to have been involved with many extraordinary people with learning disabilities, and their brave families and carers, as they attempt to navigate ever-changing health and social care systems.

Listening with All Our Senses © Pavilion Publishing and Media Ltd 2012

Foreword

To revisit books that one has written a while back is challenging. In some ways the landscapes of severe or profound disability, autism and distressed behaviour are familiar; but in other ways perspectives have been altered when viewed through the lens of subsequent experience. Two questions that need to be asked are: do they have validity for today and what, if anything, has changed in the way that I approach my work now?

In a way, I was surprised that these texts appeared to need little updating. I think this is because, although my understanding has deepened, *Person to Person*, *You Don't Know What It's Like* and *Crossing the Minefield* are based on practice rather than on theory. They contain many examples of interaction and on the whole I think that my interpretations of these still stand.

Nowadays I work mainly in the field of autism with people at the severe end of the spectrum, but no matter whether one's partners are on the autistic spectrum or not, the overall approach is based on the idea that the essence of each person is valuable and that as human beings, we are creatures who desire to communicate if we can find a common language. The latter is true, even if it may appear to the contrary in people with autism since many appear to turn away from relationships. Yet even in these cases, they tell us that they do feel lonely and do love people but cannot handle the negative feedback that they are getting from their bodies. Their retreat is not from relationships but from sensory overload.

The three books represent a progression: starting in *Person to Person* using a person's body language to get in touch with them, in some cases designing equipment based on their interests to direct their focus into our world. For example, making a styrene mirror with holes in it captures the attention of a man who is unable to engage but is fascinated by fingers waving. In focusing on a finger waved through the hole, he notices himself in the mirror and me looking over his shoulder.

At the same time Geraint Ephraim – who was my supervisor during tenure of a Joseph Rowntree Fellowship and who introduced the method that subsequently became known as Intensive Interaction (Nind & Hewitt, 1994) – pointed out to me that I myself was the best piece of equipment I had. Gradually I learned the art of listening with all my senses and responding to my conversation partner, not just to what they are doing but to how they are feeling, a skill that a speech therapist named 'intimate attention'.

The title of *You Don't Know What It's Like* is taken from the protest of an apparently non-verbal woman with autism who one day bellowed this at a colleague when it was suggested to her that she calm down. This desperate sentence set me thinking about autism: what is going on in the brain of someone on the spectrum when they appear to lose all control of their behaviour? This text tries to look at autism from an inside perspective.

Crossing the Minefield draws together the two previous books and considers engagement through body language in the halfway house of affective listening to how one another are feeling. In this way, whatever the disability, we establish genuine conversation, exploring what each other has to offer in a shared arena that sees us both 'being with' rather than 'doing to'.

In answer to the second question, what has changed for me is a deepening understanding of the nature of autism with its hyper – and hypo – sensitivities, partly as the outcome of people on the spectrum writing about the effects of the condition and partly because of research that has uncovered the role of the autonomic nervous system in response to sensory overload. A woman with autism tells us that her brain is like a dial-up modem – if you feed it too much data it crashes (WeirdGirlCyndi, 2007). A child tells us that it is like having your head in a car-crusher.

Another significant change has been the emergence of the mirror neuron story concerning a network of cells which recognises if someone else does an action that is already part of our own repertoire and fires off a motor signal in our own head in response. (If I see you yawn, my own jaw tickles, telling me I want to yawn.) While our brains have learned to suppress most of these motor prompts, the process is also activated by feeling: if one is with a person who is depressed, one may well be dragged into their unhappiness. This recognition is so powerful that the brain is drawn to the source it recognises like iron filings to a magnet. Although there is a school of thought that suggests that this system is not working in people with autism, in practice they always respond provided that the action is already part of their repertoire.

Apart from my partner's frame of mind, my own communication practice has been affected by the mirror neuron theory in that I have learned to place greater trust in my intuitive responses to my partner's affective state by listening more carefully to my own response to them. Nevertheless, as with all insights, they need double-checking against the cognitive processes.

Finally, since writing these books, through collaboration with the paediatric occupational therapist Jane Horwood, specialising in sensory integration, I have become aware of the important role played in so many people with autism, of a deficiency in their proprioceptive system, which results in them not receiving enough messages from their muscles and joints to tell them what they are doing (Caldwell & Horwood, 2007). Before one can get in touch through using body language it is sometimes essential to address this deficit with strong proprioceptive inputs.

So in my practice nowadays, whether I am working with people on the autistic spectrum, or those who are severely or profoundly learning disabled, and those who as part of their condition may have behaviour that is very distressed, I more consciously use Intensive Interaction as part of an approach that seeks both to reduce those aspects of their environment that are triggering sensory overload and distress, and at the same time to increase signals to the brain that have immediate significance, such as proprioceptive input and the use of their body language to communicate. In re-reading these books, I see that the germs of these ideas are already present.

Whatever their disability, I continue to learn from the people with whom it is my privilege to communicate. Each time I am a beginner in a process that enables us, in the deepest sense, to engage with each other.

Phoebe Caldwell DSc
Intensive Interaction practitioner
www.phoebecaldwell.com

References

Caldwell P & Horwood J (2007) *From Isolation to Intimacy: Making friends without words*. London: Jessica Kingsley Publishers.

Nind M & Hewett D (1994) *Access to Communication*. London: David Fulton.

WeirdGirlCyndi (2007) *Sensory Overload Simulation* [online]. Available at: www.youtube.com/watch?v=BPDTEuotHe0 (accessed February 2012).

Person to Person

Establishing contact and communication with people with profound learning disabilities and those whose behaviour may be challenging

Phoebe Caldwell with Pene Stevens

Originally published by Pavilion as a single volume in 1998

Introduction

For years I have been looking at innovative ways of getting in touch with those people with learning disabilities who seem to be locked into a world of their own. Broadly speaking, they fall into two groups: those with very severe disability and those whose behaviour we find challenging. Quite a number of the people whose behaviour challenges us will also have autistic features.

While it seems that, although they may overlap, these two groups have little in common with each other, our problem is the same: how can we find ways of getting in touch with people who are not able to respond to current service provision? They do not respond to our initiatives and we feel we are getting no feedback.

The work described in this book is not just about techniques but about the whole way we relate to people in all aspects of their lives. It is about the different worlds that each one of us carries and how, if we truly want to get to know each other, we must recognise and respect actualities which are not the same as our own. We need to understand how other people's realities are for them.

While some of the work has been done with children, most of the histories described in this book are interventions with adults, the majority of whom have spent long periods in institutions. Many have only recently moved into community homes and the expectation that it is possible to communicate with them is relatively new. It was easy to overlook an individual who sat quietly and rocked in a large ward or to think in terms of containment of a person with challenging behaviour. However, in small group homes we are face to face, our individual personalities more exposed. We have the opportunity and the need to be able to communicate with each other but in order to do this we have to take into account our different ways of sensing realities – I may not see things the way you do.

This is particularly true of people with autism and can be a major source of stress for them. Although autism is not necessarily linked with learning disability, a proportion of people with severe learning disabilities have autistic features. Much of what we are learning about autism is written by people who are high-functioning and the question arises as to whether or not this is applicable to people whose autism is compounded by other disabilities. My experience is that, making allowance for the possibility that what we now term 'autism' may turn out to be an umbrella term for a number of neurobiological disturbances and also for the complexity of their disabilities, in practical terms it has always been helpful to apply what we can learn from high-functioning people with autism as an indicator of the direction to take with those who are low-functioning. In this book, for all the people involved, I look at a combined approach that seeks to reduce stress at the same time as building confidence. As well as looking for a common language, I explore issues that may be contributing to withdrawal or disturbed behaviour so that we can then look at how to modify events and interactions that an individual finds painful. In order to meet their needs, we may need to adapt ourselves to their world.

This work combines my own approach – which involves finding out what an individual likes doing and discovering creative ways of using this to enlarge their experience, as first described in Getting in Touch (Caldwell, 1996) – with the work of Ephraim (1986) and Nind and Hewett (Nind & Hewitt, 1994; Hewett & Nind, 1998), which is now known as 'Intensive Interaction'. It also draws heavily on the creative insights provided by Williams (1992) and others who are able to write about their autism.

The title of this book is *Person to Person* as I want to emphasise an approach that is about relationship. It aims to shift our attention away from the problems a person presents to the difficulties they experience. Bearing in mind that current service provision is unable to reach these people, this approach is predicated on a radical change in values. In order to get in touch, we must cease trying to bend their behaviours to our world and enter into their world, as they experience it. While being aware of the dangers of projection, I want to know, as far as possible, how they perceive their world – how it feels to them. Within the parameters of where they feel safe, how can we enlarge and enrich their experience? How can we increase their confidence and help them to 'feel good' about themselves and others?

The objective of the person-to-person approach is to help individuals to feel safe and interested enough to move from the solitary occupation of self-stimulation to shared activity, from the closed loop of talking to themselves to a situation where they can explore, negotiate and interact with the environment and people around them. Then we can learn from each other.

Some of the histories in this book will be familiar to those who have read *Getting in Touch* (Caldwell, 1996), which was written as the outcome of four years' work supported by the Joseph Rowntree Foundation. Where they are offered again, it is to look at them from a slightly different and amplified perspective, to support new work or for completeness. That work which is new centres on the way we can use people's 'language' to communicate with them, not only in their ordinary daily lives but also when they are becoming distressed. It also looks at how we can support them by reducing the stresses they experience in their environment. It concludes with an appendix on training by Pene Stevens, drawing from her experience as the manager of a group of community homes. It looks at ways of setting up and maintaining such training.

Chapter 1

First steps to learning

As infants, we begin to relate to others from a very early age. We initiate signals and activities that are confirmed by the parent figure so that we are free to explore further. According to Stern (1985) in his book, *The Interpersonal World of the Infant*, we build outwards from 'core self' to 'core other'.

We do this by setting up what I want to call a 'negotiating arena' between core self and core other. I introduce this term because it is sometimes difficult to talk about that part of ourselves which is defined by where we feel psychologically safe enough to engage with the outside world. This is the border-land between core self (where we have established and integrated our experiences) and core other. Using core self as a platform, the negotiating arena is the site of that more ill-defined and sometimes impulsive part of us, which gathers enough confidence to risk tentative overtures to the world outside: the border-land where we grow or shrivel. It is the critical area where we are strengthened or eroded by the responses we receive from the outside world and it is easier to discuss the potential and variable parameters of this area if we can visualise it.

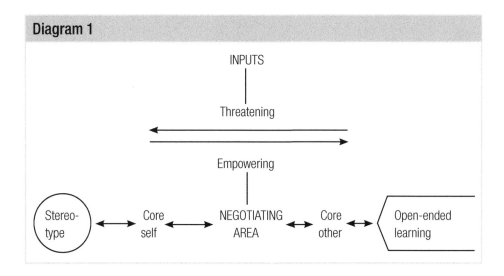

Diagram 1

INPUTS

Threatening

Empowering

Stereo-type ↔ Core self ↔ NEGOTIATING AREA ↔ Core other ↔ Open-ended learning

When we are considering relationships, the negotiating arena is critical. I want to highlight it because it is here, within this arena, that all our external interventions, all the work we do, will be helpful and empowering or unhelpful and undermining. All our inputs will have to be weighed in the balance. We have to determine, not just whether we, through our realities, see them as proper working procedures but also whether the person with whom we are working can relate to them sufficiently in order to be able to accept them. We have to be flexible in the application of our models.

How does this idea of core self/negotiating arena/core other relate to the compulsive, repetitive behaviour that we call the stereotype?

Although it may overlap, the negotiating arena is not the same as 'personal space', which can be measured by physical proximity. It has more in common with feelings of self-confidence and security; its dimensions vary depending on the state of our lives and how this affects our ability to relate to the world outside.

Starting with infancy, if our lives are going well, we feel confident and open to risk, with new ideas, people and everything which is not self. In our expanding world, the arena feels safe enough for creative negotiation with 'core other'. We use language, whatever form it takes, to explore and exchange, confirming ourselves and others so that we and they grow in the world outside.

When our lives are going badly and we are afraid of what has happened, is happening or may happen, we erect protective barriers – we shut ourselves off from a world with which we cannot cope. The stereotype is at the extreme end of this continuum. Here the arena is completely shut down and the core self is isolated. There is no potential contact with the world. Whatever language we have, we use it to talk to and confirm ourselves – nothing exists outside the boundary of core self.

Within and from the negotiating arena, we learn to adjust to the external world through a process which Stern (1985) refers to as 'varied repetitiveness': each successive variation being partly familiar and partly new. The familiar guidelines render it a predictable place that can be controlled. Provided we can connect with them, it is a safe place in which we can graft in new but related concepts to our core self.

Ephraim (undated personal communication) suggests that, for infants with severe learning disabilities, this process of adjustment appears to go wrong or never gets started. Perhaps because the infant is not ready, the parent/infant process is not synchronised. By the time the child is ready to participate, maybe years later, the parent has tried and become discouraged as there has been no response. The child makes noises or movements but the only feedback is those same sounds or feelings. What should have become an open-ended learning process becomes a closed loop of auto-stimulation, which progressively excludes external stimuli as the person focuses more deeply on their own signals. They become stereotypically bonded on themselves; their repetitive world becomes their reality.

Stereotypic behavior

Much of the work described in this book involves working through activities generated within stereotypic behaviour. The exact form taken by a person's stereotype seems to have a number of origins:

- **The core self is locked in on itself:** The repetitive behaviour has as its object part of the person's own sensory experience, for example, particular sounds and movements.

- **The core self 'hijacks' a particular object from the core other** as, for example, in people who are fixated on external objects such as doors and light-switches. Although these objects originate from the outer world, they are taken in and become part of the 'furnishings' of the core self. As above, the process of fixation excludes contact with the outside world. However, experience shows that both types of stereotypic behaviour can be used as access points to the core self.

■ **The boundaries weaken:** The person's sense of the location of their core self becomes displaced. This is much more difficult and puzzling to understand but I have come across a few people in whom their whole sense of who and where they are seems to have shifted and comes from another part of their body. It is not just, for example, that they do not feel centred and that their interest is totally centred on, say, their knee. They seem to 'come from' there. Occasionally the boundary between core self and core other is so ill-defined that the person feels totally vulnerable to contact with other people and will avoid contact by running away. In such circumstances, it has been helpful to establish a physical boundary such as a screen (discussed further in Chapter 5).

■ **Pseudo-stereotypes:** There are some behaviours that appear to be stereotypic but have quite a different origin. Williams (1996) describes how she spent two years flapping her hand to try to shake it off. It seemed to her to be an extraneous object with which she had no organic connection. The reason for this appeared to be that one of her ways of dealing with sensory overload was to switch off processing one of her senses, that is, she might switch off 'feeling' while retaining 'seeing' and vice versa. She calls this 'going into mono'. Because she could not see and feel simultaneously, the effect was to have no sense of her hand belonging to her. So she tried to get rid of it.

Because I believe that a person-to-person approach requires a fundamental alteration in perspective, I am now going to switch to the first person to give a sense of how profound our change needs to be.

Looking at the core self in its stereotypic form, from the inside it is:

■ **Stimulating:** A conversation with myself confirms me in the way that my parent might have confirmed me. It lets me know I am here.

■ **Closed down, safe inside:** My stereotypic behaviour is a fixed point, a beacon, in a confusing and jumbled world of sensory disinformation. I can refer to it and know it will be there. It is a non-threatening 'pseudo-other' which I can control. Contrasting the safety of his stereotypic behaviour with his chaotic sensory experience, Barron (Barron & Barron, 1992) says: 'I know what happens when I switch the lights on and off.'

■ **It excludes signals that are unfamiliar** and therefore potentially threatening:

'Objects are frightening. Moving objects are harder to cope with because you have to try and take in the sight, movement and further complexity of the noise. Human beings are the hardest of all to understand, they make demands on you which are just impossible to understand.' (Jolliffe et al, 1992)

I have set up a very effective boundary to keep you out and you will have to find familiar and unthreatening signals that my brain recognises in order to reach me. You will need my personal code, which you can key in. When you have learned my language you will be part of my 'safe other' and we can talk to each other.

Chapter 2

Finding the way in

How can we reach people who appear to be locked into their world, often absorbed in repetitive and stereotypic behaviours that exclude contact with the world outside their own?

One problem is that we frame our strategies on the basis of our own reality and not with respect to how the other person senses and perceives their world. We are also in danger of confusing communication with the ability to give or receive information. We want people to understand our requests; for example, so that they sit when we ask them to sit down.

Yet communication is about more than just getting someone to understand and respond to what is required of them. When we really communicate, we establish social contact and express sociability rather than specific meaning. By this type of phatic interaction, which may include language without words and more specific body language, we simply make it known that we are present for each other. We use gestures and small phrases to greet each other such as, 'Fine day today,' or 'Doing all right?', which are not really about content, but rather to let the person know we are friendly. This type of communication is also known as 'strokes'. Perhaps one of the reasons why it is so powerful is that it may be a part of language derived from 'grooming' activities, which conveys feeling rather than information (Dunbar, 1996). I need to know that you are here for me. I need to give and receive intimate attention from 'core self' to 'core other'. By 'intimate', I am referring not so much to physical intimacy but to the total attention that embraces all that the other person is and does.

This is the most empowering way that we can get in touch with each other. It affirms and confirms us in our fundamental struggle to test our existence in the world as we experience it.

The following two histories illustrate the process of getting close to two people with whom alternative strategies have been unsuccessful. The first has very severe learning disabilities and the second, severe autism.

> *Chris sits all day curled up and scratches the arm of his chair with his forefinger. He does not look up or respond to stimuli.*
>
> *I sit opposite him and scratch the far end of the arm, synchronising my scratches with his. It takes a while before he notices but when he does, he stops and listens. I do it again and gradually we are doing it for each other. We both begin to introduce small variations and take note of each other's. After a while, I introduce 'suspense' in the form of running my hand along the arm towards him and holding off before I scratch. Eventually, Chris puts out his hand, takes mine and holds it gently. He is smiling and looking up at me.*

> *Rose, a woman in her thirties with severe autistic features, lives in a community home. She sits all day and picks her head, pulling out bits of dandruff and examining them closely. She runs away if she is invited to participate in any activity.*
>
> *I sit with the table between us and place some dried flecks of Tippex on the table. They resemble the flecks of dandruff which she finds so fascinating. She appears interested and looks at them carefully. When her attention is caught, I blow them gently so they move. She finds this funny and smiles. We move into a game of blowing them round the table. Since she has visual difficulties, this is helping her to track. We move on to blowing them with a whistling straw. She tries this, too, and laughs. We move through a variety of equipment, all of which incorporates flecks, ending with rolling a ball, covered with shiny flecks, to each other. The next time I come, Rose sees me coming and, instead of running away, she comes and leads me to the place where we worked before.*

Both these histories illustrate the basic technique of Intensive Interaction, that is, we look and see what it is that the person is focusing on and feed back the same stimulus to catch their attention. In Rose's case, we are using interactive activities. With these, the signal that the person gives themselves is made more interesting by incorporating it into equipment or 'games', which are deliberately chosen to enhance the stimulus. This increases the element of novelty and hence, surprise. **Surprise is crucial.** Once we have found our way into the arena of exchange, it is surprise, presented in a familiar and therefore safe context, which extends both the potential of the interaction and the person's capacity to experience it.

Learning the language

In *Getting in Touch* (Caldwell, 1996), I used the analogy of entering a locked room. As I pointed out, this involves four stages:

1. Finding the right key

2. Opening the door

3. Exploring the treasures in the room

4. Looking out of the window

I want to explore these in more detail here.

1. Finding the right key

In order to find the right key, it is essential to develop accurate and non-judgmental observation. We are often not as good at this as we think we are. We may only notice gross activities, such as position. For example, we may say that a person is 'sitting down' or 'lies on the floor' but this overlooks the particular activity on which they are focusing. We need to know exactly what is happening.

What is this person focusing on?

It is not always easy to spot activities such as digging nails into the palm of the hand inside a clenched fist, or to notice such sounds as the jaw clicking during chewing. Even if they are obvious, we have a tendency to 'filter out' those stimuli which are not significant to us. This is a trick we learn as children. It enables us to select, for example, the voice of someone we want to talk to in a crowded and noisy room. I am often told, 'No, he doesn't make any sounds,' of a person who is sitting still, gently grunting to himself. Even heavy breathing can be a source of self-stimulus, that is, the person focuses on this to the exclusion of external stimuli.

Furthermore, there are some stimuli that we reject on the grounds that they are socially unacceptable, for example, as in Rose's history above, picking dandruff out of the hair, or grinding teeth. Support staff will admit that they forgot to mention teeth-grinding as they did not like it, so 'switched off' to it. Besides, they could not see what potential it had for communication. **We must learn not to make value judgments based on our own reality.**

When we are making observations, it is important not to jump immediately to the obvious conclusions.

> *Sarah clutches a folded crisp packet. I am told that she 'likes the noise'.*
>
> *A second look shows that what Sarah also likes very much is the 'feel', she is pulling at it regularly with her other hand. She very much enjoys it when I stimulate this area of her hand with vibration.*

We need to draw up a list of questions to ask ourselves.

- Is this person making any sound at all, including such activities as heavy breathing or grinding teeth?

- Is this person making any movement in a repetitive way?

- Does this person like particular smells/tastes?

- If this person has any speech, is it focused on one subject? Are we really listening to what they are saying?

- Is there any object or activity (however passive the latter) to which this person is attached?

In order to find the right key, we need to detach ourselves from our own blueprints of what a person 'ought' or 'ought not' to be doing and learn to observe them as they are. What is it that is important for them? Can we find a way of using this to enter the negotiating arena so that we can talk to each other?

2. Opening the door

Once we have decided on an appropriate strategy to work with a person, using a language that we think they will recognise, we have to consider how to present such an approach in a way that will be acceptable, so that they will not only notice it and find it familiar, but also non-threatening. It is very important at this stage to be aware that the person with whom we are working may perceive the world differently from the way we do.

- The person may have physical disabilities that hinder reception of the signals we send them. For example, a person with tunnel vision will not see signs made outside their field of vision.

■ The person may receive signals normally but be unable to process them, as happens with people with autism. For example, if we try to communicate verbally, the person may hear the sounds but be unable to attach meaning to them. This may happen intermittently (sometimes the processing works, sometimes not), which can mislead their support staff into believing that they are lazy or difficult. Such failure to process builds up pressure, which is described as being 'overloaded'. Williams (1995) says: 'I keep running, running, running, trying to keep up.'

■ Overload causes 'fragmentation' – images and stimuli break up. This is a painful process. In my experience, it is sometimes accompanied by overheating – the person streams with sweat. (It is difficult for us to realise that it may well be our attempts to draw an individual into 'our' world which are stressful and contributing to the difficulties they are experiencing. Again, Williams (1995) talks about the tension and stress of always having to be in 'the world' and not in 'her world'.

■ For a number of reasons, some people reject our interventions. Perhaps the most obvious is that we are physically too close to them so that they are afraid. Another reason might be, if we put out our hand to touch an object they are flicking, they feel we are trying to take it away, something that has almost certainly happened in the past. (This can sometimes be overcome by using a duplicate so that we can join in without being seen as threatening.) It is also my experience that, where people have more than one repetitive behaviour, they may use one of them not so much as a conversation with themselves, but as a line of defence in order to keep out a world with which they cannot cope. At the same time, however, most people are carrying on some form of internal dialogue with themselves and it is this we need to be looking for.

■ 'Normal' signals or even 'valuing' signals, such as a smile or eye-contact, may have a negative impact if the brain of the person who receives them understands them quite differently from the intention of the sender. (A person with autism may experience eye-contact or even direct speech as acutely painful.)

■ The signal the person receives may be correctly processed but may not connect up with familiar ideas. According to Stern (1985): 'Each successive variation must be partly familiar, as well as partly new.'

■ There must be something recognisable in our signals for the person's brain to connect with. If we offer something that is totally new, we may be introducing expectations with which people cannot make connections. This sets people up for failure. This is particularly easy to do if we offer 'blanket occupations' where everyone is offered a particular activity regardless of whether they connect with it.

We therefore need to be aware that our well-intentioned inputs may be received as:

■ indistinct

■ intermittent

■ confused

■ distorted

■ reduced

■ unclear

■ bottlenecked

■ fragmented

■ unmotivating

■ disconnected

■ positively threatening.

Intensive Interaction

In the first two histories, we referred to the technique known as Intensive Interaction, in which a person's behaviours are reflected back to them. This process is now well documented, especially in Nind and Hewett's excellent book, *Access to Communication* (1994). Further reflections on these techniques and their use with a wide range of people with disabilities are to be found in their more recent book, *Interaction in Action* (Hewett & Nind, 1998).

For the benefit of those who are not familiar with the method, I will briefly run through the way I approach the technique. I sometimes find, when I am teaching, that support staff only have a partial idea of how to go about it. They will speak of 'mimicking' behaviours and are 'not sure what to do next'.

- To begin with, the language we use is important since it determines the way that we think. Mimicry can have an undertow of mockery and uses the person as an object. There is a fundamental difference between mimicking and talking to a person in a language that speaks to their inner world in a way that they understand and with which they feel safe.

- Having decided what signals the person is giving themselves and focusing on, we start to reflect these signals back to them.

In principle this sounds simple, and it is – provided we are aware of various forms of interference that can arise.

- We may feel self-conscious – particularly when we are new to the techniques. This becomes less of a problem as we begin to get feedback and a sense of the essence of a person (rather than behaviours) in a way we have not experienced before.

- We may have been taught to work in certain ways that exclude a necessary flexibility of response. For example, we may feel that we have to 'teach' the person skills, rather than use activities as opportunities for sharing.

- We may have in mind ways of working with people with similar disabilities that have been helpful with other individuals. Such agendas can obscure the potential of the person with whom we are working – what they have to offer.

- We may doubt our ability and lack the confidence to be wholly present for the person with whom we are working, especially if we are not used to giving people undivided and what I call 'intimate' attention, something we rarely do.

- We may be trying to do too much at one time when the person needs to rest and assimilate what we are trying to do together. This is particularly true of some people with profound disabilities. Characteristically, they respond and then withdraw. We need to give people time to take in what we have been doing together. Birath (undated personal communication) points out that, after a period of withdrawal, they will quite often sigh and then resume attention at the end of the 'assimilation time'.

■ We may fail to trust the person with whom we are working. We need to empty ourselves and put ourselves in their hands – give them control.

Responses

When the person notices, they will usually stop what they are doing and look surprised. ('That's one of my signals but where did it come from?') You can see them attending.

Three points need to be mentioned here.

1. It may be some time before people notice the intervention, or at least they may notice but not respond. Even if they do, the responses may be very small, for example, a change in head movement or breathing rhythm. Using a stethoscope, Ephraim (undated) even noted a change in heartbeat rate when he was working with a quadriplegic man. Occasionally, it has been up to half an hour before I have noted a physical response, although I have kept going since I have had the 'feeling' that the person was attending – presumably through subliminal clues that were too small to identify. (I make it a rule to take note of intuitive 'feelings' and test them against practice.)

2. It is worth remembering that a 'stimulus' is sometimes the difference between the presence or absence of a signal, rather than the signal itself; for example, with vibration, the stimulus is the difference between the on/off rather than the continuous buzz.

3. Sometimes a person with hearing disability will signify their attention by turning their face away from the source of the intervention, rather than towards it. We are so dependent on eye-contact for confirmation that it is easy to mistake this for lack of interest, when it actually signifies turning their head to present their best ear. What is almost always clear is an alteration in the posture of the body towards 'alertness'.

Usually the person will wait to see if the unexpected signal happens again. After a pause, I will do it again. I will try to get us to take turns. They do it, I do it. At first I will mirror their actions, then, with touch, I may try joining in. I am trying to develop a conversation, using all the skills involved in this. Using their time-frame, I am alternating, listening and responding, giving space and adding new and related material. No two conversations are the same and I need to be totally focused on what the other person is showing me. I also need to show my pleasure in our meeting but always have respect for the way that they understand my signals. At this stage we are beginning to interact. One student said: 'It's like a jar of sweets. Each person has their own unique flavour.'

It is this flavour, this 'essence', that we need to look for and work with.

It is easy to make assumptions about people's capacities based on our interpretations of their responses or lack of them. We may suggest that a person is not motivated, when it is nearer to the truth to say they cannot connect with 'our world' but can be interested and innovative if we learn their language and enter 'their world'.

Joe, who will not normally initiate anything and seems to be completely without self-motivation, becomes interactive through using his rather complex inner language of card-sifting hand movements and sounds.

He becomes lively and experimental, introducing new movements and waiting to see if these are picked up. When they are, he is obviously pleased. He enjoys the exchanges. He is motivated and concentrates on what we are doing together for twenty minutes.

Testing the system

Having recognised the system, a person often moves on to test it. People may deliberately introduce new material to see if I am really listening and whether our new-found communication is reliable. I have been surprised by the sophistication of the techniques people have used on me to test whether they have control. The next two case histories illustrate this.

Polly screams loudly about twice a minute. These screams seem unrelated to events, they just go on all the time. She cannot be taken outside and her behaviour affects all the residents and staff in her community home.

I try screaming with her. Every time Polly screams, I scream. When she first hears me, she looks very shocked and runs upstairs. I do not follow her because she has chosen to have that space and I must not encroach on her, but I can continue to echo her screams. She comes downstairs and looks at me round the door. Then she returns upstairs. I continue to echo her screams. After five minutes, she comes down and sits at the table with me. We move into exploring her noises, louder and softer. She puts out her hands and starts a series of hand movements that are not in her usual repertoire. It is as if, having been locked into her own world, she physically starts to explore the space outside her boundary. Her arena is enlarging. We do these movements together. She is smiling and relaxed.

Her key-workers undertake regular sessions with Polly, using whatever language she is using at that time. Her screams become less frequent and she is progressively more interested in hand contact and movements. By the end of six weeks, she has stopped screaming altogether. She can go out shopping with the others. Her quality of life has improved.

Mary, in her thirties, has total visual loss. She is difficult to work with as she hits and scratches. She appears to be unhappy. She has bits of string with which she plays. When she goes into a room, she walks round kicking the furniture and then lies down and drums her heels on the ground.

Mary's most obvious repetitive behaviour is playing with her bits of string. However, when I try to touch these, she thinks I am going to take them away and so she scratches me. Next, I try drumming my feet on the ground. This immediately catches her attention. She stops drumming her feet and listens. I repeat my drumming. She repeats hers. We then alternate and she begins to smile. Next, she gets up and stamps round the room. I stamp after her. She lies down again. This time, I walk across the room slowly (stamping my feet to let her know where I am), lift my foot and step over her and walk to the far side of the room. By this time she is laughing out loud. She then gets up and introduces a game of 'Find you'. She knows where I am because I am stamping my feet. She comes up to me and gently nudges me and moves off laughing. She repeats this a number of times.

Kicking furniture is seen as 'problem behaviour' but actually Mary is doing it in order to know where she is in relation to objects, it is a coping strategy which she has developed to deal with her environment.

The next time I visit, I stamp my feet to introduce myself but, to my surprise, Mary is very cross with me. I realise that, this time, she has taken her shoes off and is scraping her feet along the carpet. By stamping, I have conveyed the message that I am not listening to her, and the new way we have set up of talking to each other is not working. When I scrape my feet, she becomes calm and starts to smile again. Later on, she introduces tapping a tin as another way to communicate.

It is crucial that we remain open to any new material that is offered to us because not only does it convey that we are listening to and valuing the person and what they are doing, it also validates the new system. It confirms to the person that they can communicate and gives them confidence to try to extend the boundaries of the negotiating arena – 'I can use my language, the one I feel safe with, to talk to, negotiate with and affect "core other".'

It is no good using yesterday's material. We must respond to what the person is doing now – and our responses should never be mechanical. (This is why recording sounds and playing them back often does not work. Although the person may show initial interest, they usually lose this quite quickly. We need to be present and responding to what the person is offering at this time.) We should feel we are talking to friends, giving them time to reflect on what is happening and responding to their innovation.

Balancing familiarity and surprise

Problems can arise if no variety is introduced, either by us or by the person. We begin to feel that the process is no longer interactive, that we are being used and somehow we have become an object built into the closed loop of the person's stereotypic behaviour. Weighed in the balance of Stern's 'something familiar, something novel' (1985), there is not enough new material to attract their attention to the outside world. They have become habituated. **Surprise has been lost and, in the model of the locked room, it is surprise which keeps the door open. It is the foot in the door that allows interaction to continue.**

Sometimes the change needed to make the shift is very simple.

> *Meg continuously drops objects in order to have them picked up. We return them to her as we feel she 'ought' to be holding them; we become part of her 'closed repetitive loop'.*
>
> *How can we get out of this and use Meg's behaviour in a way that is both familiar, so that she accepts it, and new, so that it refocuses her attention outside herself?*
>
> *If we pick her object up clumsily, play 'butterfingers' and laugh at ourselves, we introduce surprise so that we can share a joke together.*

If we take **sound** as the stimulus, we can look at it from the inside:

■ I am surprised that my sound is coming, not from me but from 'out there'. I attend and look to see what is going on.

■ Next, I notice that my sound is sometimes out there and sometimes not, it has become intermittent. The stimulus has shifted from just being an external source to the difference between 'there' and 'not there'.

■ My sound is 'out there' but slightly different: part of it is familiar – enough for me to relate to – but part of it is new – what I recognise is linked to something I do not already know. This is the beginning of the learning process, the opening out and enlargement of the negotiating arena. I use what I recognise and feel safe with as a platform to explore new territory. On its own, it would be too threatening, but it is acceptable within a safe context.

In order to maintain both contact and surprise, there is a variety of options open to us when we work. If we take, for example, a person's **hand movements**:

■ The person's movements can be **reflected back** in such a way that copies what they are doing. As has been pointed out, it may be difficult to get the person's attention by straight copying. Particularly where the stimulus is visual, they may be too locked into their inner world to notice.

■ If we have the person's attention, we can strengthen it by **making the source** discontinuous. This not only provides stimulation but allows us time to reflect on what each other are saying.

■ Where people are really locked in to a physical movement such as rocking, flapping their hands or hand-wringing, they may not notice if we mirror this. It may be more effective to **reflect the movement back in a different mode** – for example, through sound that mirrors the gesture, such as scraping a corrugated tube to the rhythm of rocking; or through touch – perhaps movement of a finger on the person's back or arm, or somewhere they find acceptable. We also need to think creatively. For example, we can enhance finger-flapping by designing a mirror with holes in it (as shown in the picture below) through which 'their' movements can be made. This equipment not only encourages the individual to look at the stimulus that they enjoy but also draws their attention to their body image.[1]

Mirror with holes

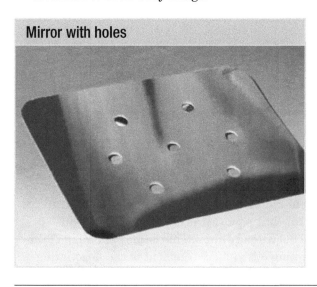

1 Stern (1985) throws light on why 'changing the mode' may be so effective. It is not only introducing variety but also empathetic. He says that if we copy a person, we let them know that we know what they are doing, but if we reflect back their actions but in a different way, through a changed mode, we let them know that we know what they are feeling.

- We can **physically join in** the movement, placing our fingers on theirs if they will allow us to do so. This is a process that requires great sensitivity and, if necessary, willingness to withdraw. Further, if touch is going to be used, then it needs to take place within the context of an agreed management strategy so that it can clearly be seen to be non-invasive. There is a difficult balance to be drawn between privacy and what may be the only possible way to establish the vital link between the person's inner world and the outside reality, between isolation and participation.

- Even rejection itself can be used as a way of interaction in that it allows the person to control the distance between us. If I am pushed away, I can stay and work at that distance. By doing this, I show that I am respecting the needs of the person with whom I am working – she wants space and I am giving her control. Even if she does not want to work with me at all, she may be intrigued by my respect for her; it will awaken her interest.

The following history illustrates the balance between habituation and surprise.

Fran, a woman with autism, has two languages, one of which she uses on her own when she thinks she is unobserved. It relates to her outer world: 'I'll go on the red bus,' or '…in the green car'. Her other language clearly repeats what has been said to her previously when she was being 'difficult': 'I'll get Sister!'

When she starts to walk round in circles and becomes agitated saying, 'I'll get Sister!', it is possible to divert her by taking elements from her inner turmoil and switching the context to her outer (if hidden) language, combining the two to draw her attention to the outside world. For example: 'You'll have to get Sister in the red bus.' Fran is silent for a few minutes while she thinks about this.

This strategy works three or four times until she gets used to it and it no longer stops her in her tracks. But switching to 'You'll have to get Sister in her green car,' is surprising again, and again Fran is diverted while she thinks about it. Each time there is a new element contained within the familiar response, something she is not expecting, the surprise defuses her rising distress. Support staff are now using this technique to help her when she is upset.

Adjusting to the individual

It is very difficult to lay down blanket guidelines. Each person is an individual with their own history. What works for one person does not necessarily work for another. We need to think more in terms of a jigsaw – as Williams puts it: 'which bits fit where' and 'how they are related' (Williams, 1995).

Richard is able to interact if his sounds are reflected back to him when he is happy, but when he switches to his distressed phases – something which happens very fast and may be related to epilepsy – trying to work with his sounds makes him increasingly agitated.

On the other hand:

Ash, who is often very withdrawn, relates through touch with his many and diverse hand movements when he is distressed, but when he is 'happy' he prefers to relate through games such as 'thumbs up' and 'give me five' which are in the nature of party tricks. These, while being an expression of his happy state, leave no room for mutual exploration.

For Ash, it may be more realistic and effective to work through his outer world, that is, his interest in boxing. For example, he enjoys looking at boxing magazines. (In the case of another person with similar interests, we used cut-out stand-up figures, as shown in the picture below.)

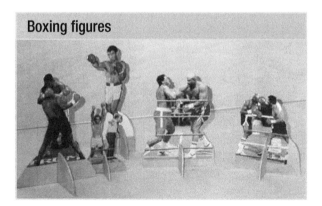

Boxing figures

A number of people with stereotypic behaviour have more than one repetitive pattern. They may move through a whole sequence and it is not always the most obvious signal to which they respond when we reflect back their behaviour. As pointed out above, some repetitive patterns may be defensive. Where there are multiple behaviours, we need to try all of them.

If the person with whom we are working shows any signs of distress or overload, we need to return to the original mode or way of presentation. We are working in an area where people have dropped their defences. We are inside their boundaries and they may be very vulnerable. It is crucial that we are aware of this and ready to withdraw at the least sign of unease. If the person becomes over-stimulated – as can happen occasionally, for example, with people with epilepsy or autism – we need to shorten the time of the intervention.

We may be trying to work with people whose disabilities are extremely complex and whose lives are a hidden history of unhappiness. It is important for them, as well as for us, that we are not judgmental about ourselves if we are rejected, since there will inevitably be times when, even if everything went well last time and the intervention has been carefully thought through, the process does not work – the person with whom I am working does not want to know me. Although we had a marvellous 'conversation' yesterday, today the person gets up and moves my chair away. It is very important that I put my feelings aside and consider what actually happened. Did I get the timing wrong? Was I too close? Despite the fact that I used their language, did I get the presentation wrong? Do I need to introduce new material? Did I miss something or were they just telling me they have had enough?

3. Exploring the treasures in the room

We have found the right key, opened the door and are looking round to see what is in the room to share with each other.

The sharing has to be mutual. We have to be open ourselves and let people explore us. It is extremely important that we allow ourselves and our pleasure to be evident to them as this gives people the confidence to exchange. Using their language, we begin to introduce flexibility into the stereotype, opening out into an arena in which the core self can feel safe to negotiate with others.

> *Sally, a child aged five with severe autism, is completely locked into the idea of her family car. All she will say is, 'Mummy's blue car.'*
>
> *I make her a blue car, two sides with a box between. I am now able to place objects in the box and Sally is able to name them. They are literally contained within the familiarity of her stereotype, which has been enlarged to admit new material.*

> *Donna, a small girl, tears up paper and stuffs wedges of it in between her fingers. She is very upset if these are removed. It is extremely difficult to focus her attention on alternative activities.*
>
> *Her father does the same. Donna watches carefully. He takes his out and sorts them into piles. Twenty minutes later, she takes hers out and sorts them for the first time.*

Both these histories show how, using the language of a person's stereotypic behaviour, we can begin to enlarge the negotiating arena, strengthening the area in which the person feels safe enough to interact. At this stage, we have not moved the person outside the stereotype in which their core self is anchored. Rather, the stereotype has become more flexible so that we are able to insert new ideas, new openings, which can be dealt with in the security of their familiar world.

Exploring the room is not only about discovering and increasing what the people with whom we work can do, but also about the more unquantifiable world of discovering who we both are. What can we learn about each other through our body language? How can we learn to trust one another and share each other's pleasure – a vital stage in making friends?

At this stage, support staff will often ask what they have to do next. This is a problem because we are conditioned to the idea that, in order to succeed, we must be moving on. There must be new goals in what appears to be a progressively upgraded obstacle race. The difficulty is that if we are locked into our own forecasts, we easily miss what the person with whom we are working has to offer. When this happens, when we miss their cues, it tells the person that their new way of relating to the world outside themselves is not effective. The outcome of this is loss of confidence and a return to their inner world. Williams (1995) suggests that we put our own agenda in our back pocket. We need to keep ourselves in the present, trust the person with whom we are working, watching for their contributions and valuing them. This is the way to empowerment.

4. Looking out of the window

Inside this new flexible arena, which we enter by using the individual's 'personal code', and in which we communicate by using their 'language', whatever form it takes, the person:

- usually becomes more relaxed, not only during interventions but also spilling over into the time between – the person becomes more adventurous with us; at the same time, we need to be aware that the person may also be more vulnerable since we are working inside their defences

- will sometimes speak – from surprise, but within a position of safety

- can use the arena as a platform to view the world outside.

George, a young man with severe autism who attends a day centre, draws road plans repeatedly on an A4 pad. He is very upset if staff try to join in or offer alternatives.

Trying to share his drawings requires sitting very close to him. I decide to give him more space and place a very large sheet of paper on the table (one by one-and-a-half metres). This gives room for me to sit at one end with George at the other. We work towards each other, eventually meeting in the middle. He begins to enjoy my contribution and I am able to move into his side and he into mine. I add traffic lights and road cones to his roads and he starts to look outside, through the window, at those he can see in the road. All goes well until we introduce some model cars and try to drive them round his roads. This is too much and he becomes upset until we draw a car park and park them in it. We are able to contain George's normally disturbed behaviour during the lunch hour by continuing to focus his attention on our joint project. The following day his mother, who has been unaware of the intervention, phones the centre to enquire what has happened – she has never seen him so calm and relaxed.

George, in spite of his autism, enjoyed working co-operatively, provided he was given enough space to do so. When he did feel threatened by the cars, we did not have to take them away, but were able to neutralise his fear by enclosing them in a car park. We were using his 'language'. Because he felt safe, he started, quite literally, to look out of the window and compare and share his inner world with what he saw outside. His enjoyment of this sharing intervention overflowed into the rest of his day to the extent that his mother, who had not been present, noticed his changed behaviour.

The arena can be used as a launch pad to start exploring the world outside.

Daniel is a young man who has recently left hospital to live with his family. He sits in a chair all day, looking at his fingers flapping. In spite of the best efforts of his family, he does not respond to their initiatives, except finger-flapping games or making animal shapes on the walls. The chair has to be tipped in order to prompt him to get up for meals, the toilet, and so on. He does like being pushed out in a wheelchair but in the winter this is not practicable as the family live down an unmade road which gets too muddy for this to be possible.

I am asked to see if I can find a way of interacting with Daniel so that, when winter comes, his family can work with him indoors. He responds to interacting with fingers; this is his language – the way he talks to himself. In order to widen his experience, I use a plastic mirror with holes (as shown in the picture on page 28). When he looks at my wriggling fingers pushed through the holes, an amplification of the stimulus he is giving himself, he also sees his face and starts to look at himself for the first time.

I also design a box with holes in it (pictured below), through which a finger can be pushed. The aim of the game is to use a transparent plastic cup to catch the finger.

So far, other than playing shadow games with him, it has not been possible to engage Daniel's attention. He needs hands-on prompt only eleven times before he is able to play by himself. He finds it very funny and enjoys the interaction. His family works with him daily. After about a month, Daniel stands up one day, picks up his chair and takes it out into the garden. This burst of self-confidence is the beginning of more normal interaction with his family. He goes where he wants to.

'Catch my finger'

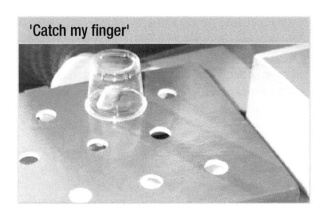

To summarise

■ When we are looking for ways of working with people who are locked into their own world, we need to observe each person's behaviours non-judgmentally in order to identify the language that they are using to talk to themselves.

- We have to find ways of using this language in order to attract their attention to a source outside themselves, presenting our interventions in ways that are non-threatening for that particular person.

- We have to be alert to any new material that people bring, and be aware of the need for surprise to 'keep the door open'.

- Above all, we need to remember that the aim of our interactions is to be present for an individual in a way which opens up the person to the possibilities of new experience. We are trying to enlarge their arena so that they become aware of a wider world outside their own and begin to see it as an interesting and pleasurable place to be. We need to share ourselves in ways the person finds safe in order to give them the confidence to explore further.

Chapter 3

Using the person's language

Once we are confident of the way we are working in the arena and understand its language and boundaries, we can begin to use it more deliberately. For example, we can enhance relationships and make it easier for others to communicate.

> *Maria, a young woman with Rett's syndrome, makes sounds and her family makes sounds back to her.*
>
> *Although Maria smiled, she wasn't really engaged until I suggested that her family mirrored her sounds more closely. She immediately 'came to life' in a way they had not seen before. A friend of the family was also able to have what she described as a most amazing conversation with Maria over the telephone. The responses were not dependent on the friend being present, only on their mutual pleasure and exploration of Maria's language.*

Defusing distress

Thinking in terms of helping a person rather than controlling their disturbed behaviour, we can sometimes use a person's language to distract them and move their attention away from their inner turmoil (where they appear to have got stuck in a stereotypic mode which feeds itself and builds up into self-injury or outwardly directed aggression) back to relating to the outside world. Since noticing this, I have been paying particular attention to ways of using personal codes to defuse distressed behaviours (which are potentially, at least, and sometimes actually, spiralling out of control) focusing the person back on the outside world.

When we discussed the relationship between surprise and habituation (see page 29), we saw how, by combining the elements of Fran's 'inside' and 'outside' languages, staff were able to divert Fran's attention from her disturbed inner state. The following histories illustrate the use of the same technique with people with disabilities ranging through the wide spectrum from profound disability to Asperger's syndrome.

Colin, who has very severe learning difficulties and severe autism, periodically gets very distressed. He shouts and becomes very agitated, sweats profusely and paces up and down.

I am asked to see Colin when he is already disturbed. Sitting away from him, I reflect back his sounds. When he hears, he becomes calmer and within five minutes he is reclining on the floor in his relaxed position. With normal intervention, it takes fifteen minutes before he calms down.

Cassie, who has Asperger's syndrome, tells me that she is making meat sandwiches for her supper. She then slips into a repetitive and increasingly agitated mode, which involves the importance to her of the number seven. Her voice rises and rises as she becomes more distressed.

I use the actual word Cassie has told me is significant to her and ask her if she is going to have seven meat sandwiches for supper. She looks at me in surprise and laughs, 'No, three.' She turns back to making her supper. I have used Cassie's language, her personal code, to enter the closed world of her stereotype and draw her attention back to the preparation of her meal.

Mark, who has very severe learning disabilities, self-injures, hitting his head. He strokes his cheek with a circular movement when he is becoming upset.

Mark shows interest when I echo his movement, first on myself and then on his cheek. When he is becoming disturbed, it is possible to distract him by drawing attention to a source of 'his' touch which comes from outside himself.

Janet, who has very severe autism, attacks people when she is upset. She speaks in a high, sing-song voice and speaks of herself in the third person. The recognisable onset of her distress is marked by her eyes becoming staring and darting about, by distinctive hum-cries and finally her hands going up as her cries get louder. Sometimes she will run and turn off the radio or TV before she attacks.

When Janet starts her eye movements and cries, I sit down and reflect her cries back to her. She runs and turns off the TV, then returns and looks at me with surprise on her face. She says to me, in a low voice, 'You be me!' (By this she means 'You copy me' as she will often say, 'Janet be Mary!' and then copy her.) I have been able to reach Janet by using her own signs that are part of her inner language. She answers me from her inner self with a voice that sounds completely different and more centred than the usual high childish voice that she uses. She also uses the first person.

Stress can build up as an outcome of a person being unable or not allowed to do what they want. They cannot control their world.

> When Majella gets on the coach to go home from her day centre, her escort is warned that she is becoming upset and there may be difficulties. She is muttering to herself about wanting to stay in that evening – she doesn't want to go out. She becomes increasingly repetitive, agitated and locked into her stress:
>
> 'I will not go out; I will stay in and turn on the TV and watch EastEnders!'
>
> At this stage, Majella usually becomes physically aggressive but her escort picks up what is, for Majella, the most important word and puts it in another light: 'Yes,' she says, 'EastEnders – that's an interesting programme.'
>
> This use of Majella's actual words, picking up the subject that is important to her in another context, catches her attention and diverts her interest to a discussion about the programme.

In her book *Autism: Preparing for adulthood*, Howlin (1997) observes that:

'Direct attempts to prevent or prohibit obsessional or ritual behaviours result in individuals becoming more disturbed, agitated and anxious. If stopped, they may develop new rituals and obsessions. As they become larger, attempts to prevent these activities become more difficult.'

However, there is sometimes the alternative of working through repetitive and some disturbed behaviours in a creative way that reduces anxiety. In particular, all the people described above responded to the use of their personal code by moving from their inner world, where they were so upset, to a more positive context outside themselves. By using their language, it was possible to enter their arena and draw their attention away from their inner distress. We were able to divert each person from their stereotype by reducing stress, even when the person was already involved in or building up to challenging behaviour, bringing them down to the point of re-entry into 'this world'.

If we are to speculate as to why mirroring a person's exact activity or words when they are becoming disturbed should offer the possibility of being able to divert them from their outbursts, we need to look back at the processes which are taking place in that person:

■ There is turmoil in their inner world. If they have autistic tendencies, we know from what they tell us that, for whatever reason, when they are stressed, their processing becomes overloaded and the images and sounds their senses are receiving fragment and distort. This is a distressing and painful process, one that some people describe as agony: *'I would do anything to stop it, run out into the middle of the road, bash my head against a wall.'* (Weekes, undated)

■ The person may be trying to cut down or control sensory input. Williams (1995) says that she cuts out processing one sense in order to be able to cope with input to others. An alternative is to limit the volume of the input, as with Janet who, when she is becoming distressed, turns off the radio or TV before she attacks.

As has been pointed out, making use of the critical words or actions on which a person is focused introduces surprise and draws attention away from their inner turmoil to the outside world. At this crucial stage, empathy is probably not enough – just saying, 'You must feel miserable', or similar words may not penetrate: the interaction must be a word or action that relates critically to the person's inner language at the present time. (It may be that when we become locked into anger and anguish – as is possible for all of us – we mentally return to the infant stage where we need a 'parent' figure to confirm our exact words before we move on.[2])

While the primary intention of person-to-person intervention is not to 'manage' challenging behaviour but to help the person feel good about themselves, where there is a relatively slow build-up to the challenging behaviour, this approach does seem to offer the possibility of a respectful and non-threatening way of intervention with some people who are disturbed. There are some indications, however, that this type of approach is less likely to be effective where the disturbed behaviour is linked to temporal-lobe epilepsy.

Interpreting sounds

We often experience many practical difficulties when trying to disentangle a language that involves a whole range of sounds.

■ What is the function of each?

■ What, if anything, is the person trying to say?

■ Are the sounds outwardly-directed attempts to communicate, to let us know what the person wants, as, for example, in screams related to events?

---

2 Far-fetched as this may seem, a friend related a parallel personal experience when locked in to a road-rage situation: it needed mirroring of the actual significant words in a sympathetic context and, hence, acknowledgement of the specific feeling, to release him from his anger.

■ Are the sounds inwardly directed, aimed at self-stimulation? Is the person talking to herself?

■ Are the sounds non-intentional, such as the clicking noise made by a person's jaws when eating?

Even non-intentional noises can be used as part of a person's language – especially if associated with a pleasant activity. The next history illustrates this point.

Hannah has severe cerebral palsy and no sight. In the day centre, she screams at dinner, when she is in the hoist, and when she is about to travel on the coach. The screaming at dinner is a particular problem as it upsets other students.

One view is that Hannah needs to be helped to learn to wait for her dinner, perhaps by finding ways of distracting her. Alternatively, we can try to see how her day looks to her.

Some people with cerebral palsy seem to be very hungry. In Hannah's case, food is the most important thing in her life. She is only really happy when her stomach is full. When she reaches the dining room, she can smell the food but, because she is blind, cannot see the preparations for its arrival. Often there is a long wait, ten to fifteen minutes. Hannah becomes increasingly distressed. By the time she is served, she is screaming loudly.

Hannah is fed by spoon and eats fast – then there is another ten-minute wait before her dessert arrives, something she particularly enjoys as she has a sweet tooth. So Hannah screams again. This is communication. She is telling us what she wants.

The situation can be resolved by making sure that Hannah is not moved to the dining area until her food is ready, and also by making sure that there is no delay between the first and second course. We then see the situation from the point of view of a person who is blind and hungry and unable to know that her meal is on the way. We adapt to her needs.

Hannah also screams when she is lifted, either manually or in the hoist. Watching this, I notice the look of sheer terror going over her face when she is lifted, even though the staff who lift her are careful and very gentle. Her reaction suggests pain and the fear of pain. The latter can be just as upsetting as pain itself – a blueprint in the mind, which, as a result of some past incident, is painful enough to cause spasm when Hannah is being lifted. (Jolliffe (Joliffe et al, 1992) says: 'Fear has dominated my life. Even when things are not directly threatening, I tend to fear something horrible may happen.')

When Hannah is eating, which she likes, her jaw makes a clicking sound. She is fascinated when I use these clicks as a way of distracting her during periods when she is normally afraid – for example, before getting on the hoist at the back of the coach and when she is being lifted – to the extent that it overrides her fear of being lifted. She is quiet during the period of departure, a time when she usually screams. The clicking is part of her most positive internal sensation – eating.

As well as her communication screams, telling us what she wants or dislikes, Hannah also has non-intentional sounds which are part of her repertoire. She recognises them and, since they are associated with her most pleasurable activity, we can use them to remind her of this and calm her when she is afraid.

To summarise

The approach that I use starts off with extremely careful and non-judgmental observation:

- What exactly is going on for this person?

- How can we learn from the person what their own true needs are, as opposed to our needs of them?

- How can we meet these needs and start to enrich their lives?

Chapter 4

Getting the balance right

There are two questions that are sometimes raised.

1. **Doesn't working with repetitive behaviour sometimes reinforce the stereotype?**

In practice, the answer seems to be 'no'. On the contrary, picking up the person's own signals and reflecting them back from outside their arena shifts their focus outward from the core self; that is, the person looks outside themselves for the source of the stimuli which they have been giving themselves. As in the infant learning process, the external source confirms the core self so that the core self is able to move on and explore further. By handing over control, letting the person lead the 'conversation', we open up for them the possibility of understanding that what they do can affect how we, and those around them, respond. If we do not give people this opportunity, they may never be able to move on from pre-intentional language, whatever form it takes, to intentional language – using their signals deliberately for communication. People need to take this step in order to break out of the stereotype.

Far from enhancing the stereotype, reflecting back a person's repetitive behaviour almost always helps them to become relaxed. As the tension eases, they slow down and become more able to be flexible and interact. The area of negotiation enlarges. As their confidence increases, they are prepared to consider and try out new activities and let themselves be opened to new experiences.

2. **Isn't it better to leave them in 'their' world?**

It is not always possible to predict the outcome of bringing a person from 'their world' to 'this world'. As they emerge, they begin to take an interest in their environment. People who empty cupboards and strip leaves from houseplants present more of a challenge to their support staff than those who sit quietly. The increasing confidence to explore, on their part, may test our resolution as we begin to learn the consequences of empowerment.

Furthermore, it is sometimes extremely difficult to disentangle 'disturbed behaviour' from the way we work with people. With the best intentions in the world, our engagements with a person may reinforce their problems. For example, it is hard not to feel singled out when someone, who does not know how to relate normally, picks on you as a particular member of support staff and follows you round all day, sniffing your hair. However, using words such as 'attention seeking' does not address an individual's need to find appropriate ways of making contact.

I want to examine the next history in detail, not because I was able to offer any startling remedies, but to illustrate how important it is to look at all of a person's difficulties from their point of view. Although the work we did with Sunita was in some ways beneficial, in others it presented staff with increased care problems.

> *Sunita shouts loudly and repeatedly and disturbs the neighbours. To attract attention, she puts her face close to staff and makes her noise. Sometimes she brings them a cup and, if they fail to take it, she drops it. She has a number of less obvious repetitive behaviours and slides from one to the next. She has a very short memory and seems to be losing skills. It is suggested that Sunita is sliding into senility.*
>
> *First, the overall impression was that, although staff liked Sunita, almost all the signals she received from them were negative because of the difficulties of being with her. For example, when she came to them, they turned their heads away. Picking on a particular member of staff was known as 'targeting', so that even the language reinforced their feeling of being a 'victim'.*
>
> *We decided to try to alter this to give Sunita the attention she so clearly desired. When she put her face near, staff smiled, said 'Hello' and, using one of her own behaviours, rubbed her cheek gently with a finger. Staff were encouraged to think of targeting as an opportunity for interaction and take advantage of it.*

It was difficult to work with Sunita through Intensive Interaction as, apart from her noises, to which she did not respond when they were echoed back to her, she had a number of different repetitive behaviours. She slid from one to another and in practice it was difficult to know whether she had stopped because she was listening and waiting to see what would happen, or if she was starting another one; it was difficult to know where she 'was' at any particular time.

We did, however, find that Sunita was sometimes responsive to our joining in with her finger-scratching, a behaviour which was not at all obvious but did go on most of the time. Working from this, I tried using vibration on the area Sunita was self-stimulating and from this was able to lead on to using a food-mixer, power-sander and vacuum cleaner, all of which vibrated in the area of her hand that she normally self-stimulated. (Previous attempts to persuade Sunita to help with vacuuming had foundered on the expectation that she should show prolonged interest in it. We have to remember that the whole point of an interactive approach is to provide opportunities for doing things together rather than teaching people to do things by themselves: it is about relationship and not skills.) Further, when staff looked more closely at Sunita's movements, they realised that while she was unable to manoeuvre the machine backwards and forwards, she could manage to push it straight up the corridor. Their careful observation turned her efforts to success.

Another activity that related to Sunita's self-stimulation of her fingers was rubbing cream into her hands. Staff found this very effective in calming her.

Looking at language, ours and hers, it was apparent that at least some of Sunita's loud noises derived from words. Staff were asked to look out for approximating sounds and encourage her if she used them. She also had some high sounds, which were happy noises from bits of song. She liked it if these were sung back to her.

Sentences needed to be very clear, for example, we used nouns and not pronouns: 'put the cup in the sink,' but not, 'put it there.'

Sunita's memory was very short. She needed reminding frequently as she would forget she was carrying a cup and drop it. If she did drop it, we picked it up, gave it back and made a game of passing it one to another, gradually extending the time she held it.

The immediate outcome of this change in care was that Sunita became more interested in her surroundings. In some ways, her care became more difficult as she started to investigate things she had never noticed before, such as taking things off shelves. Nor did her sounds diminish. However, Sunita smiled and made happy noises more frequently. There were periods when she was quiet. She was able to carry things for short distances and, with prompt, put them in appropriate places. The staff took a more positive view of her.

I have included this more detailed account because I want to highlight that it is not just enough to look at a particular behaviour in isolation. We need to look at the whole person and how we interact with each other, altering each other's behaviour.

The important points are:

- it may be difficult to succeed with Intensive Interaction when a person has a series of repetitive behaviours – as they pass from one to another, it is not always clear whether they are attending or moving on

- it may be important to take a positive view of attention-seeking and find appropriate and acceptable ways to give a person the attention they need

- it is important to analyse a complex situation from the point of view of the difficulties a person experiences rather than the problems they present

- people with short memories need constant reminders.

To return to the question of whether or not it would be better to leave people in their own world, there is also the philosophical component. Can I say, for someone else, that my world is better than their world? I think most of us would agree that we are born social animals. Evidence suggests that we do not reach our full potential if we are reared isolated.

Certainly, I have come across two people (in whom epilepsy was not well-controlled) where intervention has had counter-productive effects. For example, one woman has a severe seizure every time she smiles; her physical condition makes interaction difficult if not impossible. Such situations are, however, extremely rare. The vast majority of people respond with interest, warmth, reaching out, smiles, laughter and most often they are relaxed during and after interventions. As well as this, even people with profound disabilities, although they may get tired and need time to assimilate their new-found experiences, usually come back showing evidence of wanting to continue, both at the time and on follow-up occasions.

We also have direct evidence from Donna Williams, who has severe autism, as to what her inner world feels like. In the very revealing Channel 4 documentary *Jam Jar* (1995), she explains her poem *Nobody Nowhere*:

'Autism is … total withdrawal into yourself, the whole world is torn up and made redundant. You have replaced every relationship that you could have had with the people in the world and they don't matter any more … there is no sense of "where" and no sense of "who" and if you are compelled to live in there, you live in fear.

'The wind can grow cold in the depths of your soul,
where nothing can hurt you until it's too late.' (Williams, 1995)

These moving descriptions of her inner world not only speak to people with autism but remind us all of our own inward places, our private arena in which we feel safe but which we may also need to defend. At this end of the scale of social interaction, we have the stereotype, locked in to self-stimuli. The whole aim of the work I am describing is to reach into the core self and build up a person's confidence to the point where they no longer feel threatened and so the boundary between core self and core other can become more permeable (see page 14). On the other hand, those people who have lost their sense of boundaries will need help to redefine these (see page 14). Either way, the aim is not just to enlarge the core self (where the person has been able to integrate their new experience) but also to strengthen the person's capacity for negotiating relationship. I need to feel stronger in myself so I can reach out to you.

However, getting the balance right between leaving a person in their world and encouraging them to come to ours is not always easy. Their world feels safe, a place to which they can retreat. Williams (1995) talks about the strain of always trying to be in a world that does not understand her 'way of thinking'. The perimeter may be a place to erect defences – protecting a person from a world in which they are vulnerable. But it is also a prison which cuts out the possibility of reciprocal communication and the opportunities for giving and receiving affection, bonding and love.

Chapter 5

Finding the right approach

In order to get in touch with a person, we may not only need to take account of their language but also the difficulties they experience in processing our approaches – particularly the feelings which people with autistic tendencies may have. Such people will often be overwhelmed by what we imagine to be our normal or even valuing interventions.

How can we ensure that our presentation of a person's language is in a form they find acceptable?

Hypersensitivities

For example, what happens when we speak to a man who is hypersensitive to sound?

> Ben, a resident in a community home, is very shy and easily upset. When he is upset, he attacks people. He frequently wanders round saying, 'Shut up, shut up!'
>
> This is the sort of language of which we very often do not take much notice, thinking perhaps that it is just something the person has picked up in a previous institution – it is 'just something they say'. By thinking about Ben's difficult behaviour and relating it to shouting and loud noises, the house manager realises that Ben is using his limited language to try to get people to be quieter, that loud noise is intolerable for him. When the staff start to speak softly to him, there is a marked reduction in his outbursts.

It is very difficult for us to step outside our own sensory experience and the tight blueprints we carry around with us of how the world 'ought' to be. It needs conscious effort on our behalf and we need frequent reminding. We need genuinely to listen to what people are saying, otherwise we can get it wrong for them.

Most people who work with people with autism are familiar with gaze avoidance. The person will do anything to avoid looking at us. They turn their head away or give fleeting glances and then their eyes slip away. We need to listen to what they are saying.

'People do not appreciate how unbearably difficult it is for me to look at a person. It disturbs my quietness and is terribly frightening.' (Jolliffe *et al*, 1992)

Some people with autism find direct eye contact acutely painful. Because we are so dependent on eye contact ourselves, this is difficult for us to understand and very often we try to insist that they look at us.

The next history illustrates how respecting and being sensitive to this difficulty can make it possible to communicate with a person who appeared to be totally unreachable.

> *Paula spends much of her time in her room. She becomes very disturbed, breaking furniture and attacking people. She avoids eye contact and does not like strangers.*
>
> *When I go to see Paula, she is sitting on her bed, twisting her hair. She looks away from me. I deliberately avoid looking at her directly, gazing out of the window, and I twist my hair. After a while I say, using indirect speech, 'If I had been doing this for some time, I should want to brush my hair, and if I wanted to brush my hair, I should put my hairbrush on the bed.' She puts her hairbrush on the bed. I walk over to her and brush her hair, still looking out of the window and speaking indirectly. After about five minutes, Paula leans forward and rests her head against me. The occupational therapist, who has been trying for months to help Paula learn to make tea using behavioural techniques, uses the same indirect technique the following day. Paula makes tea with minimal prompt (she needs help to take the lid off the tea-caddy) and ends up hugging her therapist.*

Paula wants to make contact and is able to do so when we use an indirect approach, respecting the overload and fragmentation that she experiences when people look at her and address her directly. Her sensory input breaks up and her nervous system feeds back pain instead of information. Looking away and speaking indirectly is non-threatening and allows Paula to communicate.

It is quite difficult to adopt this approach and it requires practice. Support staff will say that they feel cold or rude if they do not look at the person to whom they are speaking, or if they use indirect speech or simplify the language they use (this is not the same as using childish language).

However, Williams (1992) says that far from experiencing such consideration as impersonal, she was grateful when people respected her difficulties.

Sometimes people who are hypersensitive to sound or direct eye contact, can tolerate it under certain circumstances; for example, if they know that the sound or contact is going to happen and have time to prepare for what is coming, or if we are working inside their stereotype so that the signals we are giving them are recognisable and non-threatening. Under these circumstances, the person feels safe to negotiate. They can relax and may even initiate eye contact and touch themselves.

Boundaries

Part of the same problem for people with autism is not having a strong sense of boundary, the difference between core self and other. Returning to Williams (1996), if we do not know whether our hand belongs to ourselves, since we are switching off processing one or more of our senses in order to try to prevent overload, we have no picture of ourselves. We do not know where 'we' end and 'another person' begins. Under these circumstances, it is very easy to feel invaded by another. This is a very threatening situation and is illustrated by the next history, where Jack would like to communicate but needs a physical boundary between himself and another person in order to do so.

Jack, who has severe autism, spends much of his time outside the house. He is very disturbed and runs away from people if they approach him. Occasionally he will come to the window and tap it. If anyone looks up, he laughs.

Jack's behaviour suggests that he does want to communicate but can only do so if there is a physical screen between him and other people. This lets him know where they are and where he is. He can experience their separateness and therefore does not feel invaded. We decide to use a plastic screen to see if this will make it easier to get in touch with Jack. This is very successful. On the second visit, when we were not yet ready for him, Jack comes indoors, picks up the screen from the floor, puts it on the student's lap, knocks it and laughs at her. He is coming to us for the contact he enjoys which is now presented in a way he finds safe. He can knock and feel the physical boundary between us. It shows him, in a way which he can understand, that we are separate from him. He knows where he ends and we begin.

Such containment and separation may be built into the stereotype in more obvious ways; that is, the person uses the stereotype as the boundary to protect themselves from overload.

Luke, who has autism, spends much of his time within doorways or moving from one paving stone to the next in a way which suggests that squares are safe; it is the children's game of lines and squares played in an obsessional way. In any other circumstances, he is extremely withdrawn and difficult to motivate.

On the assumption that Luke needs a frame to protect him, I make a game. This is a sheet of paper ruled with black lines in squares (as shown in the picture below). The aim of the game is to flick the pieces (flat, black lids) into the squares. If they land not touching the lines, then they are safe. If they overlap the lines they are not safe and I take them back and try again. At first, Luke controls my game by saying, 'Yes' or 'No' as to whether or not I can have a turn. This in itself is co-operation of a kind he is not normally able to show. Within twenty minutes, he is sitting at the table playing the game with us, dealing out the pieces and taking turns.

The squares game

Working creatively within the arena of the stereotype, where he feels safe, contained and not threatened by overloading, Luke is able to interact. I would suggest that this has considerable implications for the way in which care is carried out for people with severe autism. By working within the stereotype, using the individual's own language, we can reduce the tensions caused by overloading. For example, Luke (in common with a number of other autistic people) seems to feel most threatened when he wakes in the morning. His confusion is greatest then. He runs from his bed and crouches in the corner of the room and refuses to come out and put on his clothes. Although, in this case, circumstances prevented my trying it out, the approach which I would suggest that might help Luke is to provide a square rug with a black border and put his clothes in the centre, offering a clearly recognisable and safe place for him to dress.

It also helps a person if you tell them in advance when it is necessary for you to move into the area that they regard as their safe place.

> *William, who has De Lange syndrome, sits in the doorway to the kitchen and hits anyone who tries to pass through.*
>
> *William clearly feels safe when he is framed by the doorway. I suggest that he feels threatened when his safe space is invaded. Staff stand away from him and call his name to get his attention when they need to get into the kitchen, pointing out by simple gestures what they need to do. When they do this, William no longer hits out.*

When a person feels threatened by direct contact, it sometimes helps to divert their attention to equipment which contains elements of the familiar signals which constitute their language – a middle ground from which the threat has been removed.

> *Peter, who has autism and very severe behaviour problems, patrols the large day-room, licking the walls in three specific places. If this activity is interrupted, he becomes extremely disturbed and attacks anyone near him.*
>
> *Peter enjoys objects that spin. I am able to attract his attention with a spinning mirror. He is happy to sit and operate this. Although this is less fraught than his previous activity, it is still a solitary occupation. I then introduce a puzzle that has spinning pieces but also requires manipulation to complete it (as shown in the picture below). Peter is interested in the spinning activity but cannot complete the puzzle by himself so he accepts my putting my hands on his to help him. By displacing our attention from the face-to-face interaction that he finds so threatening, and substituting the middle ground of the puzzle, (which includes the activity in which he is interested), Peter is able to allow hands-on contact.*

Rotating disk puzzle

To summarise

■ It is not only the 'language' we use that is important, but also how we present it; not only what we say, but how we say it.

Self-injury

We have to ask ourselves whether or not it is possible to use these techniques with people who are self-injuring. It may be part of a continuum but – at present – I want to differentiate between those people who are self-injuring as part of a repetitive behaviour pattern and those who injure themselves as a response to current external circumstances. As with sounds such as screaming, we need to know if the self-injury is rooted in internal factors or is a response to external events.

> Tara, who has severe autism, is unable to make contact with people, except on occasional days when she follows them round sniffing their hair. She runs away from people and hits her cheek so hard that she lays the bone open. She is very disturbed.
>
> I stand at the opposite end of the room so that Tara does not feel pressured by me. Every time she hits herself, I tap my cheek. It takes about twenty minutes before she sees me. When she does, she literally drops her jaw in surprise. She waits to see what I will do, so after a short interval I tap my cheek again. She bangs hers. I mirror her and in a short while she begins to introduce new varieties of movement with her arms and hands. When I get it right, she laughs. Then I move slowly towards her, tapping my cheek. Eventually, I am able to place my finger on Tara's cheek, opposite to the one she is hitting, and very gently echo her movements on her cheek. Tara's self-harm gradually becomes more gentle, mirroring the progressive quieting of my tap. Her key-worker becomes involved in working with Tara this way. Over the following months, Tara starts, of her own volition, to bring a cushion and sit beside her key-worker in the evenings instead of running away.

I am not suggesting that all self-injuring behaviour can be modified in this way as not enough work has been carried out in this particular field. However, that which I have done indicates that it is at least worth trying.

Again, the crucial stages are:

■ finding the right language

■ finding a non-threatening way to present it.

As was the case with Tara, it may then be possible to use the person's language creatively, drawing their attention more and more from their inner locked-in world to the world outside.

Getting the level right

Some people have special interests through which one can attract their attention. If these interests have not been developed or have been allowed to lapse, a person's behavior can be very deceptive indeed – they may appear much less able than they potentially are, particularly if they have a hearing or visual disability.

An art therapist works with Josh, whose sole interest appears to be counting beads. Efforts to interest him in alternative activities have been unsuccessful.

Josh does, however, have a hearing aid which he takes off to show to the therapist. She gets him to draw around it and enlarges it on the photocopier. This is traced onto card, used as the basis of a design and projected onto material for fabric painting. Josh's designs are shown in an exhibition in the community. He is very proud of this and takes people to show them. Using the personal object in which Josh is interested, the therapist has been able to lead him to a new way of relating to this world.

Jeff, who is blind and almost totally unresponsive, dislikes being touched. He is reputed to have enjoyed walking by the sea in the past when his mother was alive. He mutters but it is not intelligible.

Jeff comes to life when he is taken for a long walk on shingle (where he has to hold on) on a day when there is a wild wind and the waves are crashing. After two hours, he is obviously enjoying himself and suggests that they 'go for a lager'.

Both Josh and Jeff appeared to be unreachable. The battle with their sensory disabilities had overwhelmed them and they had retreated from the struggle, to the point where they appeared to be profoundly disabled. Only a very strong significant stimulus had brought them back to 'this world'.

Chapter 6

Equipment and interactive activities

The actual way in which we decide to work with a person depends entirely on that individual. Either we can enter into their world and work with the non-threatening language that their brain recognises through Intensive Interaction or interactive activities, or we can try to find an alternative presentation, which is more fascinating to them than their own signals. This would override the signals that they are using to talk to themselves as, for example, when we might try using vibration to desensitise a person who is continually scratching a particular part of themselves. In either case, we are trying to refocus the person's attention on an external signal so that they look outside themselves for its source. Which way we try depends on the person's behaviours and responses. In the end, a two-pronged strategy may be needed.

There comes a stage in the process of getting close to people where it may be useful to use equipment. We can use equipment:

- to **capture attention** by enhancing the stereotype or the person's interest so as to present it in a more compelling way

- to help **engage the attention** of people who find face-to-face interaction threatening.

The first two uses have already been explored, as in the history of Rose, who was examining dandruff (see page 18) and that of Peter, who found one-to-one intervention acceptable when his attention was focused on spinning objects (see page 53).

Additional reasons for introducing equipment are:

- to provide **extra tactile stimulation** for people with visual impairment

- to encourage particular **physical movements** or activities

- to provide **pleasure**, as in hobbies

- to encourage **sharing in social activities**

- to encourage and facilitate **communication**

- to help understand **abstract ideas** such as 'time'

- to assist people to have **access to feelings** which are too painful to experience in everyday life

- containment – to help people look after **precious objects** and to help them 'hold' ideas that are frightening

- to explore **nurturing**.

Extra tactile stimulation

A large proportion of the stimuli we receive from the outside world are visual. It is not only information that people with visual impairment miss out on. They actually need extra tactile stimulation. This can be given at a simple level with Astroturf, which has a springy, scratchy feeling which is interesting to touch.

Support staff think it may help Craig, who has a visual disability, if he has some idea of his body image. He spends most of his time sitting in a chair looking at the ceiling and rubbing his hands through his hair. In order to help Craig look at a mirror, we need to alter the direction of his gaze.

This involves getting his hands down from his head. Bearing in mind that Craig enjoys the feeling of rubbing his hands through his hair, we make a mirror with a strip of Astroturf on one end (as shown in the picture below) and place his hands on it. After a few prompts, Craig brings his hands down by himself and starts to explore this new texture. He then finds the mirror and starts to compare the crisp, springy feeling of the Astroturf with the smooth, shiny surface of the mirror, moving his hands from one to the other. As his head follows his hands down, Craig starts to peer at his image in the mirror.

Astroturf mirror

Craig enjoys textures and comparing one with another. We should not have learned this unless we had stayed with his discovery of the Astroturf. It is crucial that we learn to resist the temptation to fast-forward into wider exploration. We have to stay with the person, sharing and enjoying their sense experience with them, in order to validate it.

At a more sophisticated level, tactile stimulation can be provided with three-dimensional puzzles of varying levels of difficulty.

Charlie, who is deaf-blind and very angry, comes down in the morning and hits people.

We make a difficult multi-layered three-dimensional puzzle for Charlie (as shown in the pictures below). He is totally absorbed by this. It breaks the pattern of being angry first thing in the morning, so that he has space to explore people and learn to relate to them in a different way.

Three-dimensional puzzle

Charlie completing the puzzle

The puzzle pieces

Physical movements

It is always important to work in conjunction with other therapists. Sometimes equipment can be designed to help with specific movements.

> *Matt has stiff shoulders and his physiotherapist asks for equipment which will help.*
>
> *We fit a netball ring with tubular elastic bandage, so that when a ball is thrown in, it can only be withdrawn by pulling it through the tube. Matt finds this helpful.*

> *An occupational therapist asks for equipment to encourage Roy to stretch out his arms when they come out of splints.*
>
> *The problem is to find something in which Roy will be sufficiently interested to hold onto. He likes the feeling of corrugated tube over a bar, which we attach to a rope so that we can pull on it.*

> *Callum, who has cerebral palsy, has difficulty opening his hand and turning his wrist. It is not rigid: he has just given up using this hand as it is easier to use the other.*
>
> *By laying short lengths of narrow tube horizontally on the table, I am able to encourage Callum to pick them up and turn his wrist in order to place them over vertical pegs.*

I find that when looking for suitable designs, it helps to enact the desired movements oneself repetitively. This tends to trigger related images which can be used to devise relevant equipment.

Individual pleasure

If we leave equipment with a person because they are enjoying it while we are not working with them, it loses its capacity as a vehicle of surprise and, consequently, its value as a way of getting in touch. The individual may become bored or fixated on the object.

However, there are some people with disabilities who delight in certain activities in the same way as we enjoy hobbies.

Roland, who has severe visual disabilities, loves looking through grids and perforated sheets and at patterns. They give him great pleasure and offer a new way for him to explore light and shadow. His mother says he enjoys them as much as a stamp collector enjoys his collection.

For Roland, offering new variations adds interest to his collection and to his life. It does not prevent his relating to people in his quiet way.

Sharing in social activities

Some people are physically not able to play games such as snooker or table tennis. In day centres they stand or sit near others, watching while they are playing – they are excluded by their lack of co-ordination. If they do manage to hit the ball, it goes into the net or off the table. These difficulties can be overcome by clamping a four-by-one-inch wooden batten down the length of each side of the table – the ends are left open (see Diagram 2 and the photos overleaf). These battens can be fitted to any rectangular table, or square tables pushed together. (The clamp only fastens on the underside of the table and therefore does not harm the table's surface.) Table tennis bats are used, or, if the person has difficulty in holding these at the right angle, it is easy to design bats using door- handles or special grips. Ball size is varied as appropriate – a yellow tennis ball is easy to see.

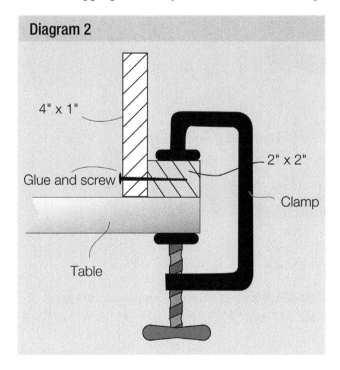

Diagram 2

4" x 1"

Glue and screw

2" x 2"

Clamp

Table

'Pushball' makes a good game which is enjoyed at many levels (see the pictures below). It can be played quickly or slowly, depending on capability. The ball is either hit straight down or spun off the sides. Pushball is useful for promoting tracking, and hand-eye co-ordination. It can be set up on dining room tables and is easy to use by people in wheelchairs. It is also great fun. It has been very helpful in promoting self-control with one individual who learned that if he returned the ball in such a way that his less able peers were able to return it, he would get a better game than if he smashed it. He learned to co-operate.

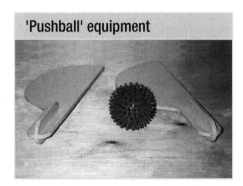

'Pushball' equipment

'Pushball' table

Communication

Before discussing the design of equipment related to communication, we need to look more specifically at the problems which people have in getting in touch with each other.

All the people who are the subject of this book have communication difficulties – for one reason or another they cannot 'talk' to us and we cannot 'talk' to them. This cuts out the possibilities of telling each other what we want or do not want, giving or asking for information, making comments or communicating emotion. Because of the frustrations involved, many people become withdrawn or exhibit what we call 'challenging behaviour' when they try to let us know that they are in situations which they cannot handle.

When we are working with people, we very often tend to focus on our need to convey information to them and lose sight of their need to tell us what they want and how they feel. It is vital, not only to find the most effective means of talking to a person, but also to learn to observe their body language so that we begin to understand what the person is feeling and trying to tell us.

To be real, communication must be a two-way process.

1. How do we let the person know our needs of them?

First, there are the barriers such as in hearing loss, or processing difficulties as in people with autism:

'They may hear sounds but cannot attach meaning to them.' (Peeters, 1997)

Also, people may not understand that speech is directed to them or even understand what speech is for:

'Speech is no more significant than any other sound.' (Jolliffe *et al,* 1992)

In actual practice, it may sometimes be difficult to distinguish between people with learning disabilities who also have severe hearing loss and people with learning disabilities who also have autism. However, the difference may be crucial when we try to communicate: people with autism may find it extremely difficult, if not impossible, to make sense of sign language – it is too abstract, they just cannot make the connection.

In his comprehensive book on autism, Peeters (1997) makes it clear that in order to make ourselves understood, we need the closest possible visual link between the gesture by which the message is conveyed and the intention we are trying to get over. In order to let a person know I want to go into the kitchen, I point first to myself and then indicate the kitchen. Peeters also points out that **the method we use to communicate with each other must be the one that is the most efficient in enabling a particular individual to make a connection with the world around them**. It should not be chosen for any other reason.

For some people, even objects of reference (object clues that relate to a proposed activity) may be too abstract if they do not relate closely enough to the message content. We may have to make our communication clues even simpler.

- **Objects of reference plus gesture**
  These should be clues from a familiar part of the proposed activity from the person's immediate surroundings rather than a representation. For example, if a person was going for a walk, the difference here might be between their coat (a direct visual clue) or some representational object such as tree bark.

  The object of reference needs to be supported by a simple gesture such as pointing from the person to the door.

- **Demonstration**
  Some people with autism cannot do something, even if they want to, unless they have a model to copy. They actually need to see an activity done. Demonstration involves actually showing a person what is required. If we take the example of making toast, the visual clue and gesture might be holding a slice of bread and indicating the toaster. Demonstration would involve actually showing the person the act of putting the toast in the toaster so that they can copy the action by putting their slice in the other side.

- **Demonstration with hands-on prompt**
  Some people will actually need physical hands-on prompt – doing it together. There are advantages to this: it can be seen as a chance for sharing an activity and so not only convey the information but also give an opportunity for 'being together'.

Some people with autism hear what we are saying but need time to process it before they can understand it and organise a reply. Jolliffe, who has autism but is very able, tells us:

'Sometimes when I really need to speak, the words won't come out and the frustration is terrible. I want to kick out at people and objects, throw things, rip things up and break them and very occasionally, scream.' (Jolliffe, 1992)

In my own experience, this time-lag, while the person is trying to process what we are saying, can be up to a matter of hours. We have to understand the struggle that people are going through as they try to wrestle meaning into sound, and be patient and admire their tenacity. Their struggle shows us just how important it is for human beings to talk to each other.

2. What is the person trying to say to us?

When people have no speech, we have to learn to watch their body language and what it tells us of their needs. This requires very careful observation.

The following is a case history of a woman with autism.

When Brenda is thirsty, she flicks the teapot to indicate that she wants tea. At her key-worker's house, although there is a teapot, she flicks the kettle as she knows that, in this house, tea is made with tea-bags.

In her bath, she tries to drink the water. When she starts, her key-worker immediately gives her a drink of iced water. This satisfies her thirst but, being cold, is difficult to gulp. She now drinks what she wants and hands the glass back, sometimes with some water left in it.

It is crucial that we take notice of people's needs, not only because it is what they need but also because it is a way of letting them know that they can affect what we do – it begins to show people what communication is for. This is something we take for granted but is one of the many difficulties that people with autism experience: they do not understand that we can influence one another by talking to each other.

Communication is not only about conveying information but also about expressing feeling. People with autism have such difficulties with this that it has often been assumed that they do not experience any feelings. What is becoming apparent, however, is that they are able to experience and express emotions if we are working in a non-threatening way inside their arena, the area where they feel safe. This is often the outcome of using Intensive Interaction or interactive activities, as in the continuation of Brenda's history.

> *Brenda, who is very anxious and often agitated, makes sounds in her throat. I copy their rhythm by knocking on the table. At first she gets up and walks around. I only knock when she is sitting. When I get her attention, I gradually lean forward and knock across the table towards her. Eventually, Brenda looks up, smiles and puts out her hand and takes mine gently. She does this three times before she has had enough and walks away.*

This spontaneous gesture is a more meaningful gesture than a learned sign with which Brenda does not emotionally connect. We need to give people the opportunities to express their affection.

Continuing this history, we can see the importance of negotiation.

> *Brenda likes to go out but she has 'good days' and 'bad days'. Some time before it is time to go out, her key-worker puts on her own coat to give Brenda the idea of going out. She watches to see if Brenda is interested or whether she fidgets and walks away. If she is looking, she offers Brenda her coat – if Brenda pushes it away, her key-worker still keeps her coat on as it is important to keep the options open.*
>
> *The key-worker needs to get the balance right between doing activities and not doing anything at all. However, negotiation does involve accepting when Brenda really does not want to go this time. This means that getting her agreement has to take priority over timetables. Brenda needs to know that when she makes it clear, through her way of communicating, that she does not want to go out today, we will take notice; what she does influences what we do and she has control.*

We may need to be very careful about the meaning we attach to people's responses.

> *Sushma, who is easily frustrated and upset, gives clear signs for 'yes' and 'no'. However, careful observation of an incident where she indicates 'no' (she does not want the foot spa but immediately becomes upset when it is removed) suggests that she is not always getting these signs right. This is followed up by further observation by staff. It appears that while Sushma knows what a question is and that it requires an answer, she is either not understanding as well as was thought or she has not attached consistent meaning to her responses.*
>
> *To help Sushma with this, staff now follow asking a question by giving her a second chance: for example, partially moving the foot spa away from her to a position where she can still see it and then turning back and asking her again. This helps Sushma to attach meaning to the question – it shows her what is going to happen.*

Negotiation is about getting agreement. It is not enough to ask a person to do something. We must frame the question so that we secure acknowledgement before we start, so that together we take part in a process with which they connect. Then, the activity becomes theirs, not something that just happens to them. Agreement may be only a flicker of the eyes or a fractional nod – but, if we can obtain it, we shall accomplish the activity in a way that is sharing and being together, rather than caring (us doing something for, or to, them).

Making choices

Difficulties sometimes arise when social ideals are translated blanket-fashion without due attention to individual need. A classic example of this is the insistence on the use of choices for some people with autistic tendencies. Unfortunately, while based on the admirable premise that such people must be given control of their lives, the very act of being given a choice can set up a painful conflict. Under these circumstances, failure to process can lead to fragmentation, the outcome of which may be self-harm or attack.

Implementing such policies can translate into staff feeling that they are obliged to insist on individuals making a choice. For example, the question 'Do you want to go shopping or swimming?' can lead to the following outcomes:

- the person says 'swimming' because that is the last word in the sentence and the only one they could decode from the jumble of sound. Actually, they wanted to go shopping and are upset when it does not happen

- there is a long delay while the person tries to process the question

- the person has an outburst because they are unable to process the question.

We need to look extremely carefully at exactly what we are doing and to what extent any particular individual can be empowered by choice. There are degrees of choice, complex or simple.

- There is the either/or question:
  'Will you wear these shoes or these?'

- Or the simple question:
  'Will you wear these shoes?' (If they are rejected, the question is repeated with another pair.)

However, there is another type of choice, which we do not always think about, which really does hand over control to the individual, empowering them because it recognises – and shows them that we recognise – their inner difficulties. It centres on the problems they have with boundaries and gives them control over where we are in relation to them and how close we come. I am talking here about those people with autism who have trouble with other people: 'People … come in bits' (Barron & Barron, 1992).

Such a situation, where an individual does not know where they end and another person begins, or which bits are theirs and which belong elsewhere, is invasive and threatening.

With a number of such people, those who are able to process some speech with the aid of gesture, I have found that letting them know that one respects their difficulties by asking such yes/no questions as, for example, 'May I come in?', pointing from myself to inside the room, or, 'May I sit down?', indicating a chair, are very much appreciated. Perhaps because it is non-invasive and prepares them for what I am about to do, this approach does not set up stress and is therefore easier to process.

Interaction with others

We have a tendency to think of communication in terms of interaction as a process that happens between 'them' (disabled) and ourselves (non-disabled). Equally important is the ability to interact with peers.

> The lives of a group of people with profound and multiple disability are dominated by the continuous and unacceptably loud noises made by one of them, Eileen. Eileen's noises distress other members of the group as well as staff – it is hard to work with the group against this background.
>
> Working interactively through a kazoo, Eileen's sounds become more cheerful; she is obviously enjoying the exchanges, pausing to reflect between sounds, smiling and laughing. A video of the session highlights the effect it is having on other members of the group.
>
> Another woman, who is quadriplegic, is sitting with her head slumped down. She is often distressed by noises. During this session, she lifts her head and starts to echo them back. She is smiling as she and Eileen talk to each other. Other members of the group start to laugh. Another woman, who is normally shy, takes the kazoo and succeeds in blowing it. She laughs when she is applauded by the group and starts to play to her audience.

The difference in the quality of interaction and the 'feel' of the room is marked; it has changed from the expression of individual aloneness to group enjoyment. People are interacting with their peers deliberately.

Visual aids

There are some communication difficulties that can be helped by simple visual aids. I want to focus here on the design and presentation of these aids, which can be crucial to success.

Laurence confuses his name with his brother's – or possibly himself with his brother.

Laurence is helped to sort this out by making a two-piece jigsaw, which is all he can manage, from a photograph of himself and his brother sitting on a wall beside each other. By this means, he can see and name himself, together and apart from his brother, and he quickly learns to name himself.

As has been pointed out, the ability to process and comprehend can be sporadic, particularly in people with autism. This can mislead support staff into thinking that a person is lazy or difficult because they understood 'last time'. Often, such people are helped by flash-cards, a visual presentation of the request, which reinforce the message. These can be made of 1mm styrene sheet which can be cut with scissors. These cards can be kept handy in a bum-bag.

A number of people with cerebral palsy have communication boards that are too large to fit in their wheelchairs. As a consequence, the boards are often left unused on shelves. It is possible to make books which contain their pictographs out of styrene or foamex. The latter is an attractive material in brilliant colours which can be cut and drilled like plywood. Designing the stiff pages with staggered flanges makes them easy to turn (see the picture below). Bound with split rings, these books can be fastened to the wheelchairs by a chain so that they are always available.

Flanged communication book

Good design must be individually tailored to the requirements of an individual. It is not only the idea that is important but how it is delivered, since success may depend on it. As well as considering health and safety issues, we need to ask ourselves which materials will be the most visually attractive, which design will be the most easily manipulated and which will be most likely to convey the message we want to help the person understand.

Abstract ideas

Many people with learning disabilities do not understand the idea of time. It is an abstract concept and without it, their experience of reality is extremely confused.

'There is no sense of "where" – I never got the whole picture of who I am today, where I'm going tomorrow.' (Williams, 1995)

'Reality ... is a confusing interacting mass of events, places, sounds and sights. There seem to be no clear boundaries, order or meaning to anything. A large part of my life is spent trying to work out the pattern behind everything.' (Jolliffe *et al*, 1992)

'When I woke, I needed to know what was going to happen or there were tantrums.' (Weekes, undated)

Peeters (1997) discusses at length the need for structure presented in an intelligible way and points out that it is not only children with autism who benefit from it: it is also adults with autism and many adults with learning disabilities who do not also have autism. They need help to know who is coming when, what is going to happen and how long it will take.

If a person has speech, it is usually quite easy to spot when time is a problem for them. Although the person may be able to say the appropriate words – such as 'summer', 'tomor- row', 'this afternoon' – they may have absolutely no concept of the linear sequence and intervals of time. However, they will ask the questions, often again and again, 'Who's on tomorrow?', 'When's the bus coming?' and so on. No matter how often their question is answered, it does not address their anxiety. The event that is uppermost in their minds is not happening and they have no way of anticipating when it will. The answer to their question does not mean anything to them that they can grasp. 'Soon' is just a sound with no meaning attached. All they do know is that there is a gap between what they need to happen – for example, the presence of someone they rely on – and the fact that it is not happening now. The person is absent or present; it is an all-or-nothing situation. People often become progressively more disturbed as their anxiety rises. The anxiety which accompanies a lack of grasp of time is sometimes at the root of behaviour we see as challenging.

In her book, Howlin says:

'Repetitive questioning is the consequence of not understanding. Sometimes rephrasing helps but more often the information needs to be supplied in a non-verbal form such as photographs.' (Howlin, 1997)

As has been already discussed under **Communication** (page 70), we may have to look for even simpler ways of getting in touch. We need to find which level of presentation helps a person most.

The specific design of equipment may be crucial to comprehension and we need to ask ourselves if the important features are visually outstanding and presented so that the sequence is clear. Will the person understand which way to follow it?

The following histories illustrate some of the ways which have been used successfully to help people who have difficulties with time.

Year

Alex, who has cerebral palsy (but not autism), is very disturbed when he hears the word 'holiday'. He thinks it means that other people are going on holiday and he will be left behind. Verbal explanations do not calm his distress and aggression.

Alex is helped to understand by using an office calendar. The months are cut out and mounted on a dark background so that each month is a separate horizontal strip. It is easy to understand which way the days are being crossed off. A picture of a suitcase is placed on the date for his holiday. Now, even if he starts to get distressed when he hears someone say the word 'holiday', it is possible to negotiate with him: 'Look, we've got to here, there are all these days until your holiday.'

We run our fingers along the days and point to the picture of the suitcase. We now have a way of negotiating with Alex which he can understand.

The backcloth to many people's lives is an unpredictable kaleidoscope of shifting changes and events. They do not know what will happen when or whom they will see today or, in fact, if they will ever see certain people again. It is not surprising that the people in the following histories are anxious.

Week

Caroline, who has autism, constantly asks, 'Who is on today?'

Caroline is reassured by a timetable that has hanging slats for each day, to which photographs of support staff can be attached by velcro. The slats can be held in separate hands – a physical differentiation between one day and another or, even more crucially, between 'now' and 'not now'.

Liz, who has autism, is acutely anxious about going home at the weekend. This is reflected in her repetitive speech pattern: 'Monday, Tuesday, Wednesday, Thursday, Friday, Saturday, go home, see Mum' – which becomes increasingly distressed.

Liz is helped by a weekly timetable made of styrene panels, one for each day, held together by wide tape. The panels are set far enough apart to allow folding, so that any individual day can be isolated and discussed at any one time. Each day shows her activities. This catches her attention. Within a week Liz can say what she will do on any particular day. Although her speech is still within the 'sequence of days' stereotype, she has slowed down, her vocabulary has increased and she is less anxious.

Day

An ordinary timetable may be visually confusing if the person has no idea of left-to-right sequence. Flashcards on a board can be made with a dark reverse (see the picture below), so that when each event is finished, the card can be turned over, and there is a very clear visual distinction between what has happened and what is going to happen.

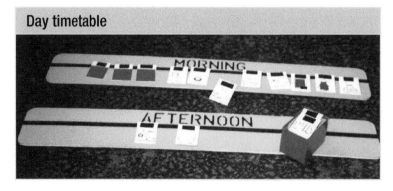

Day timetable

Another way to help people understand what will happen in a day is to mount the works of a clock on a board with a white face and remove the minute hand. What is left is the hour hand as an indicator which points to appropriate velcro-attached pictures at the right time. This is very easy to do with modern electric clocks. The parts cost a few pounds and all that is needed is a board with the right size hole drilled in it. Because the hour- hand is short, it helps if a radial line is drawn from the picture to the circumference of the little-hand sweep.

Minutes

A kitchen timer can be helpful, particularly the wind-up kind that ticks and then pings when the time is reached. People who are worried about time can hear the tick and differentiate it from the ping. It gives the brain something to focus on until the ping sounds. Marking the unnumbered part with a felt pen (as shown in the drawing below) helps a person to set their own time, long or short. This gives them control.

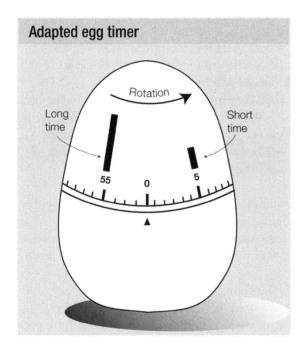

Adapted egg timer

Waiting

Some people are extremely thirsty, they are fixated on drinks. Sometimes it helps to give smaller drinks more frequently but, if they cannot understand time, the question they ask themselves and us is, 'When am I going to get my next drink?'

This becomes extremely stressful, especially so if the person has autistic tendencies. In a fragmenting world, teatime is a fixed point. ('I know what is happening and what I am doing when I am drinking my tea. I can relax.') As soon as teatime is past, tension starts to rise until the next teatime. 'When is it going to happen?' The brain asks this question over and over again. It may be an addiction to tea but it is compounded by not understanding time. 'Soon' or 'later' or even 'in five minutes' have no linear meaning, but hearing the tick of the timer ('not now') helps me to wait for the ping ('when I can have my tea'); it helps me to know where I am so that stress does not accumulate so easily.

We might also use the 'clock' described above, with a picture of 'their' teacup at the appropriate times.

It also helps to try to find an interesting occupation to fill in the gaps to divert the brain from its repetitive message. For example, with a more able person, one might build, hand-over-hand, shelves to hold their mugs and tea-caddy.

Sometimes a person with very severe learning disabilities may not be able to tolerate a long wait, even with the aids described above. Two hours can be broken down with the aid of a jar, eight wooden balls and a fifteen-minute egg timer. Each time the timer pings, a ball is put in the jar. Attention is held by the tick and anticipation of the ping. Time is negotiated by the number of balls still not posted. If the person cannot count, even one ball left indicates that the two hours is not yet up – a concrete way of distinguishing between 'now' and 'not now'.

When behavioural difficulties relate to the absence of structure in people's lives, it is crucial that where behaviour improves as a consequence of introducing this structure, the structuring elements are not discontinued. This can happen easily: 'She's better now, I didn't think we needed to go on.'

This is a misunderstanding. It is the changes in a person's environment and not in personal behaviour that have brought about a reduction in reactive behaviour. The reduction does not mean that anxiety and confusion have gone away. They will reappear if the structure is withdrawn and the person is once more faced with unanticipated events. Consistency and continuity are vital.

Working with feelings

'Feeling' is a word with a wide range of meanings. It can be used in the sense of touch, emotion (what we feel), perception (what we sense others are feeling) and insight. For some of us our emotional lives have such dark undertows that we find it difficult to acknowledge them, and this link can lead to rejection of the perceptual and empathetic aspects of our work. (In this respect, we should remember that although we may not be able to rationalise why we empathise with a particular course of action, we can measure outcomes.) We need to ask ourselves if the method we are using is working in a way that benefits the individual. This is the key question.

In practice, the dynamic of 'feeling' interactions is complex. There are our own feelings about ourselves, our work and the people with whom we are working. If we have not assimilated our own feelings, we may project these on to the people with whom we are working – as is common in many of our relationships. We need to be aware of this possibility.

However, there are times when we appear to be genuinely filled with an insight into, or an awareness of, how another person is feeling. Although it is difficult to understand how this occurs, it happens most frequently when we have come empty-handed to an encounter, perhaps sufficiently emptied of ourselves to pick up subliminal clues and attitudes which would normally be masked by our own agenda. This is illustrated by the next history.

> *I meet a woman I do not know and, telling her my name, ask what hers is. She hangs her head and says, 'I haven't got a name.'*
>
> *My reaction to this is, for me, quite unexpected. Instead of trying to jolly her along (maternal instinct: trying to make things better – a process which would not have valued how she felt and therefore would not value her as an individual), I feel myself, quite literally, being sucked into an abyss of being so non-person that I haven't got a name. I hear myself say, 'Is that how it feels sometimes, not even having a name?' She looks up at me and laughs: 'Yes, my name's Jane and you're a lovely lady.' Naming her feeling releases a flood of cheerful conversation and interaction.*

I find that, where it is possible to achieve it, an attitude of emptiness that is both alert (to all the activities and potential of the person) and detached (from my own agenda – particularly what I feel I, or the other person, 'ought' to be doing), is the most helpful position to adopt.

Very often when working with people with profound disabilities or complex challenging behaviour, it is only when I have exhausted my own resources – the preconceived ideas or equipment I have brought with me – even when I am turning away, in this void, that I begin to see the dynamic of what is going on and the person begins to respond. It is as though what I personally have to offer can actually block fluid interaction. The characteristic of these insights is that they are both surprising and fleeting. The moment needs to be grasped quickly, both for the person we are with, so that we can show them that we value them, and for ourselves, so that we can scrutinise the insight and evaluate it, beginning to unravel its implications. Evaluation against practice is one of the ways to distinguish between insight and projection.

It is at this level of feeling that my 'self' can truly share with another person. In terms of the locked room, this is where we can jointly open the window, lean out and enjoy the new view together. It is the moment when we say 'yes' to each other.

This therapeutic approach can lead to entanglements with a management system which demands benefit evaluations and asks: 'What will be the outcome of six weeks' intervention?'

Unfortunately, empowerment and growth do not lend themselves easily to cost analysis. One of the reasons we have actually been failing to get in touch with people who are locked in their own worlds is that our own agendas have masked the ways – in many cases, the ingenious ways – which people with severe disabilities have developed of understanding and relating to the realities they face.

After we had worked together with people who experienced great difficulties in their lives, a speech therapist said, 'I see that I have to put aside my language and learn theirs.'

We have to learn to put aside everything – preconceptions, philosophies, rules, 'occupations' – and focus on who the person is, aware of all they do and are, present for them so that nothing else matters.

Flexibility is the key to this way of working and outcomes can only be measured in retrospect. All we can do is create optimum conditions, which experience has taught us are likely to promote success. Whether the person will smile, laugh, relax and begin to relate are questions we cannot answer until we have tried.

Some of our experiences – and the emotions which stem from them – are too painful for us even to be aware of them. We forget or bury them in order to shield ourselves. Asking directly about them is counter-productive but sometimes we can bring about situations in which people feel safe enough to allow these feelings to emerge so that we can speak of them. One way of going about this is through the design and use of therapeutic games.

Ron, a man with severe challenging behaviour, is unable to say why he attacks people. If asked, he becomes genuinely distressed and tearful.

Working on the premise that we all have different parts of us that act in conflicting ways, we design a board game with a format that resembles Monopoly. Each player has two pieces, a 'goody' and a 'baddy' who go round the board in opposite directions. (In order to make it clear that the game is not about being 'good' or 'bad', the characters are deliberately stereotypic – there must be no moral verdict on behaviour.) Each square is a situation with alternative outcomes – for example:

You are at the dentist and afraid. Do you:

a) tell him and ask him for an injection?

b) bite him?

If the 'goody' and the 'baddy' land on the same square, specially designed dice are used to decide the outcome. The aim of the game – where both players have an equal chance of the 'baddy' coming out on top – is to stimulate conversation, laughter and being with each other in a way that feels safe and accepting enough to talk about how we feel. It is alright and normal to feel angry, unhappy and frustrated. We all do.

We play for several months. One day Ron says, 'You know, I'm not going to get better while I feel so angry.'

This is a breakthrough for him. Although the situation is still complex, he is able to start caring for his parents who have become disabled.

This is a man who is totally unable to understand or communicate why he feels impelled to attack people. Ron cannot feel his anger – it is unknown to him – but he is periodically overcome by situations that he sees as life-threatening, so he responds accordingly. He describes it as 'a black cloud moving up through him' – more of a physical description than an emotion. It does not appear to be related to epilepsy.

Some people appear to try to protect themselves from others coming too close to them by using repetitive speech patterns.

> *Carol, a woman who seems closed off from others, uses a very tight pattern of three sentences about a famous personality. Trying to ignore this or override it results in her becoming increasingly agitated.*
>
> *We decide to use a poster of 'her personality' to work with Carol. We place the poster between a transparent plastic sheet and a white backboard. Using a large felt pen, we draw round the head and remove the photograph, leaving the outline. I suggest she adds more hair. Carol picks up the pen and adds some. In subsequent sessions, she starts to talk more about the personality. After another two sessions, she suddenly becomes extremely angry. She expresses this by scribbling very hard on her picture and telling us how she feels about her life. After this incident, Carol is able to talk more freely about normal things such as wanting to go shopping.*

Some more able people are able to express themselves and talk about their feelings through a keyboard when they cannot do so through speech. An indirect approach is essential: use of the third person and statements rather than questions are less threatening. It may be possible to contain and hold feelings in the computer, which otherwise feel dangerous and overwhelming.

It is not only extremely important that we try to create a space in which people feel safe enough to express their feelings but that, when they do, we really listen to what they are trying to tell us. When I told staff that the woman had hung her head and said she had no name, they said she always did that. But Jane was not trying to say that she had literally never been given a name; rather, she was trying to tell us what it feels like to be so under- valued and powerless that she does not feel she qualifies as an individual. The anger of Ron, with whom I played the game 'goodies and baddies', is so powerful that if he allows himself to feel it as an emotion, he fears it will destroy him. For whatever reason, Carol, who talks about the well-known personality, feels so vulnerable that she cannot bear meaningful interactions with other people.

Individuals who are living in these types of situations are experiencing stress. Sometimes they are able to devise coping strategies to protect themselves but more often the pressures build up into outbursts, which are either self-destructive or aggressive, situations which we experience as 'challenging behaviour'. The challenge for us is to look for ways in which we can ease their tension. We have to try to examine all aspects of their lives from their point of view: how does their life feel to them? This is the subject of the next history, which is about a man who was very disturbed indeed.

Precious objects

Jim who has severe learning disabilities and challenging behaviour, is admitted to hospital when his parents can no longer manage. He breaks up furniture on a daily basis and eats plastic. He is unable to relate to people in any positive way and is heavily sedated to the point where he is unsteady on his feet and often falls. He does not speak meaningfully.

In a new ward, the team leader and I take a look at the cycle of Jim's behaviour. He breaks furniture to obtain plastic bits, which he then eats, as they are otherwise taken away. As he no longer has his plastic, he breaks up more furniture looking for replacements.

I take Jim to my workshop and, using power tools with hand-on-hand prompt, together we make a box for him to keep his bits in. He understands its purpose perfectly and keeps it by his bed. He stops needing new bits and therefore stops breaking furniture.

X-rays show that the number of pieces of plastic in his stomach is reduced from thirty-five before the intervention to one a month later. Because his behaviour improves, Jim's medication is reduced. He can now walk and run. His motivation is improved and he can now make his needs understood using speech. With his key-worker, Jim now goes to evening classes in woodwork and, when we meet, he shows me with great pride a construction he has made.

Trying to keep objects that are precious to a person may lead to their walking around with them or even eating them. It is not only that they feel the need to keep the objects safe but sometimes they feel as if their own safety depends on the presence of their particular things.

Jim's bits of plastic are extremely precious to him. In spite of all the trouble they bring him, his need to keep them is overridingly powerful, almost like our early need for transitional objects when, as children, we cling to the safety of a loved blanket, which is our half-way house to independence. We resist vigorously any attempt to remove it.

Taking it away is equivalent to separation from a parent. Jim's need is that strong. In order to give him confidence, we need to find a way of helping him to protect his things instead of taking them away. Again, this shows that we value what he values and by implication, that we value him.

This technique of making boxes to hold what a person values has been used with a number of disturbed people. It can be extended to making (together) shelves to hold people's precious objects. Doing it together is crucial. Even if the person is only able to pass the screws, they are taking part, it is theirs.

The outcome has always been beneficial. Once a person knows that their objects are safely contained and that they can control them, their need for them usually diminishes and they can move on to other activities.

Nurturing

Not everyone can speak. One of the roots of distress, which seems to affect some women, is the lack of opportunity to give birth and bring up babies. These women often respond very positively to life-size images of babies, enlarged photocopies mounted on plywood (as shown in the picture below).

Catherine sits in her chair and hits anyone who comes near.

I show Catherine images of babies and she puts out her hands and says, 'ahhh.' She becomes creative in her 'play' with the 'baby', putting it behind a mirror with a hole in it so that just the eye shows. She laughs at it. Her key-worker works hard using it with her. Not only is she interested and involved with the images but over the next three weeks she learns to greet visitors with a hug instead of hitting them. This instinctive empathy response is hormonal. It appears that repeated experience of the empathy response has changed the way Catherine was able to relate to people.

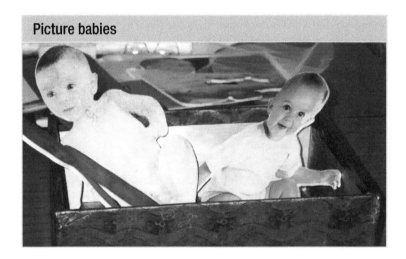

Picture babies

We have learned to pay attention to the sexual needs of the people with whom we work but little, if any, to their need to nurture. We know that the absence of opportunity to give birth and raise children can cause great pain. In spite of this, it is not generally a factor that is taken into account in the lives of women with severe learning disabilities. It is absolutely essential that we learn to show that we respect these feelings, to make it clear that they are meaningful to us. At the same time, we have to be careful not to raise expectations which cannot be fulfilled and for this reason I find it preferable to work with representations rather than dolls – pictures seem to be enough to introduce the idea and work with the feelings without inspiring hopes that cannot be met.

Chapter 7

Empowerment and respect

How do we help people to feel good about themselves when, even if they have received loving care, their perception of what it means to be a human being is of living in an environment which is at best puzzling, but may be very frightening indeed, and one in which they have no effective control?

Before we can answer this question, we have to put ourselves in their place and look at their situation from their unique point of view. We find ourselves in a world that is, for one reason or another, stressful. We are unable to let people know what we need and we are, to a large extent, dependent upon the basic signals afforded by body language.

A dual approach

Looking from inside outwards enables us to see that we, as supporters, need to adopt a combined approach of **stress reduction** and **confidence building**, considering both the outer (environmental) and inner (personal) elements which affect an individual's life. We should address those things in a person's life which increase tension as well as working through people's personal language to refocus their attention on an outside world which they can experience as friendly, welcoming, interesting and supportive.

Stress reduction

Stress reduction is often accomplished by paying respectful attention to some aspect of a person's life which may seem very minor to us but is extremely important to them. The following list of areas to which we should be paying attention does not include the issues of loss and bereavement or the anger that some people may express, if they are able, towards their disabilities and sometimes towards the non-disabled world in which they live. How does lack of ability feel in a world based on competence?

Hypersensitivities
As we have seen, a person's experience of sound, or being looked at or spoken to directly, may be different to ours and even painful. We may be able to address their needs by speaking softly or by indirect communication.

Non-confrontational body language
We need to remember the difficulties that a person may experience with boundaries and use non-confrontational body language. This involves the realisation that some of our gestures and behaviours, which are unintentional or even well-intentioned, may be perceived as frightening or even painful. We need to think about how our movements and positions and proximity appear to others; a person who stands over them or too near them or even, in some cases, looks directly at them, may be seen as intimidating and the person responds as though they are under threat – by withdrawal or attack.

If it is difficult for a person to hold together a stationary image, how much more difficult is a world and people which move?

Valuing feelings
Every opportunity should be taken to help people express how they feel and to be sensitive to their feelings. We need to value people and also show that we value what they value devising, if necessary, ways of helping them to contain their precious objects. We need to be sensitive to the deprivation which may arise from their lack of opportunity to nurture and raise children.

Negotiation and control
We need to develop the skill of negotiation so that we can help people increase control over the conflicts that really affect them – those concerned with relationship, their inner lives and the tensions which arise out of expectations based on realities different from their own. For example, it is hard to relate to people if they appear as fragments, and you do not know what they want.

Structure
If people do not know what is going to happen when and have no sense of order, time, interval or sequence, we need to help them by introducing

timetables, timers, visual aids and objects of reference which are specifically designed for that individual so that they can be understood. If the person cannot understand these, we can sometimes still help by being present for the person in a way that respects their difficulties.

One support worker who has particular sensitivity to the person with whom she works says that when this person is feeling bad she sits in the next room with the door open. She can then be seen but is not invasive.

We must try to make it possible for people always to be able to know what is going to happen when and the difference between 'now' and 'not now'.

Environment

We need to remember that certain people are unable to cope with environments that are small and noisy. They may find other people intolerable. All these factors contribute to stress. Peeters points out that some people may also not be equipped to cope with the ideal of community living:

'Although social interaction is difficult for people with autism, the accent in group homes is put on group experience and group activities.' (Peeters, 1997)

For example, we may expect that all residents will go swimming, although the pool may be echoing and noisy for an individual who is hypersensitive to sound.

Building confidence

At the same time as trying to reduce stress levels, we need to work on building confidence through getting in touch by improving relationships. This book has addressed in detail the possibilities of Intensive Interaction (using a person's own language) and interactive activities (activities with which an individual can connect). We also need to pay particular attention to valuing what the person values and finding ways to hand over control. We need to try to help people build an internal picture of themselves as having individual lives.

This can be done with photographs (enlarged on a photocopier to A4 size) of all aspects of their lives and activities which can be presented in plastic display books. It is important that these are not just portraits but pictures of the individual 'doing' things in order to encourage conversation about them and their lives, to recall the good times and give opportunities to explore the sadder times. We need something to talk to each other about. Audio and video tapes help revisit an experience and reinforce the person's part in and relation to it.

An equal partnership?

In his contribution to the book *Making Connections*, Robinson says:

'Fundamentally, we need to develop a philosophy which provides a sound basis for valuing and respecting all human beings, including those with learning disabilities, regardless of their capabilities, performance or appearance.' (Robinson, 1989)

I am sure that most of us would concur with this. If this is so, why, in spite of our best intentions and positive mission statements, is it not happening for some of the people with whom we work?

Perhaps the first thing we need to look at very carefully is: what are the underlying implications of saying that we respect and value a person?

The rationale is that each person is unique. While some of us come wrapped in better packaging than others, what we all have in common is our humanity.

Sometimes humanity can be hidden behind disabilities and challenging behaviour, however. We feel cut off from the person. We get no feedback, or negative feedback, from them. When this happens, it is easy to allow more immediate feelings to determine the way we relate to the person.

> *Mick crouches in the corner of the room. If approached, he gets up, rushes through the centre, hits anyone he comes across and then returns to a corner. Support staff have tried every way of getting his attention – he will not focus on anything.*
>
> *I stand away from Mick so as not to disturb him and look at him very carefully. He is, in fact, concentrating very hard on one particular activity – digging his fingernails into the palm of his closed fist. It is not easy to spot: all you can see is the tendons moving on the back of his hand.*
>
> *I hold my hand up in the air so that he can see it and reflect his movements back to him. It takes about twenty minutes before he notices. Once he sees what I am doing, he begins to attend to me and focus on the movements of my fingers. I stop. He waits to see if I will start again. We start to alternate. I gradually bring down my hand and walk across to him, continuing with our 'conversation'. When I am near, he lets me place my hand on his and join in his movements. He starts to smile. Within ten minutes we are 'playing' all sorts of hand games, which he initiates. We are laughing together and feel a bond between us.*

If I had been asked, before I started to work with him, whether I valued and respected this man as an equal, rationally I should have said, 'yes'; but if I had been totally honest, then I should have admitted that my overriding connection with Mick at this time was the feeling that I was afraid of him. He behaved like a wild man. His humanity was obscured for me by his behaviour. It was difficult to stand back and view him other than through the spectacles of my own timidity. Once we were engaged with each other in a shared activity, which we both enjoyed, the perspective shifted. We were two people who were present for each other in every sense of the word.

More subtle than our immediate responses are the blueprints that we all carry with us: for example, the ways we related to our parents; our need to control; or, for some, the need to 'mother' with all that this implies. These are the walls we place round ourselves and they obscure for us who the other person actually is.

The mother of a woman with severe epilepsy and autism said that until she had learned to work interactively with her daughter, she felt that she had only been able to relate to her as a child who needed to be looked after, **but now she could relate to her as a person and talk to her all the time**.

When we work interactively, we work from inner person to inner person in the context of total respect for who the other person is, not who we feel they ought to be. Far from treating people as children, we are enhancing their dignity as individuals. We are taking part in a process that transcends disability and age.

> *Mehmet, who has severe cerebral palsy, has the use of one hand.*
>
> *Mehmet learns to use a sewing machine handle and together we make cushions and a quilt for his bedroom. He is very pleased with these. One day when I come in, he leans across and with great difficulty manages to grab a cushion and pass it to me. I say, 'Yes. We made that together, didn't we?'*
>
> *But it is not the acknowledgement that he wants. Mehmet wants me to be comfortable. It is something he can do for me. I realise that in all the years I have been working with Mehmet, I have been so focused on my own contribution to our partnership that I have not allowed him room to be himself, to feel about me as I do about him. I have not valued his feelings as a man.*

In order to relate to people, we need to empty ourselves of our own programmes and become vulnerable, so that we can learn from the other person as well as they from us. This is the equality that allows us to respect a person for who they are. We need to be able to enter their world on their terms so that they can relate without being afraid.

As Williams says of a relationship, describing a photograph of herself and her partner:

'This is me in "my world" and him in "my world", not always having to struggle to be in "their world".' (Williams, 1995)

This is respect, the respect which values another person enough to give them space to be their true selves, not 'respectability' with which it is so often confused. Respectability seeks to conform a person to 'our world' without giving value to their worth as an individual. While image is important in that it has a bearing on how a person is perceived and treated by our world, equally important is how a person is able to view themselves. Being socially acceptable is not enough if, at the same time, a person feels isolated – a prisoner in their own world. We need to learn to share our enjoyment and pleasure in each other's company so that people can grow in confidence and begin to reach out, on their terms, to a world beyond the private place in which they have been locked. This is how we can empower people and give them confidence. This is a beginning, the freeing-up of potential.

We need to ask ourselves if the interactions we are having with a person are enriching their lives. Does what we are doing enable them to be closer to their true selves and live more freely and confidently, at whatever level?

Finally, whatever our theoretical standpoint, is what we are doing working for this person? If we cannot answer 'yes', we need to re-examine our premises.

We must be able to answer: 'yes'.

Appendix

Training

By Pene Stevens

All over the country, services are having difficulty getting in touch with a small but significant proportion of clients who are not able to respond to the services which are provided for them.

Enough work has been done in this field to show that use of the techniques discussed in this book is an extremely effective way of empowering many of these people and transforming their lives. It usually costs very little but, because the work is relatively new and sometimes introduces premises that do not always sit comfortably with other approaches which have been tried, it requires thought and training.

If it is to be successful, the approach must be understood by senior management and incorporated into the structure of individual houses. Because it requires frequent interventions and embraces all aspects of people's lives, the only practical way that this work can be carried out is by unqualified staff, supervised and supported by senior qualified staff and therapists who are familiar with the techniques.

Obviously, all the people involved are going to require training at the appropriate level. Experience suggests that this training is best done in situ, working with the people with whom the support teams are having difficulty. Staff are far more likely to be convinced and given the confidence to try these techniques themselves if they have seen them work with people they already know.

Training presents enormous problems. One is the very high turnover of staff. Another was highlighted recently by a training officer who commented that in a group of eighteen unqualified staff who came recently for training, three were unable to read or write. In another group was an individual who spoke no English at all. In the same groups, there may well be graduates. The range is extensive.

On top of difficulties with understanding, there is the equally important question of emotional sensitivity. What are the qualities we are looking for? We may need to employ people on the grounds of availability who, in their own lives, have never had the security which enables them to abandon the more traditional position of control. In addition, they are almost certainly not familiar with the practice of being able to stand back and assess their own attitudes and interventions.

Against this background, how do we go about setting up an interactive approach in a group home, the aims of which will include reducing stress so that residents feel secure and building up their confidence?

Setting up such an interactive approach breaks down into three main areas:

1. How do we train staff?
2. How do we put training into practice?
3. How do we ensure that this style of practice is maintained?

1. How do we train staff?

Training needs to be experiential to enable staff to feel what it might be like to be the person with whom they are working. Role play and active exercises encourage relevant reflection and insight. For example, many people with severe learning disabilities have some degree of visual or hearing loss. Exercises using blindfolds or earmuffs, which mirror these disabilities, help staff to understand more clearly the kind of support people need – a person with visual loss finds it easier if they know where other people are in relation to them.

How does this apply to Ella, a woman with severe tunnel vision, who spends much of her time wandering round the fairly busy hallway? The 'blindfold' exercises highlight for staff the difficulties Ella faces in understanding what is going on round her. Feedback from this exercise includes remarks such as:

■ 'it was frightening'

■ 'I couldn't work out where I was although I knew the layout'.

This enables staff to understand why it is important actually to tell Ella where they are and what they are doing: 'I am just coming past you to go and turn off the washing machine.'

A light touch values Ella as a person and includes her in the activities that are going on in her house. She knows what is happening.

Sometimes, however, Ella is jostled by other residents and becomes confused and upset, throwing herself to the floor, screaming. Now it is staff who need to know what is happening. To help them understand, another training technique uses brief case studies describing similar situations and invites staff to reflect on why the person might be behaving in such a way and what would be the most helpful response.

In Ella's particular case staff need to:

■ recognise that she is upset and why

■ empathise with that feeling instead of trying to jolly her along

■ take action to show their support, that is, lie on the floor beside her until she is calm and ready to get up instead of trying to get Ella to her feet while she is still upset. Support staff are often surprised to find that this approach works.

This experiential training enables staff to move from their instinctive reaction to pull Ella up, to the perceptive response of reflecting back her state of mind in a way that values her, a response which has a successful outcome. The staff are working with Ella rather than against her.

This formal training needs to be set alongside and reinforced by in-house demonstration of techniques. It can be greatly helped by periodic evaluation of videotaped activities.

2. How do we put training into practice?

Training that helps staff to understand the best ways of supporting people, reducing stress and helping them to feel secure, needs to go hand in hand with techniques for building up their confidence such as Intensive Interaction and interactive activities.

Ella responds to rhythms of music she hears. Picking up on this, staff focus with her on drumming, at which she becomes very proficient. She begins to smile and laugh out loud in a way she rarely has before. Through watching video recordings, staff notice that Ella's posture changes from being hunched up to an upright position, and her gestures become more open and expansive. At the same time, since she is getting more one-to-one interaction, and therefore staff are talking to her more frequently to explain what is happening, Ella's speech and vocabulary improve. Staff can see that she is becoming more confident.

Underlying all these approaches is the importance of teaching staff careful and accurate observation skills. House leaders need to take the lead, spending time with residents, pointing out to staff what they see and initiating discussion. Staff need to know that their observations will be valued and considered by house leaders. Time must be set aside for staff to practise such skills. More importantly, staff need to feel that observation and 'being with people' is a part of their role. Domestic chores, while they may provide an important source of interaction, should not be allowed to assume dominance, as they so often do.

3. How do we ensure that this style of practice is maintained?

Given that the house leader is aware, in the ways discussed above, of the needs of their residents, what are the factors that result in effective implementation of the approach in one house but not in another? For example, most homes have individual care plans but they are not always carried out.

The structure needs to be clear. In the author's service, which consists of homes for people with severe and profound disabilities and extra support needs, small key-teams have been developed around each person, consisting of a leader (in this case a qualified nurse) supporting and supervising two support workers who key-work an individual. These teams meet regularly, with each member of staff having an individual supervision session every month between meetings. Every six months, all staff take part in a study day.

Staff need to be clear what is expected of them. House leaders need to emphasise that the main work centres around the individual and their care plan. Significant interactions must be recorded on daily checklists. Staff need to know that their work is going to be examined in depth, both in supervision – where the emphasis will be on their skills, thoughts and feelings about their key-resident – and in client care meetings – where the emphasis is more on the resident.

While the key-worker is responsible for an individual, the team will be involved when the key-worker is away. The key-worker is accountable for the carrying out of the care plan and so exerts peer pressure on any team member who is not performing to standard.

The quality of the care plan is vital. Records need to be carefully designed so that staff see the need for keeping them. They must know that relevant information will be used: it will be evaluated and used as the basis for updating care plans at client care meetings. House leaders must check every aspect of the care plan. New needs and relationships will be supported.

So what makes one house effective and another not? It is evident that clear and informed leadership is crucial with high expectations and good communication. The more that people understand what is expected of them, the less need there is to chase them on an individual basis.

The benefit of this style of working is a more interactive team with increased motivation which focuses on enabling rather than caring and on empowering rather than controlling. The emphasis is on the resident and, as their skills increase, there is more job satisfaction and therefore lower staff turnover. The purpose of the paperwork in such a process is clearly seen and understood by all staff.

In order to train sufficient people, including where necessary introducing the relevant techniques to house leaders, it would help in large service areas to employ one or more practice development officers, whose duties would include visiting each of a group of homes or residential units once every week to pick up exactly what is going on. In this way they could highlight the needs of individual service users, picking up on particular difficulties; for example, how is it best to work with a man who is hypersensitive to sound? Practice development officers would then come back with video analyses and role play, spending time with individual support staff and helping the whole team to develop better and more effective ways of communication and interaction.

While practice development officers would need to include shift work in their remit, so that they can reach the whole team, they should not be regarded as an extra pair of hands. Their role should be to stand back, observe and train. In order to attract the right calibre candidate and so that such training is seen as fundamental to practice by management, the practice development officer would need to be employed at the level of an H-grade nurse, depending on their profession. This would ensure that a nurse, for example, could be research-based. A person would not have to leave clinical practice in order to pursue their career.

While this may seem impractical for small agencies, it is important to remember that the approaches outlined above can be cost-effective, as well as transforming the lives of people who have, until now, been seen as beyond the reach of our skills. However the service is delivered, to be effectively embedded it must be seen as being valued by management.

References

Barron J & Barron S (1992) *There's a Boy in Here*. New York: Simon and Schuster.

Birath G [no date] Personal communication.

Caldwell P (1996) *Getting in Touch: Ways of working with people with severe learning disabilities and extensive support needs*. Brighton: Pavilion Publishing/Joseph Rowntree Foundation.

Dunbar R (1996) *Grooming, Gossip and the Evolution of Language*. London: Faber and Faber.

Ephraim G (1986) *A Brief Introduction to Augmented Mothering*. Playtrack pamphlet. Radlett, Hertfordshire: Harperbury Hospital.

Ephraim G [no date] Personal communication.

Hewett D & Nind M (1998) *Interaction in Action*. London: David Fulton.

Howlin P (1997) *Autism: Preparing for adulthood*. London: Routledge.

Jolliffe T, Lansdown R & Robinson C (1992) Autism: a personal account. *Communication* **26** (3) 12–19.

Nind M & Hewett D (1994) *Access to Communication*. London: David Fulton.

Peeters T (1997) *Autism: From theoretical understanding to educational intervention*. London: Whurr Publishers Ltd.

Robinson T (1989) In: A Brechin and J Walmsley (Eds) *Making Connections: Reflecting on the lives of people with learning disabilities*. London: Hodder and Stoughton.

Stern D (1985) *The Interpersonal World of the Infant*. London: Basic Books, Harper Collins.

Weekes L (date unknown) *A Bridge of Voices*. Radio programme. London: BBC Radio 4.

Williams D (1992) *Nobody Nowhere*. London: Doubleday.

Williams D (1995) *Jam Jar*. Film. London: Channel 4.

Williams D (1996) *Autism: An inside-out approach*. London: Jessica Kingsley Publishers.

You Don't Know What It's Like

Finding ways of building relationships with people with severe learning disabilities, autistic spectrum disorder and other impairments

Phoebe Caldwell with Dr Matt Hoghton

Originally published by Pavilion as a single volume in 2000

Introduction

Ever since I first started working with people with learning disabilities in big hospitals, and subsequently in the services that succeded them, I have been looking for ways to develop relationships with people who are difficult to reach. Such people may have severe learning disabilities and are often very withdrawn, or have behaviour patterns which separate us from them. In either case, there is a gulf between us – a gulf of confusion, or perhaps anger and fear – that leads them to reject us and may lead us to reject them. The relationship between us becomes distorted – mothering or control may replace respect and solidarity. We do not know how to bridge the gap.

This book is a companion volume to *Person to Person,* which was the outcome of freelance work following four years of work supported by the Joseph Rowntree Foundation. It explores innovative ways of getting in touch with people who are difficult to reach. While its focus is on individuals with autistic spectrum disorder (ASD), it also includes reflections on other behaviours that we label as 'challenging' or 'maladaptive' behaviour. Not everyone with ASD has learning disabilities and, where an able person has severe ASD, this can mask their ability – they present as much less able than they are. However, there are people with learning disabilities who also fall within the autistic spectrum; it is this group that I shall mainly focus on in this book.

The book takes up the theme that each individual perceives the world differently but that this may be especially true of people with severe learning impairments whose behaviour we find difficult to work with. It does not set out to be an exhaustive manual. Rather, it is a series of reflections on the ways we think about and work with people with a wide range of disturbed behaviours. In all cases, it tries to look for creative ways of working which are based on understanding **what a person is experiencing** and **what it is that their behaviour is trying to tell us**.

One of the book's starting points is a series of questions I was asked during a training day for managers of community homes for people with severe learning disabilities. The first questioner asked what I would do about a person who greeted the speaker every morning with personally offensive names. Would I agree that one should ignore undesirable social behaviour? The second said that, living as we do in a world where we are liable for our actions, should we not be thinking in terms of training the people we work with to take responsibility? The final questioner asked if I believed in punishment (as in punishment and reward). In the course of this book, I hope to address the attitudes that underlie these questions.

The other starting point is an incident that happened more than 20 years ago. I had just begun working with people with severe learning difficulties and challenging behaviour in a long-stay hospital which has since closed. A woman with very severe ASD was extremely upset. A colleague suggested she sit down. She put her face close to his and shouted:

'You don't know what it's like! You don't know what it's like!'

She was unable to elaborate on this cry for help – it was the only time we ever heard her speak – but I can hear her now. What she said has remained deeply engraved in my mind and periodically I have reflected on it.

Two different realities

At one end of the spectrum we meet the language of control and at the other, a cry for help, a window opening on a landscape of desperation. These two different realities stand in stark contrast to each other. On the one hand, we have our need to contain a variety of behaviours which may be unacceptable for one reason or another. On the other hand, we have an individual's cry for help which, in spite of goodwill, is not always being heard within the services we offer to people with learning difficulties/ disabilities and disturbed behaviour.

Contemplating this divide, a colleague said: *'We need a new paradigm for working with challenging behaviour. We need to see it in a different way.'*

Reviewing recent work on the 'theory of mind', Dunbar (1997) reminds us that although we are born egocentric, by the age of four we are able to understand that others may think and feel differently to ourselves.

The problem is that, in spite of this intensionality – our capacity to know that another person can have a different point of view from our own – we do not always act on it. When I am teaching, I find that one of the things people find most difficult is to take into account that others may perceive the world we all share in a completely different way. In our day-to-day interactions we make enormous assumptions, based on our own sensory intake, about the way others are perceiving and processing their experience. This mind-set can also get built into strategies for care which, although well-meaning, do not allow for the ways in which a particular person encounters their world.

For example, a person with severe learning disabilities who also has ASD may find it extremely stressful to handle change – they do not have the flexibility to cope when an event turns out to be different to that which they had anticipated. They cannot marry the two different images, what they expected to happen with what is actually happening now. Nevertheless, we frequently persist in programming in opportunities for change on the grounds the person will 'get used to it'. However, this throws the person into an impasse and can be a trigger for rising stress and consequent 'difficult' behaviour. The situation can be stabilised by reducing the incidence of change and, if the change is predictable, working out ways of letting an individual know that it is going to happen so that they have time to work through the idea.

The purpose of this book is to help us set aside our own reality and enter into worlds which people are struggling to interpret, worlds where people respond to completely different sets of sensory perception to those which we experience in our so-called 'normal' world.

Subjective language and experience

An enquiry of this nature immediately runs up against the difficulties of how we can transfer our perceptions of feelings to each other, since the only language we have to describe them accurately is subjective.

As adults, we view the behaviour of other people through distant eyes – we see it from the outside, forgetting that it is also part of the range, or at least within the potential range, of our own responses. For example, those of us who experienced temper tantrums as children will recall the all-embracing explosion that can be triggered by conflict with reality. Nothing exists but over-the-top blind rage. Our response to frustration is as if we were life-threatened – and indeed the ego does feel itself to be in danger of extinction. We are swamped with adrenaline, we have 'become' our feeling. We are not accessible to reason.

It is interesting to put this insider's view of a temper tantrum alongside Bennett's analysis of the 'fight response' (1998). She describes the physical effects of adrenaline that accompany this and charts the build-up to aggression. In particular, she discusses the impact this has on crucial areas of functioning: the effects of adrenaline interfere with the ability to communicate, respond appropriately and think rationally, amongst other impairments. Bennett shows how we can identify the various stages of build-up through our observations of physical behaviour and discusses appropriate techniques to aid de-escalation.

Why then, if we can chart the progress of a difficult behaviour so accurately, should it also help us to know how it feels to experience it? For example, isn't it enough to 'know about' autism? Why should we need to know about what it feels like?

Part of the problem is that the word 'feeling' has different meanings. For some people, it is such an emotive word that they reject insight and empathy as ways of perception. Throughout this book, I use 'feeling' in the sense of how we experience sensory intake. I find it helpful to know how the person I am working with sees, hears, touches and is touched by the world, and if they perceive it differently from the way I do. I need to know this in order to avoid basing remedial and therapeutic strategies on the false premise that we are both operating from the same sensory model.

In this book, I want us to try to look at difficult behaviours from the inside – to walk into subjective experience deliberately, with our eyes wide open. We can then begin to view problems not just from a distance but to know what the people we are working with are feeling.

I am suggesting that, although this can be a dangerous path since it embraces the risks of projection, if we are not prepared to empathise in its deepest sense, we risk the equally hazardous alternative of omnipotence and control. To share feeling, even the attempt to share it, enlarges and deepens our understanding. At the same time, however, we have to monitor our perception, trying always to bring together the rational and the empathetic approaches. If we achieve this, we may uncover questions to be answered which we would have missed if we had maintained a detached standpoint.

Enhancing empathy

Because attempts to share the subjective experience of others can lead us into situations that are fraught with painful relationships, and also because to change a person's gender in the pursuit of disguise might render interactions psychologically untrue, I have used a variety of ways of presenting personal material. Wherever possible, permission has been sought. Where it has seemed that it might be damaging to raise the issue of permission, and where there are groupings of behaviours, I have made use of imaginative reconstructions, sometimes to the extent of complete personalisation, standing in for an individual, putting myself in their place. However, I must emphasise that all the encounters relayed in this book are factual, and actually happened.

While being aware of the dangers of projection, (grafting my feelings onto other people) and introjection (taking on board the feelings of other people and failing to distinguish between these and those which properly belong to myself), this approach has the advantage of enhancing empathy. Using material which is generally available (particularly that written by high-functioning people with ASD about their experiences of the world they live in), and ideas gained from talking to people who have some insight into their condition, together with fragments from my own work with individuals, I hope to be able to build up pictures that allow us to see how the world might be for others. I shall approach this task by asking such questions as:

- What messages is an individual getting from the world in which they live?

- Which of these messages has meaning for them?

- Which of these messages do they perceive as frightening, and is this is leading them to behave as they do?

- Can we meet their needs? If not, can we modify their environment?

Summary

In this section we looked at:

- the two points of view – society's need for control versus an individual's cry for help

■ intensionality – the capacity to see another person's point of view

■ the need to set aside our own reality

■ the possibility of calling on our own experience, such as with temper tantrums

■ the benefits of knowing what ASD feels like as well as knowing what it is

■ the value of an empathetic approach

■ sources of information about 'feelings'.

Chapter 1

'Is he one of us?'
The consensus of acceptable response

Whether we have impaired faculties or not, each one of us carries round a different version of 'reality' – our own point of view of the world we inhabit. The way I see things is the outcome of what I inherited from my parents, plus the whole pick-and-mix pattern of my experience and the unique way these two have interacted. The way that I react to particular circumstances is largely, if not wholly, determined by how my brain assesses the current situation in the light of previous experience. However, this assessment is also dependent on how well my senses are functioning and, even if they are functioning correctly, whether their intake is being properly processed.

Although we all have different 'realities', most of us operate within the consensus of acceptable response. We identify with people who are, by our standards, predictable – we know roughly how they will respond and are surprised and put out if they react in an unexpected way. The phrase 'Is he one of us?' encapsulates this idea. We form social, political and cultural groups on the basis of what we have in common. Conversely, we exclude those we find unpredictable.

Impairment and disability, by definition, may cause separation from the norm of experience. Although we all inhabit the same world, if my senses are impaired, my perception of what others experience may be not just a different viewpoint, I may be looking at the landscape through a totally different lens – and one that is physically damaged. For example, I may be limited by sensory deficits such as impaired vision or hearing. I may find it difficult to follow what people are saying and be 'slow on the uptake'. However, whatever the limitations of my sensory intake, or the difficulties

I have in processing it, I am still a human being. Although my perception may be different, the world itself is just as much mine as yours.

Detaching ourselves from our own vision

Those of us who are working with people who are disabled often find it extremely difficult to put aside our own reality and always remember that John, for example, has tunnel vision and cannot see any signs that we make to him outside his visual field. However much we know what his difficulty is, in day-to-day interaction our brains may persist in superimposing our version of reality on his, so that we are unable to make the necessary imaginative leap to see the world through his restricted eyes. There is no tube in front of his eyes to remind us. Sometimes he responds and sometimes he cannot, and it is easy for us, making judgments from our standpoint, to see him as lazy, or worse, as stubborn ('he will not'). From where we stand, we may feel he is deliberately trying to manipulate us, to 'wind us up'. In fact, few people with severe impairments are manipulative. Although it may appear to us, from our viewpoint, that they are being so, most of their responses are instinctive rather than calculated. The blindness is ours and is the result of us projecting onto a person our sensory version of the world. It cripples our freedom to ask the crucial question, 'Why?', 'Why is it that John will happily respond sometimes and at others is completely uninterested?'

We may feel that this is very obvious but, in one form or another, this projection of our own sensory experiences onto the people we work with is a very easy trap to fall into. For example, a member of a support team may be berated because she has allowed her key-person to be mildly untidy, regardless of the fact that the house belongs to that individual. The team leader carries blueprints which are overly concerned with tidiness. She cannot distinguish between the restrictive blueprints which she carries from her own upbringing and the need to empower the individual. Her feelings of how the world 'ought' to be override her understanding of a situation where it is more important for the person to feel at home than to live in a 'super-tidy' environment.

I have laboured this point because it is crucial that we learn to detach ourselves from our own vision of what 'ought' to be, in favour of what will most empower the individual concerned. This also applies to particular methods of working. Faced with a difficult scenario, it can be easy to cling to a specific approach in the teeth of evidence that it is not working, sometimes for years at a time. Yet if we think about intractable issues in a creative manner, we have the opportunity to come up with new and possibly more effective ways of getting close to an individual.

The barriers of language

We often reinforce our one-sided view by using language which is biased in favour of confrontation. We talk about 'challenging' behaviour, a word which immediately sets up expectations and resonances of opposition. If we look at the associated words in a thesaurus, we find 'provocative', 'exciting', 'rousing', 'stimulating', 'galvanising' and 'defiant', next door to 'incitive' and 'inflammatory'. In other words, we associate the word 'challenging' with processes which involve an adrenaline 'high' and not with calm. This is no way to prepare ourselves to engage with someone whose behaviour may be the outcome of inner disorientation and distress.

We may actually approach our work in the frame of mind of 'us' and 'them', so that no matter how much we consciously intend to take an approach based on sharing and equality and empowerment, we are being master-minded by ideas of control and separation. We set ourselves apart so that we can 'manage' and 'contain' behaviours, isolating them by using such terms as 'targeting' in a way that sets us up as 'victims' and does not recognise the opportunity presented for interaction. Similarly, we talk about 'attention seeking' in a way that does not address an individual's overwhelming need, for whatever reason, for contact.

This emotive and adversarial language focuses on the problems that a person presents rather than the difficulties they face. In some cases, the language may be positively misleading. For example, if we say that someone is 'selectively deaf', the immediate implication is that the behaviour is of their voluntary choosing. Similarly, we may speak of a person with ASD who will not move as 'posing', when in fact what they are probably experiencing is a failure of the processing system, which leads to an uncoupling of the motor system. They are unable to move. (As discussed in Chapter 3, this may be one of the consequences of emotional overloading (Williams, 1996).) The immobility is not purposeful, but a form of evasive action devised by the brain in order to protect a person from the pain experienced in the process of fragmentation, which is brought on in response to 'feeling' the nervous system cannot handle. But if we see it from our own viewpoint, it makes it difficult for us to search for a creative way to move through their particular emotional difficulties.)

Clinical language helps us to analyse and contain situations we may find frightening or bizarre, but at the same time it separates us further from the person whose behaviour makes it difficult for us to be with them. For example, the word 'maladaptive' expresses our perspective; we see the behaviour from our point of view. We box ourselves in and are unable to take account of the psychological or perceptual obstacles and the whole raft of neurobiological discontinuities and distortions which may be part of a person's daily life (such as the variety of hypersensitivities and sensory distortions that people with ASD experience). Our responses become reactive rather than therapeutic. The more we can clarify both the therapeutic and neurobiological possibilities, the more likely we are to be able to assist the person we are trying to help.

The benefits of a more open approach

To illustrate the possibilities of a more open approach, I should like to return to the first of the three questions presented in the introduction: 'Would I agree that one should ignore undesirable social behaviour?'

The speaker described how he had had to face a daily barrage of name-calling for several months. I asked him whether he felt that ignoring the barrage had proved effective and he replied that it had not. Yet the same ritual was still being played out. Because the approach that was being taken (ignoring unacceptable social behaviour) was received wisdom – a respectable and well tested strategy – it was difficult to accept that in this instance, it was not proving effective.

We have to assume that this individual wanted to communicate but was unable to do so appropriately. It is probable that his pay-off was not the negative reaction (ignoring it) that he was getting from the person he was tormenting; almost certainly, at some earlier stage, he had raised a laugh from a third party. He wanted that positive and inclusive input again – it made him feel good. But he was going about it the wrong way. The way out of this type of impasse is not to continue giving the negative input of turning away to distance oneself, but to turn the interaction round so that the person feels included. Recalling some work I had done in a similar situation, I suggested it might work better if he gave the individual in question a big grin, agreeing and, saying something such as, 'Yeah, just my bad luck to be a… [whatever it is].'

In the similar situation, my 'holding' of a young man's inability to communicate in an acceptable way with older women, for whatever reason, was completely effective. It unblocked the impediment to communication and we became good friends. Had I clung to the idea that I should not tolerate such rudeness, we should never have moved beyond our mutual separation.

In his contribution to the book *Challenging Behaviour*, Emblem says,

'I have come to realise the limitations of ignoring the bad and rewarding the good. If you are really good (in the sense of skilled at your job), you can accept the bad and use it for good.' (Emblem *et al*, 1998)

The second question, which was a starting point for this book, about whether we should be training people to take responsibility, hinges on the word 'train'. In the sense that it was asked, 'training' is about power: I decide what someone shall learn and I arrange a programme to ensure that they do so. It is not about empowerment, which helps the person to understand what is going on and motivates them to want to take part. (A history that illustrates this, and the possible use of images that resonate for a person, is that of Mary in Chapter 7.)

Similarly, the third question, about punishment and reward, is also about control. Although the intention may be benign, the effect is separation. I hope that it will become apparent throughout this book that such an approach makes it very difficult for us to ask such vital questions as:

- What is happening in this person's brain that leads them to behave like this?

- What can I do to support them?

- Is the strategy we are using working for this person?

We have to be non-judgmental. We should not be thinking about what people ought to be doing but what they are doing and what it is telling us.

Summary

Suggestions for support staff in this section include:

- avoid stereotyping and labelling

- move beyond mutual separation

- if possible, accept 'bad' behaviour and use it for good.

Chapter 2

'I know what I'm doing'
Repetitive behaviours

At present, support staff are not always clear about why they are being asked to pursue particular programmes, especially some of those associated with people with ASD. It is easy to say, 'Oh he's autistic, therefore we work with him in such and such a way,' without knowing exactly what is going on in that individual's life and thus missing the urgency of a particular strategy.

What is it that Brenda is doing, for example, when she spends her days endlessly drawing houses – three windows and a door, terrace after terrace, street after street? Or when Jane draws tigers, always the same, endlessly stalking across the paper, wild faces turned towards the onlooker? It is easy to label this as repetitive, compulsive, fixated or stereotypic behaviour and dismiss it. From our point of view, this behaviour is a barrier to communication; it may make it extremely difficult for us to get in touch with a person. Not only do they ignore us in favour of their chosen activity, but they may also become extremely upset if we try to interrupt.

The degree of attachment to a fixation was brought home to me by Ed, a child who stored leaves in boxes. When the lawnmower drove through a pile of leaves, he rushed past distraught, shouting 'they are cutting my friends, they are killing all my friends.'

However, if we could learn more about such behaviour and understand something about what people are getting out of it, we might be able to use that understanding to get closer to them and work with them more effectively. To do this, we need to look at what able people with ASD say about what repetition does for them and why they need it.

The comfort of repetition

In her interesting and useful book *Nobody Nowhere*, Williams describes the onset and growth of her fascination with coloured specks in the air, how she first noticed them in dreams and how she gradually began to see them floating everywhere. She tells us how she focused on them and how doing so became her overriding occupation to the extent that she learned to exclude people in order to pursue them. She says that she was happy when she was with her spots and resisted being 'dragged back to understanding' when people spoke to her. As she grew older, she became afraid. She collected bits of coloured scraps and held them tightly, 'so she could fall asleep securely' (Williams, 1992).

Some people suggest that Williams' ASD is atypical, sufficiently unusual to make it difficult to generalise from her insights. As discussed in *Person to Person*, in practice I have always found it helpful to build on her experience, even when working with people who are low-functioning or whose ASD is genuinely linked to severe learning impairment.

Donna Williams is an exceptional human being, exceptional in the degree to which she has been able to reflect on her condition and make her insight available, unique in the depth to which she has explored how she feels. Because we find people with ASD so difficult to reach, it is easy to assume that they do not have access to the subtle world of feeling. From our standpoint of an ability to exchange, most people with ASD do not appear to experience feelings because they do not show them to us. As we shall see, this is because they find the world they live in too threatening in sensory terms. In practice, however, many are able to cope with reciprocal interchange of emotion if we work with them inside the secure world of their stereotype where they do not feel threatened.

Williams has made it possible for us to follow her into her world by her 'inside-out' approach, as she calls it. In her film, *Jam Jar* (1995), she uses metaphor to lead us through experiences which are acutely personal but also universal. Her coloured specks have become a jar of glass beads which sparkle in the light. She groups them by their similarities to show how they are related. She is a different bead and alone. With a breathtaking leap of imagination, she breaks out of her isolation by becoming 'a traveller who likes to visit'. Her body language changes and she laughs in her new freedom. This contrasts very strongly with a later sequence in the film, where she is playing with the beads and where, although she may be partially in control of this 'as demonstration', she gets caught up in the game she is playing – in her inner world. Her voice is that of a child who is lost in a game, for whom the game has taken over. The inner world is all that there is.

The fixation that Williams describes so clearly is visual – and it emerges that she is hypersensitive to vision (1992). What she was looking at as a child was particles in the air – perhaps as we should see motes in a dusty sunbeam – but the range of sources that can be used repetitively is endless, from innate self-stimulation through touch, sound and vision, to complicated rituals involving objects and activities from the outside world. Jenny, for example, endlessly runs small pebbles through her hands. It is not a question of intelligence. Professor Temple Grandin, who has described her ASD in a number of books and interviews, speaks of her own fixation with running grains of sand through her hand (Grandin & Scariano, 1986).

Thérèse Jolliffe says:

'Up to the age of seven or eight, I spent hours enjoying running my fingers over and scratching on the edge of my pillowcase, which had embroidery around it. I still do this now with different surfaces, especially if they feel good and make a small sound.' (Jolliffe *et al,* 1992)

Sometimes it is hard to identify the activities on which people are focusing. They may be hidden, such as digging fingernails into the palm of a clenched hand, or so unremarkable that we would discount them, such as a breathing rhythm. They may be what we would regard as socially unacceptable, such as picking dandruff from the head and looking at the white flecks; or they may be uncomfortable sounds such as teeth grinding, which we ignore. However, laying aside their exact origin and the exact form that the repetitions take, the most direct clue as to what an individual is getting out of them appears in Sian Barron's account of his childhood autism. He says:

'I loved repetition. Every time I turned a light on, I knew what would happen. It gave me a wonderful sense of security because it was exactly the same each time.' (Barron & Barron, 1992)

For those of us not in his position, this sounds strange. However, I have highlighted this because it is extremely important and I shall be referring to it again in this book (and do constantly when I am working and teaching.) While we need to explore the role of repetitive behaviours in producing endorphins in the brain which reduce the pain that is the outcome of sensory fragmentation (see Chapter 15), for now it is crucial to remember that when a person is using stereotypic behaviour, in a world of sensory chaos, **they know what they are doing**.

We should find doing the same thing, over and over again, boring. In order to see what is going on, we need to switch out of our own reality and move into the sensory world that a person with ASD is trying to process. We need to see why it is that a person should have an overwhelming need for repetition and security to the extent that they may become deeply disturbed if attempts are made to move them out of the world they are locked into. Why, when we can look round and see and hear and feel and understand our experiences (what is going on for us), and when there is nothing wrong with Sian's senses (he could see, hear and feel normally), why does he say that he found it comforting to know what was going on in his world? What is it that is so different and threatening for Sian about the world we share with him?

Summary

Suggestions in this section include:

- look carefully and non-judgmentally at what a person is doing, even if it has no immediate significance or seems bizarre

- ask yourself what they are getting out of their behaviour

- think about stereotypic and repetitive behaviours in terms of security in a world that does not make sense.

Chapter 3

'A whole lot of confused jumbles'
What ASD 'feels' like

Many of us have been taught to think about ASD in terms of a triad of impairments:

1. A deficit in language and communication

2. A deficit in ability to form social relationships

3. An impairment of the capacity to think flexibly and use imagination.

This is our point of view, a diagnosis that tells us how people with ASD appear to us – what to expect – but it doesn't tell us much about how such people feel, how they experience reality. There is a gap between how we as carers experience the difficulties ASD presents us with and what it is that people with ASD and other difficult behaviours are living through.

In recent years a number of people have written and spoken eloquently about how they experience autism – what it is like for them. Considering the extraordinary breadth of manifestation of autism, their accounts paint a very consistent picture. Of course, the authors are self-selected, being high-functioning and able to write, but in practice, even from this narrow base, it has proved extremely helpful to think about what they are saying when working with less able people. Unfortunately, their accounts are rather scattered so it seems useful to draw some of them together for the benefit of those who do not have access to all of them.

Sensory overload

This is Lindsey Weekes, speaking on a radio programme about his childhood:

'I'd always had problems with getting a sort of coherency out of the world unless I could be in somewhere I was very familiar with like my room, in my space, because it's very easy in autism for the world to fragment under pressure.

'If I get a lot of sensory overload then I just shut down … you get what's known as fragmentation … it gets really weird, like being tuned into forty TV channels at once.

'You just get this whole overload of sensory impressions – if you get that when you're four, it's total panic. You're going to run full tilt into a wall or into the traffic, anything to stop the sensory overload happening because I'd much rather have pain … it's one overriding sensation rather than getting a whole lot of confused jumbles. When you're adult it's freaky enough, but when you're a kid it's really bad.' (Weekes, undated)

And again:

'If your senses start to become fragmented or if you start to feel reality slipping away from you, you want to focus on something. Sometimes they don't focus exclusively on pain like smashing into a brick wall, it's just as easy to flick a light on and off very rapidly, like strobe lights at a disco and you just focus on that.' (Weekes, undated)

Thérèse Jolliffe says:

'The world of the non-verbal person with autism is chaotic and confusing. A low-functioning adult who is not toilet-trained may be living in a completely disordered sensory world. It is likely that they have no idea of their body boundaries and that sights, senses and touch are all mixed together. It must be like seeing the world through a kaleidoscope and trying to listen to a radio station that is jammed with static and has a faulty volume control all at once.' (Jolliffe *et al*, 1992)

How can we possibly put ourselves in this position? Searching for an image that meets the above descriptions, I should like to borrow the phrase, 'landscapes without landmarks', used by Grant in the completely different context of dementia (1998). In ASD, it is not that the landmarks are being eroded or erased as they are in dementia (and in the case of profound disability, they may have never been there). Rather, the description fits because a person's sensory perceptions of existing landmarks are being progressively shredded so that they are unrecognisable. Under this bombardment, the floating bits merely add to confusion as the individual gropes not only for destination but also for starting point – where they are now.

> *Jilly bangs her head on a particular shape of carpet pattern when she is overloaded, holding on to the one piece of coherent reality she can identify.*

It is clear that what we are looking at is a battleground, not only with the physical senses but also with tumultuous emotional experience – what Williams calls 'a love-hate relationship with oneself' (1995). A colleague has remarked that the emotions can be completely labile: 'You reach out for sorrow and get despair' (O'Brian, 1988).

A struggle is in progress between the order that we take for granted in our world and disintegration. Survival is the issue and victory is by no means assured.

According to Grandin, whereas low-functioning people may not understand what is said to them and therefore be unable to reply, high-functioning people with ASD may grasp what is said to them but still be unable to organise a response. She speaks of the appalling frustration this caused her (Grandin, 1995). Similarly, Jolliffe says:

'Sometimes when I really need to speak and can't, the frustration is terrible. I want to kick out at people and objects, throw things, rip them and break them and occasionally to scream.' (Jolliffe *et al*, 1992)

Trying to process sensory intake seems to be like a conveyor belt going faster and faster. Williams says: 'I keep running, running, running, trying to keep up (1995).

It helps if we use the model of a bottleneck. The visual images, sounds and touches come in undistorted, but are unable to pass through the narrowing neck. The pressure builds up and the images fragment.

We, the outsiders, can get a little idea of the extraordinary lengths to which the human spirit will go to bring order into chaos when the question we ask of a person with ASD today is answered perfectly tomorrow. For the person with ASD, it has taken that long to process the reply. We dismiss the endeavour which keeps going for that length of time, battling to assemble the fragments into a pattern, because we cannot see it. The only evidence we have of the heroic struggle is that the person we want to talk to takes an irritatingly long time to respond. We see it from our viewpoint and the gulf between our world and theirs widens.

The first thing we need to understand is that **the most likely explanation for an outburst in a person with ASD is that they are unable to cope with the sensory overload they are experiencing.** They are not 'just being difficult'.

The senses

Distortions and break-up of incoming stimuli can occur in any of the senses and, according to Gillingham (1995), are mainly related to hypersensitivities; for example, a person may find certain sounds acutely painful. Again, we can get some idea of what they are experiencing from their accounts.

Seeing is difficult. Objects tend to jump around and slide away. The brain focuses on particular detail rather than on the whole. Williams says:

'I never see the whole. If I see the leaves, I don't see the tree.' (Williams, undated)

In the film *A is for Autism* (1992) a small boy says:

'It is difficult for me to concentrate on things, particularly if they are important. The more important they are, the more they seem to slide away.'

We know now that this type of visual disturbance, which is the effect of scotopic sensitivity, can sometimes be markedly reduced by wearing tinted lenses. Williams (1996) gives accounts of the beneficial effects of Irlen lenses.

I had wrongly assumed that the difficulties of testing would make it impossible to work in a similar way with people with autism who also had very severe behavioural or learning disabilities – until recently, as the following history describes:

Jake clearly has severe learning disabilities as well as ASD. He sat with his head down and eyes screwed up in a way that suggested he found vision difficult. When staff tried a pair of green lenses on, he pushed them away. But when they followed this with pink lenses, he kept them on, his head came up and he started to look round the room in an interested way. This reaction has now been noted with a number of clients.

It is important to realise that the actual colour that works to correct this dysfunction (scotopic sensitivity) can be very specific and needs testing as it differs from individual to individual. The suggestion is that individuals require a particular frequency to adjust the input so that it is more in synchronisation with the capacity to process. This may mean speeding up or slowing down the input, so different and very specific colours are required to correct the dysfunction of each individual. The work described above does not constitute a test for scotopic sensitivity, it was only an indication of possibility, which has to be followed by a professional test.

Regarding the visual dysfunctions experienced by some people with ASD, there is no guarantee of continuity. As a colleague put it: *'Mummy in a red dress can be a different person to Mummy in a blue dress.'*

Also, dimensions can shift. A room that appears to be of normal size one minute can collapse the next. This is a life-threatening scenario. Almost all childhood accounts of people with autism speak of terror or of terrifying situations. It is not surprising that they react with such desperation, as Jolliffe says:

'I am frightened of so many things that can be seen: people, particularly faces, very bright lights, large machines and buildings that are unfamiliar, my own shadow, the dark bridges, rivers, canals and the sea.' (Jolliffe *et al*, 1992)

One of the most difficult things is to look at people. Williams describes eye contact as acutely painful (1992) and Jolliffe says:

'People do not appreciate how unbearably difficult it is to look at people. It is terribly frightening.' (Jolliffe *et al*, 1992)

We get the same story when we look at touch and sound. Weekes says:

'I don't particularly like being touched, touch is not pleasant for me at all, unless I'm warned in advance that I'm going to experience this sensation. Otherwise, I don't like it.' (no date)

Speaking of his childhood, he says:

'People were touching me and pulling me around like they do with all kids and I was reacting badly to it.' (no date)

Grandin, who is hypersensitive to touch, says that light touch is like a cattle prod which fires off every nerve in her body. She may be able to feel the scratch of uncomfortable clothes a fortnight later. On the other hand, deep pressure may be helpful. In her book, *Emergence: Labelled autistic* she describes how, when she was quite young, she built herself a pressure machine which helped her to desensitise her skin (Grandin & Scariano, 1986).

Many sounds, particularly high-frequency sounds, are extremely painful and frightening. Again, we may have a life-threatening situation, when a toilet being flushed may sound like an express train about to run one over. But the painful sounds may also be very small, for example, the click of a ballpoint pen. Voices at normal level may hurt. In *Person to Person*, it was noted how the incidence of Ben's attacks on people dropped markedly when support staff deliberately spoke in very soft voices (see page 49).[3]

People and emotional overload

According to Williams, it is not just sensory information from the outside world that can cause overload, but also the bodily feelings generated by emotional contact which may be perceived as hostile. The brain just can't process the information fast enough and people have problems keeping up. Internal physical feelings become disconnected from the events that set them off. Instead of giving emotional information the feelings may come in terrifying gusts which are unrelated (in time) to their inception. Williams says:

'Where meaning and significance connect so rarely in the context that provokes them, the emotional feelings that these cause may be felt extremely, yet out of context. Without comprehension to make sense of them, the effect on the body may be so extreme that it is too much for the body to sustain.' (Williams, 1996)

She goes on to describe how intense, out-of-control physical sensations may be wrongly perceived as danger and an attack on the body: 'An adrenaline rush puts the body on hyper-alert' (Williams, 1996).

---

3 For further extensive information and examples of hypersensitivity, see Gillingham (1995).

To defend themselves, people may attack others or self-injure. The brain may become dissociated – switch to 'autopilot'; there may be a systems shut-down of communication and/or movement, or there may be hypersensitivity. If the brain learns that emotional experience causes overload, this can lead to avoidance, which becomes an integral part of a person's identity. In an effort to cut down on emotional overload, the brain may cut off from the motor system, so that the person freezes and is unable to move (Williams, 1996).

Sometimes a person can be helped out of this evasive action by powerful but non-threatening visual 'clues'. Since the person is frozen, it is important to place these clues squarely within their visual field – they must be able to see them without moving.

> *Beth, who has ASD, gets locked into a 'loop' of laughing which is persistent. It can go on for twenty minutes and has nothing to do with finding a situation funny. Her hands and head are tilted at the ceiling. She likes coffee. Offering her coffee and showing her a mug does nothing until this is placed above her head in front of her eyes so she can clearly see it. She comes out of the loop at once and accepts the drink.*
>
> *It seems possible that, in order to be successful, the 'clue' has to be presented through a channel other than that which is blocked. In Beth's case, although she can hear, her hearing does not appear to be operational when she is offered coffee which is out of her line of sight. This does not mean she does not want it. As soon as the coffee is put where she can see it, she can take on board what is on offer through her unblocked sense of vision, so she stops at once. She has made the move, from the inner world she was locked into, back to the outside world.*

The need for clues may be so great that a person is unable to proceed until they have actually seen someone else do an activity. Even 'objects of reference' (objects which are an integral part of an activity used as prompts) are not enough, the person must have a role model so that they can copy the whole sequence of the activity.

> *Jeff is unable to comply when his key-worker shows him a slice of bread and points to the toaster. Eventually his key-worker tires of waiting and puts his own slice in. Immediately Jeff puts his in. He is not unwilling but unable to make the necessary movements until he has a behavioural template to copy.*

Sometimes the effect of shut-down may be less severe. The person starts activities but comes to a halt and stands waiting for help. This is sometimes interpreted as laziness but it is not. The person needs visual clues to re-establish the connection between the brain and the motor system.

Thérèse Jolliffe explains how the complexity of increasing stimulation affects her:

'Objects are frightening. Moving objects are harder to cope with because of the added complexity of movement. Moving objects which also make a noise are even harder – you have to try to take in the sight, movement and further complexity of noise. People are the hardest of all to understand because, not only do you have to try to cope with the problem of just seeing them, they move about when you are not expecting them to, they make various noises and, along with this, they place all sorts of demands on you which are just impossible to understand.' (Jolliffe *et al*, 1992)

Warburton says:

'I like reading about inanimate objects – human beings are too complex. I never know how to behave when they are around. I feel like a foreigner in an alien world except when I'm on my own.' (Warburton, undated)

Eye contact is a particular problem. In *Person to Person* I describe the history of Paula who is extremely disturbed and has frequent outbursts against people and property. However, she becomes able to make close physical contact if I look away while I speak to her. She clearly enjoys this occasion and also other interactions which use an impersonal approach.

If people are avoiding eye-contact, it is better to look away when talking to them and it may also help to use indirect speech. This makes it much easier to for them to respond and interact; it takes off the personal pressure which leads to stress so that they can process what is going on more easily.

A more able person may prefer to write rather than speak. Weekes explains:

'Writing is my preferred method of communicating with the world…because it's impersonal. I don't have to have anything to do with the person I'm writing to, I can express myself better, the pressure is off. Sitting here talking to you, you're a presence…you're there. [It feels like] another person invading my world.' (Weekes, undated)

A person with ASD may not even understand their connection with other people. Jolliffe says:

'I cannot remember ever thinking about where my mother, father, brother and sister were, they did not seem to concern me. I did not realise they were people and that people were supposed to be important.' (Jolliffe *et al*, 1992)

While Barron remembers: 'I didn't know what people were for' (Barron & Barron, 1992).

For us, this is an extraordinary statement with its implication that it is possible to pass through at least part of one's life in a state that is totally disconnected from other human beings. This is an aloneness which is beyond our comprehension.

A sense of self

We can also consider the question of how people with ASD perceive themselves. Some of the accounts of high-functioning people bear witness to a strong sense of self and of themselves as separate from others. Weekes realised other people were different but assumed he had got it right and they were all wrong (Weekes, undated). Williams says it was late in her life that she realised that others had a different perception to hers, (Williams, NBC film). Weekes says that he likes himself as he is and would not wish to change and Grandin agrees:

'If I could snap my fingers and be non-autistic, I would not – because I wouldn't be me. Autism is part of who I am.' (Grandin, 1995)

In a particularly moving interview, Williams, who also likes herself, expresses her sorrow at being unable to use all her senses in an integrated way; that is, to process all of them simultaneously (Williams, NBC film).

It is probably not helpful to try to generalise, as people with ASD have as wide a range of experience as those outside it. However, what we can say is that they may have a very poor sense of boundary which affects their sense of who and where they are. For example, Williams describes how she spent two years trying to shake off a hand that she did not realise was hers. It was a floating object in front of her. This seems to have been because her brain, in an effort to cope with more sensory input than it could handle, had learned to switch off either 'seeing' or 'feeling'. She calls it 'going into mono' and when she is in this state, she only processes one of these senses at a time. As she only saw or felt but never did both at the same time, she never got the idea of organic connection between her hand and the rest of her (Williams, 1996).

Some confusion arises from how we define 'self' – whether we define it in terms of physical limits, 'where my skin ends', or as my inner feeling of myself, knowing 'who' rather than 'what' I am. They are not the same thing. For example, I know who I am – and should I be unfortunate enough to lose an arm, I should still be that same self. But I might well be wrong about my boundaries since my phantom limb might be giving me incorrect information about its presence. Even for those of us without ASD, our sense of boundary can be very elastic. If I am in my car, it becomes part of me in a sense, and the boundary of me is my wheels on the road. With ASD, you may have no idea of which bits of yourself are you and what belong to other people. This can be intensely invasive and it is not surprising that so many such people deliberately seek solitude.

Thérèse Jolliffe says:

*'Reality to an autistic person is a confusing, interacting mass of events, people, places, sounds and sights. There seem to be no boundaries, order or meaning to anything. **A large part of my life is spent trying to work out the pattern behind everything.**'* (Jolliffe et al, 1992)

It is possible to speculate that, in the future, we shall view failure to perceive boundaries (and, where it arises, to have a clear sense of self) purely as the outcome of dysfunctional processing of sensory intake. Sometimes this can, potentially at least, be partly corrected by use of Irlen lenses where the user finds them physically acceptable. A positive physical reaction has been strongly marked, even in people with severe behavioural difficulties or who have severe learning disabilities in addition to their autism.

Richard, who has ASD, has also been labelled as showing psychotic behaviour (and has been severely withdrawn as well as challenging). When he starts walking round with a smile on his face and looking at everything in a new and interested way, one can only speculate at the life-changing relief he is experiencing. Before wearing his tinted lenses, he would frequently start an activity and then come to a halt, needing someone to show him how to complete it. Although it is only two months since he received his new lenses, it appears that he can now usually complete tasks. He is much more relaxed and interested in his surroundings.

When she first received her new maroon coloured lenses, Ivy took them off and put them on frequently but she now wears them much of the time. She decides when she wants them on or not. (It is as if at first she needed to compare her new world with her old.) Ivy is now calmer and spends much of her time with her head up looking round instead of looking down at her fingers as before.

Time and routine

In the world of sensory confusion, there is another flickering dimension to contend with, that of time. In her film, *Jam Jar*, Williams says:

'I was totally caught up in every moment. I never ever got the whole picture of me, I never got the whole picture of who I was yesterday, who I am today, where I am going tomorrow. I never got the whole picture of even a whole day or who anyone was in relation to anybody else and so that is a huge turmoil inside of a person.' (Williams, 1995)

If we consider this, we can begin to see why it is that people with ASD find change in routine so difficult to handle. In the middle of incoherency, they sometimes just about grasp a pattern. All their energy is focused on this, trying to hold it together and then suddenly, meaning slips away and they are plunged back into chaos. The anticipated picture that they have pieced together in their mind does not marry with the visual image of the situation they find themselves in so they become stressed. No wonder people react as though to catastrophe – in their sphere of perception this is exactly what they are experiencing. As Lindsey Weekes puts it:

'Autistic people like sameness, simply because they know what's coming next, things are more coherent. I liked [as a child] to wake up and know what was going to happen to me on that day as far as possible – otherwise there were tantrums for them.' (Weekes, undated)

The sanctuary

In this kaleidoscope world, we begin to see why people with ASD develop rituals that may appear bizarre to us, but which for them are refuges, safe places where they feel they are in control.

Is such an approach really so foreign to us? If we look back at our childhood behaviour, we may see snatched pleasure or security derived from activities such as running a finger over corrugations or a stick along railings, counting endlessly to the point where counting becomes obligatory (otherwise something dreadful will happen). We play games which ritualise our fantasies – 'Lines and Squares', hopping from one paving stone to the next, never treading on a line or the horror will get us, whatever its form. We daydream, going off into worlds of clicks and hums and repetitive words. A child whose family circumstances entailed constant house moves, licked the walls of her room so that it would be safely there for her to return to, ensuring its permanence.

What difference is there between this behaviour and that of Ray, who has to lick every lamp-post he passes? He is also looking for permanence in the turmoil of his chaotic experience. The child was lucky. Her background contained enough stability for her to grow through her uncertainty but Ray's environment continued to behave in an unpredictable manner. He found it comforting, and later compulsory, to continue his rituals in order to hold himself together.

For the person with ASD, it seems that these behaviours, whatever their origin, do represent security. They are signals the brain gives itself, which do not break up and therefore present no threat – in the midst of chaos they are reassuring and calming. The person knows what is happening when they are involved in them. We can think of them as hard-wired into the brain. As Jolliffe says:

'What other people call 'odd' hand movements and grimaces are not meant to annoy, they give a sense of control, safety and pleasure.' (Jolliffe *et al*, 1992)

After describing the extremely painful sensation of fragmentation, Weekes goes on to talk about an autistic person's fascination with strobe lights, how, at a disco amid all the noise:

'They just watch the strobe lights – really cool – in the middle of the whole thing – it just coheres.' (Weekes, undated)

If we look back at Williams' account of her fixation with specks of light (Chapter 2), we see that not only does the behaviour cut out painful input, it also becomes interesting in itself so that all attention becomes focused on it. Some people cut out altogether. Jolliffe also says she used to pull a big blanket over her head as it made her feel safer (Jolliffe *et al*, 1992).

In her moving poem, *Nobody Nowhere*, Williams tells us how lonely it can be:

'And the world can grow cold in the depths of your soul,
when you think nothing can hurt you until it's too late.' (Williams, 1992)

From our standpoint, because they are unable to share their feelings, we say that people with ASD do not experience them. Jolliffe would disagree – describing her own feelings she says: 'People with autism can be lonely and can love' (Jolliffe *et al*, 1992).

My own experience of working with people with ASD is that they almost always respond warmly and frequently show affection if one can speak to them in a language that their brain recognises as non-threatening, one that is based on the signals they give to themselves. This is illustrated in the following history.

I am asked to find a way of working with Vera who has severe ASD. This is the first time we have met. She finds people difficult, particularly strangers. She has a number of ways of 'cutting out':

■ *she puts her hand over her face*

■ *she puts her fingers in her ears*

■ *she puts your hand over her face*

■ *she turns her back on you*

■ *she becomes totally absorbed in rustling and folding a crisp bag, examining its shiny surfaces.*

I ask if I may sit next to her, pointing to myself and then the sofa beside her. She gives me a fractional nod of agreement. When I sit down, she turns her back and starts to fold her crisp bag but does not get up and move away. Moving into her language, I also start to play with a crisp bag. She can hear its characteristic rustle although she is not looking at me. After a few minutes, she looks over her shoulder. We start a conversation with each other – she rattles her crisp bag and I follow. Suddenly she flings herself across my lap and lies there, looking straight up at me and laughing as we talk to each other. This interaction goes on for about 20 minutes and ends when she loses my attention as I start talking to support staff about what we are doing. She sits up and turns away from me. I accept this, say goodbye and leave her.

Vera, who cannot bear people, particularly strangers, is perfectly able to let me know that she enjoys my company when I use 'her' language. It does not threaten her with overload and fragmentation and she and I are able to share our pleasure in each other.

Summary

What is it like to live in a landscape without signposts? Using the accounts of high-functioning people with ASD, it seems that they are experiencing the world we share in a different and often extremely frightening way:

■ they may be unable to cope with the sensory overload

■ they may be unable to handle feelings which become detached from events

■ they probably have no clear sense of boundary or of time

■ overload and fragmentation may lead to outbursts.

We can reach them in a non-threatening way if we use their language.

Chapter 4

'When's the bus coming?'
The uncertainty of time

How does it feel to live in a world governed by time and yet not be able to understand its dimensions? The idea of 'time' is part of our life-support system and we take it for granted. As we grow up, learning to tell the time is a landmark on the journey from dependence to independence. From that point on we can, at least potentially, organise our lives. We have learned that events happen in order and that there are intervals between them. We know what will happen and when – and we can predict what will happen in the future. Using time as a platform, we can take an overview – we are both attached to and participant in our lives.

Once we are aware of time, it is very difficult for us to visualise what life would be like without it. We cannot take it away and, although it is ever-present and we refer to it constantly, we hardly give a thought to it. Like the air we breathe, we take it for granted. It is hard for us to be aware of the tensions and anxieties that accompany an absence of this structure.

If we now put ourselves in the position of those for whom time is incomprehensible, we are not able to grasp the length of the intervals, although the same pressures are present for us as for the people in the world who do understand time. We may know, for example, that we have to catch the bus home – we shall be in trouble if we do not; someone will be cross with us or we will have to wait, or walk and maybe lose our way. Our life fills up with threatening unknowns. Double bind.

We learn clues to attach to our departure: maybe we have grasped the sequence and know our departure is after coffee, but we do not know how long after. We misread this clue and go and stand by the door with our coats as soon as tea-break is over, focusing on the bus coming. Better safe than sorry. Someone pushes past. Interrupting our theme disturbs us and throws us into uncertainty, underscoring our anxiety. We hit out, or hit ourselves.

This description of the anxiety that surrounds time is one that most readers will be familiar with in one form or another. It is easy enough to recognise: endless questions about who is coming when, or what is going to happen. We cannot answer these questions adequately because it is not possible for the enquirer to attach meaning to our reply – even if they can repeat it themselves, our words are sounds, empty of content.

The only way we can really appreciate the emotional impact of what it feels like to not understand the structure of time is to place ourselves in a situation with which we are probably all familiar: in this case, it is not that there is no structure, but that the structure as we know it fails. Let us suppose that we have invited our friend Nick to come over tomorrow afternoon. We predict with reasonable certainty that he will turn up after lunch. What happens if he fails to come?

We might wait a bit and then start to ask around. We telephone people we think might have seen him. Niggling worry builds up as we follow false trails. What's happened to Nick, the Nick we depend on? Has he had an accident? Our anxiety about his safety mingles with wondering about how we shall manage without him; he is part of our life-support system – that intricate web we weave round ourselves to nourish our existence. By following this scenario, we begin to understand that to live in a world which is governed by time but not to understand it, is to go through day after day constantly being topped up with anxiety about what will happen. As we can see, such anxiety can move swiftly from minor worry to panic.

A similar anxiety can be found in the lives of people who are more able but whose physical impairments prevent their taking charge of their lives.

> *Tom has cerebral palsy. He lives at home and is in a state of acute anxiety because he is not being supplied with the information he needs – no-one has thought it necessary to involve him in planning his timetable or to tell him of their decisions or even, perhaps, that these have not yet been made. As far as he can see, his day-service provision is slipping away. Assumptions have been made about his ability and preferences because his speech is not always easy to decode. However, he manages to describe how he sits at home and listens for the phone to ring from his college, to tell him what the next term's programme will be. It's all he has to do and the anxiety affects his behaviour. Once we have understood what is worrying him, he tells us that he is more confident now that we have listened to him.*

It is easy to generate anxiety and tension by failing to supply adequate information in a form that a particular individual can make sense of. Our immediate response has to be to try to diffuse the anxiety and distract the person from any disturbed behaviour. One technique which is effective in many cases is the use of non-threatening surprise in the context of intensive interaction.

Beth is worried about catching the bus home. Towards the end of the afternoon she starts to show this anxiety by running out to see if the bus is coming and banging her head. Once this has started, her support staff are unable to stop her – she is completely locked into her self-injurious behaviour. I suggest that they try knocking the wall in time to her banging. She is surprised that her sound and rhythm are coming from outside herself and she stops and does not restart. The internal 'loop' in which she was trapped has been broken and she is able to step out of it. She is intrigued by what is going on round her.

However, important though it is to be able to distract the person at the time of their anxiety, it is even more urgent to search for ways to relieve the underlying stress.

In the history of Tom, looked at previously, those involved have not considered the impact that anxiety about his future may have on Tom, a young man trapped in his body and unable to take charge of his life himself. In effect, failure to listen to him and failure to give him necessary information – or even to tell him that the information he needs is not available yet and give him a date when it will be – is to treat him as a child with all the vital decisions in his life being made over his head. He feels desperate and angry.

Presenting information about time

In order to be less dependent, we all need information, and it needs to be presented in a way in which we can handle it. It is perfectly possible to design 'clocks' that relate intervals directly to events. For example, one engineer designed a moving light beam to relate to pictures. Another method is to use an electric clock which has been simplified by removing the minute hand: the hour hand lines up directly with the pictures (or objects of reference if that is what is required). Kitchen timers also help people to understand intervals and the vital difference between 'now' and 'not now'. We can design various forms of timetables, as described in *Person to Person* (chapter 6), to assist in understanding sequences so that people know what is happening, when and, even, what is happening now.

In this respect, the educational approach of TEACCH programmes (see Resources, page 211) appears to be very helpful in introducing structure to children's lives. Every task is programmed and coded in such a way that the child always knows what they are doing. They can also programme in for themselves time to opt out to their safe places when they need to do so.

However, within that security, they also need to learn to develop their emotional capacity – an outcome of the approach known as Intensive Interaction. We need to use a combination of techniques: on the one hand, making the ways of our world clear to people with ASD; on the other, developing their ability to relate so that, within their new security, they begin to feel safe enough to enjoy being with others. Above all, we have to put aside our certainties and recognise the uncertainties which beset those whose existence is pinned to an environment that is, for them, without structure.

Summary

We can:

- appreciate anxiety in a world where a person does not understand the intervals of time

- relieve anxiety by presenting intervals in ways that people can understand.

Chapter 5

'The man who walked backwards'
The validity of individual logic

> *Dave, who has Asperger's syndrome and occasionally has severe outbursts of disturbed behaviour, has what is seen as a baffling habit of walking backwards at times.*

One school of thought is that he should be made to walk forwards. Another way to look at it is to ask what it is that he is getting out of this habit. What does it do for him? We need to remind ourselves of Donna Williams describing the turmoil in which she lives, where she never has the whole picture of where and who she is (see Chapter 3).

Putting myself in Dave's place: if I don't know where I am, I might try to backtrack, that is, retrace my steps – walk backwards to see if I could recover where I was/am. This would be logical within the framework of my distorted perception, even if it was inexplicable to an observer. Most habits are logical if they are viewed within an alternative framework. In order to see what an individual is getting out of a habit, an outsider has to assume the validity of their logic. It is not the person's reasoning which is incorrect but the premise in which it is rooted. We need to be able to backtrack with them to see where they are coming from.

Suppose I have entered Dave's world and decoded what he is doing – where does that get me? How does it help me to help Dave?

From my point of view, it is less irritating for me if I know the reason why he is doing it. (As human beings, we tend to find it disturbing if someone is behaving in a way that seems nonsensical. It niggles us, questions our behaviour, and we feel the need to obtain conformity. We say that people will laugh at the person, but we may also be afraid of being associated with the bizarre behaviour – that we shall also be made to look silly.)

Observing Dave's behaviour through my reaction to it prevents me looking for a less coercive way of helping him. I need to see if I can reduce the stress in his life. He will then have less sensory confusion to struggle with and will therefore be more able to perceive his environment in an organised way – to have more idea of who he is and where he is at any given time.

> When Dave goes home he walks upstairs and paces up and down a long corridor. His mother says that if she calls him, he will sometimes come but sometimes mutters to himself, 'She's not going to hurry me.' He comes down when he is ready and is not upset.

What is interesting is that Dave behaves in a comparable way when he reaches his day centre. He does not come in but paces round the centre, sometimes for a considerable length of time. When he is ready, he comes in.

Taking each behaviour in isolation, it might be difficult to see what is going on. However, when put together, they suggest that when Dave, who is very able, is subject to changes, he needs time to sort out what is happening for him. He knows this and takes active steps to sort himself out before joining other people. Far from trying to hurry Dave, we need to give him space to manage himself.

Knowing that Dave, although he can read and write well, needs time to process information, staff at the centre he attends have devised a system to help him participate more fully in meetings that concern his life. Without help, Dave finds it difficult to keep up with what is being said, so an assistant sits beside him and takes notes. These are transferred to a card index system in a box. This allows him to go through the information with his assistant at his own pace at a later time and pick out anything that he wants to clarify. He also has a small box in which he can take a selection of relevant cards to a meeting. As well as this, he can help to control the agenda of future meetings by picking out and laying out in order his priorities when his affairs are discussed (Eardley, 1998). (Although one might think this type of difficulty relates to auditory processing, this is not necessarily always so. Visual input takes up 70% of our processing capacity and Williams says that when she wears the coloured lenses, her capacity to understand speech is improved (Williams, 1996). Presumably, she has more time to focus on it when she is not struggling with overwhelming visual problems.)

When we are working with people with severe sensory complications, we must look at the whole picture and ask ourselves what it is the individual is experiencing. We need to respect the coping strategies that people have developed in order to help themselves.

For example, a woman who turns off the TV or radio when she is becoming disturbed is trying to cut down on sensory confusion – she is trying to help herself. The proper response is to try to provide her with a quiet and undemanding environment so that she can feel secure and continue to work on herself. At the same time, we can provide a way of interacting that she finds non-threatening through Intensive Interaction and activities based on her own language and preferences.

Summary

This section discussed ways of helping people with ASD:

■ cope with change

■ keep up with the flow of conversation.

Chapter 6

'A safe place inside myself'
Two worlds

One of the concepts I find helpful when thinking about behaviour, not only in relation to people with ASD, arises out of the way that Donna Williams refers to 'my world' and 'their world'. She talks about the strain of constantly having to be in 'their world' (Williams, 1995). To make this distinction clearer, I shall call these the 'inner' and the 'outer' worlds.

In fact, however aware of it we are, we all live in two worlds and have an inner personal and private world. How our lives develop is at least partly dependent on how we are able to balance this inner world with the demands of the public world outside. We function best when there is a bridge between them and they inform and enrich each other. If all is not well in our public world, we may, particularly as children, retreat to our inner world, the place where we started off as infants and where our whole experience of the world was an extension of ourselves. We felt safe. Under stressful circumstances, communication between public outer and inner personal world may break down and the bridge become a drawbridge. We cannot talk to the world and it cannot talk to us. We are turned in on ourselves.

Describing her difficulties with the demands of a public world which thought she was stupid because people did not understand the difficulties she was experiencing, Williams says that all the turmoil this brought her made her decide: 'the only safe place was in myself' (Williams, 1995).

> Rachel, who has ASD and learning difficulties, is locked in a private world where she focuses continually on rubbing her face. This makes her difficult to communicate with.
>
> It is breakfast time. Her key-worker asks Rachel to take a spoon and stir some sugar in her cup. She goes towards the cup but keeps breaking off as her key-worker's suggestion is overridden by her compulsion to touch her cheek. She wants her breakfast and opens and closes her mouth, clearly thinking about food as she moves towards the cupboard, but her brain keeps diverting her back to 'scratch', 'touch', 'scratch' and she gets lost again. She cannot cross the bridge between the compulsion of her inner world to the 'real' outer world with its need to organise her meal, until her attention is caught by her key-worker reflecting back to her, her movements. This establishes the contact she needs with the public outside world. She is able to start preparing her breakfast.

At this stage, we need to look at what we mean when we speak of inner personal and public outer worlds, the relationship of these to unconsciousness and consciousness, and where the autistic inner personal world links in.

Inner and outer feedback

It is generally accepted that all of us, when we were infants, made the journey from an undifferentiated world (where we existed in the illusion that everything was part of us) to the outside world of reality (Davis & Wallbridge, 1990). This progress from 'me' to 'not me' Stern calls the movement from 'core self' to 'core other' (Stern, 1985). The transition takes place through 'reality testing', a process whereby the child learns to relate what he or she does to the effect this has. This process is facilitated by the parent figure who confirms the infant's struggles to emerge from the insulated and isolated state. This process is often painful – In Winnicott describes the assault of reality as an 'insult' (it may threaten our existence – an anxiety- provoking scenario). Winnicott goes on to point out that while our inner psychic reality is largely unconscious, the feelings that arise from it are not (in: Davis & Wallbridge, 1990).

For example, we may use our hand repetitively to sweep back our hair; in a world where we have a poor self-image and are not sure of ourselves, this gesture makes us feel attractive. For a millisecond we reassure ourselves, we have the feeling that we are all right. We call this activity a habit and we may not know we do it. If someone points it out to us, we feel surprised and at the same time we may feel a small flicker of shame. Our feeling of 'needing to be attractive' is exposed like a raw nerve.

Until this point, our behaviour has been beyond our control since we have not known what we were doing. Now that we have become aware of our feelings and actions, we have a choice: we can alter our behaviour or continue – but in the latter case we feel uneasy because we are now aware of our exposed position. In order to change, we need not only to know what we are doing, but we also have to address our underlying weakness. In the previous example, we cannot just stop feeling unattractive. We may need help and support to do this, otherwise, half-knowing, we may add guilt to our shame. **In order for us to take responsibility for our actions, we may need someone to help us feel good about ourselves.**

If we turn our attention back to our inner personal world, we may know what we are doing but still be at the mercy of repetitive messages from the brain which are outside our control. Even though we are semi-aware of them, they dictate what we do. We might call it a state of automated consciousness. The more we cut ourselves off from the outside world, the more vulnerable we are to compulsive processes since we no longer have external standards to verify our behaviour. (We may feel that we are not subject to this type of compulsive thought but we are all familiar with activities such as biting our nails or wriggling a foot. There are also the endless compulsory reruns experienced by those who have been through the powerful emotions of separation and loss.)

The effect may be compared to that which results when a computer has received an error in programming that leads to an invalid repetition instruction. This gives rise to an infinite loop which, paying perfect attention to itself, blindly refers back to and responds to an inappropriate command. Like the image in two facing mirrors, consciousness has become locked into itself.

In order to keep track of itself, our brain needs to know what it is doing and it is feedback which tells it this. The question is whether the feedback is coming from the inner world, in which case we may be locked into a loop, or is from outside, encouraging us to explore and measure ourselves against the external world.

A sense of self

How can we know what being caught up in the inner world of another person is like? To begin with, we know that being locked into an inner world is not exclusive to people with learning disabilities. Many of us know about daydreams and how we can become swallowed up in fantasies. The following history explores the experience of a child who had no impairment, to see if we can get a closer idea of what it is that can seduce and trap us into an inner world with its personal fixations.

> *Biddy was five when a woman came to look after her while her mother was unable do this. Her previous job had ended when Rose, the child she had been looking after, became ill and died. In her grief, the woman talked incessantly about Rose. Biddy, now adult, looks back and describes what happened:*
>
> *'One day it dawned on me that it would be much better for me (I should be the object of her love) if I was Rose since it was Rose that my carer was evidently attached to. Somehow I felt myself merging to the point of becoming her – there was a definite sense of movement from 'being me' into 'being Rose'. Thereafter, I refused to respond to any name but hers. This period lasted for about six months and I remember my sadness on leaving her when my Mum was finally able to get through to me. I forgot all this until, as an adult, I found a letter to my mother copied by me and signed, 'Rose'. Enquiring who it was, my sister explained to me. I felt a small flicker of shame at having my inner life so exposed.'*

Biddy's search for security led her away from reality and into a closed world which prevented real growth in relation to the world outside. It wasn't until she was able to relinquish her introjection (the unconscious adoption of another person's ideas) that she was able to continue growth and development. However, we have to acknowledge the strength of the feelings that led her into this trap. This was not a conscious decision, it just 'came about' as a response to her need.

Even now I find it difficult to write about Biddy, for she was myself. This is how I know what she felt. I have introduced this personal history because it brings home to me how it is possible, not just to have fantasies, but actually to deal with the bewildering idea that my boundaries might melt so that I, who feel myself to be myself, might 'be' other. In this condition, my centre feels itself to operate from that other place. It is one thing to read about introjection and projection and another to experience the movements and feel their power – processes which we discover in retrospect and then only if we are lucky.

We know others through ourselves – the capacity to dwell on our own relevant experience, however painful, can help us when we come across people caught in similar or analogous situations. Pertinent exploration helps us to make connections, so that behaviour which might otherwise separate us is actually a bond. Their experience is no longer foreign to us. We 'know' from personal experience that when an outer life situation becomes unbearable, our inner lives can construct an escape route – a fantasy. But we also know that this shift is into a cul-de-sac which does nothing to address our circumstances. While we are in this dead-end, we cannot grow through our difficulties, whatever they are. Empathy takes us to understanding where rationalisation may not be able to reach. (At the same time we must stand back and think about our insights: we have to learn to dovetail empathy and cognitive processes.)

In the following examples, I am able to recognise when a person's sense of themselves is displaced:

> *John's sense of self seems to be located in his foot, Jo's in her left shoulder. It is not just that they find these supremely interesting but, working with them, I get the feeling that they seem to operate from these parts of themselves. This is where they are centred. In both cases, paying attention to the relevant area and using a physical mode of approach (massaging John's foot and applying gentle but firm pressure to Jo's shoulder), enables them to move gradually back to a more normal centre.*

The world that Donna Williams, who has ASD, describes as her 'inner world' is by no means totally unconscious, even though she is describing it through retrospective spectacles. She describes it as a retreat from an outer world whose demands were intolerable, given that the world took no account of her particular sensory experience of it. This clash between impossible expectations, which failed to understand her disorientated perception, and her own struggle to make sense of her environment led to withdrawal into a world that seemed safe. In order to survive, she returned to her inner sanctuary. However, this is not the same place as the inner undifferentiated world of the infant. It has its own problems:

'Everything in the world is torn up and made redundant – all the relationships one might have had are made with shadows.' (Williams, 1995)

The question that the autistic brain has to answer is how to retain differentiation in a world that has shut off connection with the 'real world' outside – how to avoid slipping back into unconsciousness. For me, part of an answer is given by a child who, when asked by her doctor why she banged her head, replied that she did it 'to know she was there'.

The child was maintaining her status as a person through physical sensation. If stereotypic behaviour can be said to have a positive function, retaining meaningful contact with consciousness must be one of them:

'While I do this, I know who I am as what I am doing.' Feedback in the form of recognisable sensation from the body to the brain connects me with myself. In a related sense, it is also a defence against anxiety, the anxiety of being overwhelmed by chaos. By focusing on repetitive behaviours, people cut out the sensations which threaten to overload them. When a person is trapped in a loop of stereotypic behaviour, it is not that they are unconscious: the location of the dialogue has shifted from contact with the outer world to their inner world (see Diagram 1 below).

Even if the stereotypic behaviour relates to something from the outside world, the fixation has, in a sense, hijacked the object and is using it as part of the conversation in the inner world. In this place, the individual is paying total attention to the instructions from the brain saying, for example, over and over again, 'scratch, scratch'. They 'become' this particular feeling in a way that excludes the will to reach out to alternatives. See Diagram 1 below.

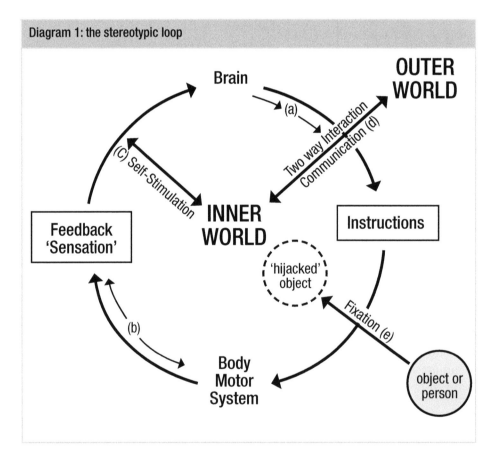

Diagram 1: the stereotypic loop

a) The brain feeds instructions to the body motor system telling it what to do

b) The body responds, giving feedback to the brain in the form of sensation (sound, movement, etc) which triggers another round of the stereotypic loop. The brain and the body are having a conversation with each other. There is no connection with the world outside

c + d) Instead of self-stimulation within the inner world (c) we are trying to establish two-way communication with the world outside (d)

e) In the case of fixations, the inner world hijacks an object or person from the outer world and 'uses' them as part of the furniture of the inner world of stereotypic repetitive behaviour. There is no tone interest in the world outside

When we are trying to gain access to the inner world of a person, we may have to relinquish our own talents and approaches. The reason for this is that an individual may have learned to 'bang a drum' or 'do a jigsaw' in a way that misleads us into thinking that the activity has meaning for them. In fact, they may be doing it in a way that is entirely mechanistic. (This is certainly true of many autistic children who have enormous facility with puzzles but are totally uninterested in the picture or its relation to the real world.) Such facility does nothing to bridge the gap between our world and theirs. It is only when we come empty-handed to a person that we are in a position to enter their inner world, reach them and be with them in a way that gives them confidence and helps them to begin to move out through us. However, this is not the same as feeling we 'become' the person we are working with, in which case we would be no more than a hijacked object. We need to be present in ourselves so they may use us as a bridge to the world outside. They need to be aware of us as an individual as well as our being a vehicle of their language. They need someone to interact with.

Summary

A useful model is to think in terms of the inner and outer world:

- we may not grow fully from the inner to the outer world

- we may retreat back into our inner world

- reflecting on our personal experience may help us enter and respect the inner worlds of other people

- in order to enter private worlds, we may need to relinquish our own agenda.

Chapter 7

'The lady with the knife'
Resonant imaging

In this section I want to consider an approach I call 'resonant imaging'. By this, I mean putting oneself empathetically alongside an individual and deliberately using one's own experience as a starting point to generate images which resonate with and give meaning to their lives.

For example, starting with a feeling of my own, I might ask myself: 'What happens if this feeling takes over – how does it feel? Does this present any pictures or images that might be helpful to the person with whom I am working?' (Experience suggests that what resonates for one person may also be resonant for another.) This lateral thinking approach, which allows the mind to drift and throw up related suggestions, requires intuition, flexibility and the ability to discern if an image is helpful or not – since not all will be relevant. Where images and ideas arrived at in this way are seen to 'speak to the person', the outcome can be extremely empowering, establishing creative links and growth where more conventional approaches have been unsuccessful – as the following history illustrates.

> *Mary is a young woman who lives in a community home. She is able, not autistic. She is extremely volatile, frequently having outbursts when she attacks anything she is near – cars, people, and so on. In discussion with her team leader, it emerges that she has a very poor image of herself and she most often becomes disturbed when she feels 'put down'.*
>
> *This led me to reflect in personal terms on the fragility of poor self-esteem and how, under these circumstances, anything which I perceive as diminishing may threaten to overwhelm me. I see it as life-threatening and my threshold for extinction is very low. I get trapped in an*

instinctive response over which I have no control. Trying to stop me reinforces the terror I am experiencing in my inner world and drives me on. I am fighting for my existence.

The team leader and I talked about instinctive responses in terms of how we get locked into them, how under certain circumstances we may still find ourselves prisoners of our biological past when we lived in caves and needed to be able to defend ourselves physically. Groping for ideas, we moved from this image to the possibility of combining it with something like a yellow-card system, introducing visual surprise to try and capture Mary's attention when she was upset. The team leader decided to talk to her about the old times when people used to live in caves and how, in those early days, men and women would have needed to be able to fight and defend themselves against enemies and wild animals. She pointed out that when situations become threatening nowadays, we do not need to prepare to do battle for our lives as we can talk about it. She asked Mary if it would be a good idea to have a picture of a cave woman to hold up when she or her support staff felt that things were getting too much.

Mary understood very well and at this point something astonishing took place – she became conscious of the implications of her behaviour and took on the responsibility for herself. She said, 'No, not a cave woman' and went to her room and brought back a picture of a beautiful woman carrying a knife. Since she knew what she was fetching and exactly where it was, it had obviously struck her as significant when she first saw it, as she had kept it. It already had meaning for her which resonated with the behaviour that she and her team leader were discussing.

With her agreement, her picture was enlarged and laminated. On the back was written in large letters, STOP, THINK, TALK. All staff and Mary had access to it and Mary kept control by ensuring that all new staff were provided with a copy. They held it up to attract her attention when she started to become disturbed. In the following three months, the incidence of Mary's outbursts fell dramatically from several times a week to two episodes during the whole period, which occurred when bank staff were on duty. It was possible to talk her through these using the image.

The degree to which Mary understood the process was illustrated when she saw a fight on TV and said to her team leader that maybe the people involved needed a card system. (She seemed to be unaware of its origins in football.) What she did understand was that people who were caught up in disturbed behaviour could be helped by visual intervention, as she had been.

I have already mentioned a number of situations where an individual may feel themselves to be under life-threat. We know that, under similar apprehensions, we react instinctively. At a biological level, the most fundamental of all our tasks is self-preservation – whether we like it or not, we are dedicated to preserving our identity, existence and the package we have been issued with known as the selfish genes. **But, in our different realities, we may have completely different thresholds of what constitutes a life-threatening situation.** If our sensory perception of the world starts to disintegrate, or if our feeling of well-being in ourselves is minimal, we will feel ourselves under attack very easily and will do battle to preserve ourselves at all cost.

We need to look at how we can help people towards alternative ways of responding – to direct the brain away from trigger-happy reactions towards stability.

Creating new pathways

One possibility is to use the techniques of behaviour modification. This approach is extensively discussed by Lovett. It aims to train people that if they respond in a certain way the consequences will be costly, or there will be a pleasant outcome to 'good' behaviour. Unfortunately, this approach sends a very dubious message to the inner self, that is: 'I'll love you if you are good, I will not love you if you are bad, therefore you are not worth loving for yourself.' This is not the message we are trying to get over to someone with a poor self-image. Interaction should never be tied to a reward scheme. It will increase a person's feeling of impoverishment and undermine self-esteem (Lovett, 1985).

When we are working with such difficulties, we need to undertake a creative search for what one might call 'trip-mechanisms' which will interrupt the dead-end loop in which a person is trapped and open it up, bringing what they are doing within reach of cognitive processes at whatever level. As already suggested, surprise, presented in a respectful way and in the related context of a person's own behaviour is non-threatening and, as such, is often successful. In Mary's case, it involved finding the right image which chimed in with what she already in one sense knew – that is, it was already present in her brain. We just needed the right link. (In neurobiological terms, we needed to establish better neural pathways between the thinking and the emotional emergency response parts of the brain.) We had to find an approach that established a link between inner personal and public outer worlds so that Mary could see that she was not in danger and take charge – take on the responsibility for what was going on for her in her life.

The more we can give people a sense of competence and control, the more likely we are to reduce their feeling of vulnerability which keeps their inner and outer worlds separate. In this quest, a direct approach is most often counter-productive. When they are upset I cannot appeal to their rational mind since links with it are being actively suppressed by the action of adrenaline. Such appeals may threaten the person's unconscious defence systems during confrontation. All I can do is try to understand what is their reality and speak to it in such a way that it grabs their attention. We need to look at the factors in the intervention with Mary that were helpful to her.

■ The intervention was based on the premise that because Mary had such a bad image of herself, she was easily thrown into the need to defend her existence if she felt slighted.

■ When the team leader, a person she trusted, discussed this with her using visual images and language she understood, it clearly 'rang a bell' – to the extent that she recognised the implications and underlying feeling at once. She was able to link these with an alternative representation of difficulties that she had already noted. You could say that at this stage she took it on board, it all 'came together'.

■ The next stage was for Mary and the team leader to set up what might be called a 'game' with rules – when she was becoming upset, she or staff could hold up a card. It is worth pointing out that the mere existence of the game, with rules that Mary had contributed to, provided a support and safety net, so that her behaviour improved without the need to use it frequently. Her underlying problems were now in the conscious domain – we may surmise that pathways had been set up which gave improved access from the thinking part of her brain to the place where her instinctive responses originated.

The key factors which gave Mary's inner feelings a chance to speak were:

■ understanding the particular problem she was having

■ finding a visual image that addressed her underlying difficulties in a significant and non-threatening way.

Furthermore, Mary's contribution was being valued and she was taking control of her own life in a meaningful way.

I should like to end this section by referring to Bill, whose story appears in *Person to Person*. He also attacked people, although not for the same reason as Mary. When he was asked why, Bill would shake his head and say, 'I don't know, I don't know', and it was obvious that he did not. For months we played a game which was especially designed to help him accept the parts of himself that he felt were so bad that he could not accept them. It was called 'Goodies and Baddies' and was based on the premise that we all have good and bad parts in ourselves. It did not approach this subject directly but did aim to make it easy to talk in a light-hearted way about awkward situations we could all get into. One day he said:

'You know, I'm not going to get better, am I, while I feel so angry.'

He was as surprised as I was. After this, his outbursts decreased.

Resonant imaging has been used to help people with ASD and those whose behavioural difficulties stem from other sources. In *Person to Person*, the history of Luke illustrates the feeling of being contained safely by squares – in his case, patio titles (see page 52). Luke never trod on the lines. I put myself back in the feeling of being a child playing 'Lines and Squares' and from that designed a game based on flipping a circular piece onto a board marked in squares – aiming to land in a square where it would be safe. It spoke to him at an emotional level and, for the first time, he sat down and joined in.

Culshaw and Purvis stress the need to develop a person's feelings of self-worth and self-esteem (1998). This is not always very easy since the factors underlying a person's low self-image may be extremely deeply embedded. One possibility is to use images with the person that resonate in their individual consciousness in order to try to set up situations where the person feels sufficiently secure to talk about the unspeakable things, the things that they may not even be able to acknowledge to themselves. There is some evidence that simply involving people in helping to identify and manage their own behaviours may assist them, even if they do not fully understand the management strategy (see Chapter 11).

To refer back to the question asked in the Introduction as to whether or not we should be training people for responsibility, it is difficult for any of us to take responsibility for our conduct unless we address the difficulties that lie behind it. We can be trained to follow a set of rules but, as pointed out above, this does not motivate us or help us to feel better about ourselves.

Summary

This section reminded us that:

- people with poor self-image may have a very low threshold for triggering the fight- flight response to what is wrongly seen as a life-threatening situation

- we need to give people a sense of competence to reduce the vulnerability which separates their two worlds

- we may be able to help by finding an image which addresses the emotional content of their inner world

- the image may be contained in a 'game' with clearly defined rules

- there is a difference between 'training' a person to take responsibility, which is unlikely to add to their feelings of self-worth, and helping to motivate a person – which does.

Chapter 8

'May I come in?'
The idea of control

The idea that we 'need' to control people is insidious and deep-seated. It raises itself in ways we can overlook. For example, the word 'carers' puts us in a dominant position. Substitute the word 'assistant' or 'companion' and we immediately think of ourselves in a different way.

Recently, I was talking about the use of gesture and how we can use this to alert people to what we intend to do, giving them control over whether or not we do it. For example, Bob has severe ASD and finds people very difficult. I said that before I entered a room that Bob was in, I paused at the door, pointed to myself and then to the room, and said, 'May I come in?' I was asked if I would have accepted it if Bob had said, 'No.' Would I have gone away? I answered that I would.

Letting a person know that they could control me was more important than my entering the room. Their agenda was more important than mine.

So, what is happening here? I want to go into the room so that I can observe Bob, see what he does and how support staff interact with him. This is my agenda. However, if I am focused on this, I miss the fact that Bob has a different one and that his interaction with me starts when he sees a stranger at the door.

I need to think about Bob's perception of me. In his fragmented world, I may appear not as someone but as something or even as bits of things. He may not know which bits he sees are me and which are him – they float about and the more he tries to focus on them, the more they slip away. Furthermore, as discussed in Chapter 3, apart from the physical perceptual difficulties of processing, Bob's brain may have learned that people are emotionally overloading and be taking steps to avoid this. Bob may not even connect with me at all. Whichever is the case, **I need to reduce my potential as a threat so that Bob can learn that it is safe to connect with me.**

The problem here is that, as carers, we sometimes have a built-in fear of letting the people we work with take control. The question I was asked assumes that this was what the interaction is about. But the interaction is not about who is boss, who is who in the pecking order. What Bob needs to know is that, in his kaleidoscopic world, there is something or someone he can connect with which will not cause him pain. He is engaged in a survival struggle. In order to make that connection, he has to understand that what he does or says will effect change in me, that he is part of a world over which he can, to some extent exert control. This will make him feel safer. It is like being thrown a life-belt (Williams, 1992).

If I had really needed to come into the room, I might have come back a bit later and asked again. Now that Bob knew he could control me, it would have been safer to let me in. He could predict that I would be sensitive to his difficulties.

I followed this tactic with another person, Luke, (in *Person to Person*, see page 52) when playing a game designed around the idea that Luke found squares 'safe'. Letting him control whether or not I made a move by saying 'Yes' or 'No', moved him swiftly from the position of being unable to interact, to sitting up and participating.

It may be more important to let the person have control than to carry out our own agenda.

Summary

We need to:

- think of ourselves as assistants rather than carers; this shifts control to the person we are working with

- respect the individual's agenda.

Chapter 9

'Intimate attention'
The empowering force of Intensive Interaction

Most people want to communicate. It is part of the condition of being human.

There are relatively few people who do not respond to an approach in their own language, and Intensive Interaction (echoing back to them a person's own behaviour) is now a well-established technique for getting in touch with people who are hard to make contact with otherwise (Ephraim, 1986; Nind & Hewitt, 1994; Hewett & Nind, 1998; Ware, 1997; Caldwell, 1996). This is illustrated in the following two histories, which relate to two very different disabilities.

Jenny has very severe learning disabilities and sight impairment. She spends her day in her wheelchair with her head down. She screams when she is unhappy. Support staff at her resource centre say that they are unable to make contact with her. She makes a little but quite regular noise, sucking her saliva. When I listen to this and echo it back, she pays attention and starts to smile. She sucks hers in a definite rhythm and waits to see if I will copy this. We alternate her sounds. She puts her head up and laughs out loud. Three members of her support team try this with her and she enjoys the interactions for over an hour.

Moving to the second history, Janice has very severe ASD.

Janice is in her mid-thirties. She has become very withdrawn since the death of members of her family. When she comes to the centre, she gets stuck at the gate, looking out between the slats of the fence. Efforts to persuade her to come in can last for over an hour. When she does come in, she stands by the glass door and looks out. She stays there all day. It is difficult to persuade her to move into the dining area for a meal. She stands on the threshold of the dining room rocking backwards and forwards. By the time she is ready to move in, her dinner is cold and has to be taken away to be reheated. When Janice sees it disappear she concludes that dinner is over and returns to her post by the door. The whole process has to start again.

Surprise presented in the context of an individual's own language is one of the key elements, which enables a person to shift from their inner world to the world outside. Starting at the gate, her key-worker and I used this as a technique: Janice's key-worker went outside and looked back at Janice through the slats of the fence. This immediately shifted her attention from her inner world to an intriguing situation which had arisen in the world outside – something that falls within the 'looking through the slats' behaviour (which is part of her experience) is now different. She starts to smile and when her key-worker comes back through the gate she is able to take advantage of Janice's attention. Janice immediately takes her arm and comes inside.

Once inside Janice takes up her customary position by the door. Her body language is, as usual, completely negative, arms folded tightly across her chest, looking out of the door. Occasionally she rubs her chin on her shoulder.

Her key-worker points out that behind her folded arms she is constantly engaged in rubbing her fingers. This is the way she talks to herself. We start to do the same, showing her what we are doing. This captures her attention, she likes it and smiles. I move into making a game of touching thumbs. She unfolds her arms and reaches out to do it more easily. Eventually I ask if I may rub her shoulders, as she does to herself when she rubs it with her chin. We move into sharing this form of interaction. She pushes her shoulder forwards for me to rub. By now we are interacting easily with each other. After about an hour I have to move on but during the rest of the morning, whenever I pass her, we touch thumbs. It has become our way of saying 'hi' to each other.

Looking at the problem of how to manage dinner, we decide that her body language is telling us that the room is too noisy and full of people for her to come in. We wait until the others have finished and moved out before inviting her to come and eat. Her key-worker brings the plate to her where she stands by the door and offers her a mouthful. However she still will not come in until I ask her if either the little soft dog she clutches or her thumbs would like some dinner. (This is an indirect approach through her acceptable point of contact and is therefore non-threatening). She nods and comes at once, sits down and eats her dinner. When she has finished she asks for a cup of tea. She then asks to go to the toilet – something she has not done before. Staff continue to use her language with her and three weeks later she was still in contact. They know how to talk to her and she is responding. (At this point it is crucial to remember that if we develop a successful strategy with people with ASD we must not remove it when they improve. We have not 'cured' the ASD – only modified their environment.)

Why does Intensive Interaction work so well? What is it about it that makes us feel good, that helps us to feel confident? Why is it so empowering? One of the objections sometimes raised when I am teaching is that 'It's too easy, it can't make that much difference.'

In essence, to reflect a person's behaviour back to them is a very simple idea, yet time and again it does make a difference. Sometimes that difference appears very quickly. A person who we would say is completely 'switched off' comes to life almost immediately, and those who have been indifferent to their surroundings become alert and attentive. After he had been watching a session of Intensive Interaction, a support worker – who had been finding it very difficult to make contact with a man who was very withdrawn – said: 'Today I saw the real person.'

So why does it work – and what do we mean by 'the real person'? What are we tapping into that makes it so effective a bridge between a person's inner world and the world outside, the world of 'me' and 'not me', so that a person begins to find the confidence to move from solitary self-stimulation to shared activity?

A depth of mutual attention

Deep down, we all feel vulnerable. We live behind some sort of mask, hoping it will shield our lurking vulnerabilities from the world.

But suppose I have very severe learning disabilities or ASD or both? If the world I live in is confusing and fragmented and I am not sure which bits of it are 'me' and which 'not me', the only place where I have a sense of my own identity is in my personal inner world. I cannot connect to the world outside. If I engage in stereotypic repetitive behaviour, these signals are hard-wired in, they do not break up. In this way, I can talk to myself and know who I am. It is only by using the repetitive behaviours of my stereotype that you can talk to me without threatening my sense of identity. This ties up with observations that individuals may be capable of understanding more complex speech than normal when one is working within the stereotype. Increased confidence puts less stress on the processing system so it operates more efficiently.

Ephraim (1994) suggests that the processes involved in Intensive Interaction are the same as those in the infant learning pattern where the parent figure confirms the infant's sounds and signals. At the same time as the infant brain recognises the confirmatory response, it is also surprised that this did not come from itself and begins to look outside itself for the source. (I have witnessed this surprise on the face of a woman who realised I was echoing back her self-injurious behaviour. Her jaw literally dropped as she took in that I was tapping my cheek every time she hit herself.)

As pointed out in the history of Janice, surprise is a very important element in the process. If we think of the model of trying to open the door of a locked room, surprise is both the hand that opens it and the foot in the door that keeps it ajar – it allows the process of interaction to flow.

When we were working together, a speech therapist said, 'I have worked for many years on a one-to-one basis but I have never experienced such intimate attention as I do when I see or use Intensive Interaction.' I was intrigued by the phrase, 'intimate attention', not really having thought through the physical bonding that is the common denominator of this type of intervention.

When I work, I am having a conversation with someone, a conversation without words. We are wholly present for each other, nothing else exists. All our attention, everything we are, is focused in the other person. That sensory sensation is overtaken by a feeling of total mutual trust to the extent of shared experience – we become lost in each other. We examine each other with minute attention, giving weight and value to every movement, sound and sensation. All sense of self is transferred to the activated part. Although both participants are 'present' it also feels as though they have 'become' the sensory area of interaction. Links are formed which bypass the cognitive processes. We shall never feel quite the same about each other as before the intervention.

Intensive Interaction addresses the emotional state of a person. For both of us, it is a creative opportunity where we can let each other know how we feel – and also test each other out using the simplicity of body language, without the complications of misunderstanding which are the downside of using words.

It is important to realise that this experience of total awareness of other/self has nothing to do with like or dislike. It is totally non-judgmental. The intellect is not involved – it is pure sensation.

This sensation feels good, it is very empowering and often extends beyond the time of interaction. Apart from enjoying themselves, participants usually become relaxed. A person's compulsive behaviour may slow or stop while they appear to drift in the experience.

It is important to emphasise that this dynamic is not dependent on the type of intervention; that is, it is not just the outcome of touch, of movement or of sound, or of sharing some particular fixation. Rather, it is the depth of mutual attention through which we let each other know that we have understood each other – that we can talk to each other and delight in doing so – that is so powerful.

A 'first friend'

I want to compare this experience with one which is common to all of us – how we behave when we move into a new situation. Although we appear to be social animals, we live with the paradox that when we first move into a group of people who are new to us, we do not immediately identify with the group. Instead, we weigh up the individuals, looking for a potential friend. This friend will be our ally in what, however much we want to be part of the group, is potentially a battleground because it is unpredictable. We do not know our way around and it is easy to get things wrong and upset people. Our success in the group depends on our finding someone who, as we say, 'speaks our language', so that they can 'show us the ropes'.

What I am suggesting is that, in order to be able to move more freely from their inner personal life to the new situation of taking part in a public outer world, non-verbal people also need a 'first friend' who will act as their ally and bridge. By learning a person's language, we can act as that first friend so that, gaining confidence through us, they can begin to look at the world outside.

Returning to Jenny, described at the beginning of this section, after three weeks of inter- vention using her sounds, she now sits with her head up more frequently. Staff say that she is both calmer and more alert. Now that they know how to talk to her, they feel confi- dent working with her. Now that she is able to get a response, she is finding it worthwhile to hold up her head and look at what is happening round her.

A month after the intervention with Janice and continued use of her language by staff, they reported that she was still making progress – 'it seems like a breakthrough'. They now know how to talk to her and she is responding.

Summary

Using Intensive Interaction can be a powerful way of establishing communication.

- Using a person's inner language enables us to communicate with them directly in a way that they understand and which is non-stressful.

- The respectful use of surprise within the context of the language helps the interaction to flow.

- Mutual attention is crucial.

- Our role is to act as a 'bridge' from a person's inner world to the outer world, and also as the 'first friend' who helps them to cross over.

Chapter 10

'Speech may be sound without meaning' Communication and comprehension

In his book on management thinking, DeBono points out that communication requires both parties to have similar languages of perception:

'If the receiver's language is known to be totally different, the communicator must know how to switch into that language. This obviously applies when the word language is used in its direct sense but it equally applies when it is used symbolically for perceptions and values.' (DeBono, 1983)

In other words, it may not only be that the person we are trying to communicate with does not understand us, but that they see the world in a different way. He continues:

'Too often we try to teach the other person our language and concepts and then communicate with them in this language. We do this because we fear that [their] language may not contain the sophisticated concepts we need in the communication.'

He concludes that we should always communicate in the other person's language. This also applies to our attempts to communicate with people who are non-verbal. They almost certainly do see the world differently and the language they use to talk to themselves is one we do not recognise as having meaning. So often we talk about communication as though it were a simple process of exchanging information. While this is true, it is only part of a much more complex and subtle process which involves social assessment and reassurance: I need to know where I stand and who will support me, be my own ally. Apart from letting each other know what we want, communication is a delicate probing of feelings using facial and body language in the hope that you will feel good about me so that I can feel good about myself. It is about security, both internal and external, and is essential to our well-being.

When we are working with people who are difficult to reach, we usually focus exclusively on trying to get them to understand what we want and giving them ways of letting us know what they want – an exchange of basic needs. Yet even here, we frequently present information in ways that people do not understand. As Peeters points out in his book Autism, the most essential aspect of any attempt at communication is that it is presented in the way that is most likely to be understood – people must be able to take on board what we are offering. This applies both to our attempts to communicate with people through their inner personal language and also how we try to inform them. **We need to use the system which is most likely to be effective for that individual** (Peeters, 1997).

It is no use, for example, using signs with a person who is unable to cope with abstract concepts and who thus cannot attach meaning to them. Yet, knowing this, we sometimes spend years trying to get people to use systems which will always be incomprehensible to them. They may eventually make a sign for 'please' and 'thank you' but still not understand what they are doing. It is just a motion they have to go through, for example, before they get their tea. (Incidentally, in the context of age-appropriateness, insisting that someone say please and thank you is something we do to children, not to adults.)

This is not to undervalue systems of signing which can be liberating when used appropriately; it is their blanket misuse in inappropriate situations which can be counterproductive. We sometimes have to suspend our attachment to specific strategies and look realistically at the cognitive difficulties people face which may make it impossible to use a particular way of getting in touch. In such situations we need to explore alternatives and those alternatives are wide-ranging. We need to look at the whole repertoire of a person's body and facial language, how they move, and the sounds they make. Even if the language consists of incidental grunts, or clicks which are non-intentional, these may relate to activities which the person enjoys. (For example, as described in Person to Person, the clicks made by Hannah (see page 41) when eating food she enjoyed, were used to distract her when she was afraid.)

We must also take note of anything external to the person in which they show positive interest, such as tearing paper, or the wind blowing in their face. Surprisingly, we often find that an individual's personal language offers us a wealth of ways to express and enrich feeling. There is also the downside – sensory stimuli which cause a person stress and trigger off negative responses. These also are part of the person's language – in metaphorical terms, the 'bad words' which may disturb them so much that their world breaks apart. The person feels under attack and responds accordingly.

> *Liza cannot bear the word 'pull' and attacks people when she hears it.*

We can only speculate as to the origin of Liza's distress but it is real enough. She behaves as though she needs to tear the world apart, it is so bad.

Finding the right language

On the practical level, if we are going to communicate, first of all we need to attract a person's attention; in getting this, we need to be sure they have no physical impairment. In spite of improvements in services, it is surprisingly common to encounter adults with severe learning disabilities whose deafness is undiagnosed, or whose hearing has not been tested recently. Particularly, deafness in one ear is often unrecognised. A person cannot respond to voice if they do not hear it.

> *Thomas stands by the door at the centre all day, watching everything intently with a slightly puzzled look on his face. He is wearing a T-shirt printed with a steamship. I tell him I have sailed on it. Since he does not respond, I make the deep sound of its siren. Immediately, his face clears. I have made a low-frequency sound he can hear. He follows me about hopefully for the next two days, waiting for that precious sound.*

We also need to present our communication in a way that a person can handle. People with severe learning disabilities who have little or no sight frequently curl up and cut off from the world completely. Their experience of the world may have been hazardous, particularly if they have been in large institutions. 'Touch' has been bad news. They do not want us near them. At the same time, they are desperately in need of input to replace their visual loss (which is about three-quarters of their total sensory uptake).

Such people usually provide themselves with a substitute language; this may take a number of forms, such as rocking or rubbing their own fingers.

Since they cannot see and very often dislike touch, it is difficult to reflect these movements back to them, to speak to them in their own language. But it is possible, for example, to reflect rocking back to a person by banging your feet on the floor in time with their rocking movements so that they feel the vibration, or to scratch the material of a person's chair in time with their finger movements. If a person is also deaf, we may be able to reach them by sitting on the far end of the sofa and bouncing to their rocking rhythm. This type of intervention is frequently successful, shifting a person's interest from self-stimulation to the unexpected source of the echo. People uncurl, lift their heads and start to smile with recognition. Once a person is interested, it becomes easier to interact; they are not in a threatening situation and will begin to be more tolerant of touch, so that movements may be echoed more directly – on a person's back, for example.

If all is well on the sensory front, we still need to be sure that a person is really attending before we try to communicate. We have to look at their language, how they talk to themselves. We need to use this, sometimes in an exaggerated way, to hold their interest.

Picking out exactly what a person will respond to can sometimes be complicated, as is illustrated in the next two histories.

> *Val, who is very withdrawn, makes humming noises but does not respond to these when they are echoed back by staff. Listening to her carefully suggests that these sounds are in fact part of a cycle of breath holding – inhalation, hum, hold, breath out. Focusing on the explosive exhalation which ends the cycle and copying that sound on the kazoo does catch her attention. Val starts to sit up and smile and listen, waiting for me to echo her.*

> *Don, who has little speech, tugs at his collar to emphasise things. Sometimes his support staff feel he is just saying, 'This is me, Don.' At other times, he grabs people's collars and won't let go. This behaviour is discouraged as inappropriate and uncomfortable. However, in order to get and hold Don's attention, I make use of his gestures, waggling my own collar in an exaggerated way. He thinks this is extremely funny. Moving from rejecting me, we begin to laugh together and become good friends. It stimulates him to try to engage his peers – pointing from them to me and showing them what I was doing. His good humour spills over and is infectious in the group.*

From isolation to integration

It is important to reiterate that in order to get in touch with people who are difficult to reach, we have to learn their language. This is because not all staff are aware of the crucial part that developing relationships plays in communication. It is at least as important, if not more so, as exchanging needs-information. Dunbar points out that letting each other know how we feel about ourselves and each other may have been an important factor in the evolution of language (Dunbar, 1997). We can use it to bring affection and security into an imprisoned world.

Some of the questions staff ask about Intensive Interaction are about the mechanics of it – how long and how frequent should sessions be? Because of the way it arose initially, through school periods or therapeutic sessions, we have tended to use limited times. However, in community home settings, more and more staff are saying that they want to use it as a way of communicating whenever it seems natural, just as one might chat to friends. This is precisely what Intensive Interaction gives us the option of doing – it is a way of expressing our enjoyment of being with another, of being at ease together. Mutual trust and confidence start to build and difficult behaviours frequently diminish as the person no longer feels isolated and defensive. There is often a marked change in how staff feel about their work. Everyone is able to take a more relaxed attitude. The group dynamic has improved.

Sometimes staff are concerned as to how this type of interaction will be viewed by the general public. It is possible to argue that some directions suggested in this book are so individually based as to lead away from social acceptance. If we learn a person's language and use it with them, will it not isolate them rather than move them towards integration?

We need to take a hard look at exactly what we have in mind when we talk about 'social integration' for an individual with profound disabilities or very severe autism. These are people who may have completely rejected their environment because they find it confusing, hostile or frightening. Further, our world may have rejected their overtures to us, the only way they have of getting in touch with us.

If we are not careful, our expectations may lead to conformity rather than communication, respectability rather than respect, and valuing a person for what we think they ought to be rather than what they are.

At a community home for children with profound disability and multiple impairment, it was suggested that communication was not possible and therefore staff focused on reducing inappropriate behaviour so the children would be able to take their place in public. With the best intentions, what was being aimed at was conformity. The effect, however, was somewhat contrary to that intended. Suppression of such behaviour as raspberry noises, for example, seemed to lead, not to compliance but to other forms of 'naughty' behaviour such as grabbing at people or objects – anything to get attention.

By ignoring or erasing a person's own language, we may cut off the one way they are able to interact with us – we seal up their prison.

While not suggesting that socially inappropriate language should be wildly and exaggeratedly used in public, it is quite often possible to develop shorthand reinforcers which maintain contact with a person without attracting unwanted attention. We should ask ourselves if we see a group of people as more 'adult' when half are sitting in dulled conformity while the other half chat amongst themselves, or when all the group are participant and enjoying themselves – when we see people with impairment truly being valued for themselves. To change attitudes, the public needs to see people with impairment who are self-assured and with whom communication is being taken seriously.

One technique used to keep in touch is the 'running commentary', with the aim of letting people know what we are presently doing with them. However, if we watch a video of ourselves doing this, we very often see that we are engaging in a monologue – we are saying things without involving an individual personally; we are thinking about what we are doing and not about them. For example, we may be talking to a person about putting their socks on while ignoring the grunts they are making. This does not engage their attention; in other words, our running commentary ignores their signals since it is fixed on what we are doing. It is not meaningful enough to promote response. To communicate, we need to pay attention to who the person really is instead of who and what we want the person to be. We can sometimes help with this by watching the person's face very carefully while we speak and exaggerating facial language to accompany what we say – for example, raising our eyebrows and smiling. (This is not an appropriate technique if a person is avoiding eye contact.)

Finding a point of contact

There is also the problem that what a person is doing very often has no meaning for us. It is so easy to say, 'they are not doing anything'. We may also find a person's language to themselves very off-putting. Excess noise is only irritating when it is not seen as communication. Once it is recognised for what it is, it becomes a potential point of access rather than a barrier.

The fact that two people are not really communicating may be because neither is doing anything which has meaning for the other. This was illustrated for me by a woman with autism who was locked into delayed echolalic speech.

Jill gets locked into a particular sing-song phrase which she repeats endlessly. She is very tense. It is not possible to break into the phrase or divert her into some more meaningful speech. Even when I repeat her phrase back to her, she takes no notice. I recall a clip from a video interview of Donna Williams talking about how speech may be sound without meaning. She shows a clip of a child repeating the shape and noise of his teacher's sentence without words. I try this with Jill, just using the pitch and rhythm of her speech but not her echolalic words. She becomes relaxed, leans forward and is deeply engaged in what I am doing. Her echolalia ceases.

I could make no relevant sense of Jill's echolalia and, when I was talking to her, Jill could make no sense of the sounds that came from me – they did not 'speak' to her in a way that engaged her attention. However, when I removed the confusing element of words, she could recognise what she heard and knew that it related to her. She responded with interest. A member of her support staff commented that the interaction between us became very intense in a way that was unusual for Jill.

We may sometimes feel that a person is doing nothing which we can latch on to. However, careful observation reveals this is rarely so – almost everyone pays attention to something, even if it is simply breathing. The techniques of Intensive Interaction give us ways of setting up true communication through the simplest bodily activities.

Summary

■ In order to get in touch with a person, we need not only to use their personal language but also to try and understand their perception of the world.

■ If a person cannot understand abstract concepts, they may not be able to understand signs.

■ If we ignore a person's language, we may never be able to get in touch with them or they with us.

■ We may need to look at all the ways a person talks to himself or herself, not just through their repetitive behaviour.

Chapter 11

'Yes or no?'
Making choices

Helplessness may be learned as well as innate. If we are to have a say in our lives, we need not only to be able to make choices but also to be given the opportunities to do so. Guess (Guess *et al,* 1985) presents a spectrum of progressive empowerment, moving from choice as preference (which may be expressed non-verbally in a receptive reactive environment), through choice as decision-making and selection of alternatives, to choice as self-advocacy and taking charge of one's life: 'I need to be able to tell you what I want and I need you to listen to me and act on my request.'

In this section, I focus on choice as preference indication and look at some of the ways in which we may facilitate this. I also want to examine the special situations that may arise when people with autism are unable to process information or organise responses, which may lead them to experience 'choice' as positively disempowering. In such situations, overloading leads to fragmentation and the person can become seriously disturbed.

First of all, it appears that, regardless of whether or not the person has fully understood and is making the correct choice, the very act of being involved in choice may in itself be empowering.

Williams and Jones describe a study where the effect of self-monitoring behaviour on reducing agitated/disruptive behaviour in community group homes was measured. A woman with learning disabilities who was aggressive was asked, after each incident, to tick on a chart whether she had handled or lost her temper. The chart had appropriate faces on it and, she was asked to tick the appropriate column. She co-operated but was not able to evaluate herself correctly. Nevertheless, the number of aggressive incidents dropped by 40%. This suggests that facilitating the participants' engagement in the process of developing verbal rules has a reinforcement potency in itself (Williams & Jones, 1997). As with 'the lady with the knife' (see Chapter 7) the very fact that the woman was involved, and her contribution was valued, increased her feelings of self-worth and elevated the threshold at which she was overtaken by aggression.

Secondly, we may be able to take active steps to facilitate understanding so that the individual is more involved – they know what they are saying. In the following history, a woman who is often disturbed appears to be able to make choices.

> *Jane nods her head clearly for 'yes' and shakes it for 'no'. At the centre, she shook her head when offered the foot spa but when it was removed she immediately became very upset. It was clear that she did want it but had indicated 'no' when she meant 'yes'. Subsequent observation suggested that she quite often got her answer wrong but she did know that she was being asked a question that required a response, so she said 'yes' or 'no'. As there was a 50% chance of being right, it had been assumed that she was able to indicate preference but in fact she was frequently incorrect. Not getting what she wanted was one of the more frequent triggers of her outbursts.*

Swain (1989), reviewing learned helplessness and empowerment through choice, points out that successful working with choice-as-preference is directly dependent on the sensitivity, empathy and responsiveness of support staff. In Jane's case, staff followed a suggestion that after she had indicated 'No', they partially removed the foot spa so that she could see the consequences of what she had said, then gave her a second chance by looking at her enquiringly to see how she responded. This enabled Jane to make an informed choice and the outbursts that had been related to misunderstanding diminished.

Negotiating choices

The skill of negotiation demands that we observe what causes a problem for a particular individual and work out ways of meeting the difficulty. As a colleague observed, we need to think about what we are doing all the time. We think we do this, but very often we are thinking about how the situation affects us and not about the difficulties which the individual concerned is struggling with. We need to put aside what we see – in this case, distressed and disturbed behaviour which is difficult to handle – and, having observed what the source of the problem is, look for creative ways of resolving it. We need to look for the underpinning causes of challenging behaviour rather than working directly with it.

In order to negotiate successfully, we need to be sure that: firstly, we have a person's attention; secondly, that we present information or choices in a way that they understand and find non-threatening. The latter particularly applies to people with autism who may find direct communication far too confrontational and demanding to handle. Only if we find a 'safe' way of offering information will they be able to process it. Because of the danger of overload if our approach is not understood, once we have got their attention, we may need to accompany our speech with secondary clues. The mode we employ will depend on an individual's level of understanding. It may be that the person can cope with pictures. For example, the PECS system – where a child has to take pictures Velcroed into a book and hand them to their teacher/parent (who says the word at the same time as receiving the picture) – helps the child to associate words with interaction; it puts meaning into the verbal exchange. Preliminary work suggests that this system can be very effective with pre-school children. Not only does it help them to understand that exchange is involved in communication, but they also learn to initiate contact. A greater proportion have been developing speech than could have been forecast. Some work has been done with adults and, although they have not developed speech, their ability to communicate is improved (Baker, 1997).

Simple gestures and perhaps objects of reference that a person can feel also help. Quite often a person with autism will start to do something and then get stuck (their motor system becomes disconnected from their brain) and they stand waiting. The person can become very stressed at this point, torn between an expectation that they will do something and an inability to perform. They need a 'clue' to reconnect. Even people who are quite able can benefit from gestures and objects of reference, especially if they find it difficult to look at pictures. (Even if the person is high-functioning they may, in order to process at least some of the incoming signals, have switched off hearing or seeing. Offering a signal to an alternative sense may get through to them so that they know what we are going to do.)

Jolliffe says that she found things so much easier to understand through touch and feeling (Jolliffe *et al,* 1992) and Williams (1995) also describes how she developed sensing through feeling.

If we have managed to help a person understand, we need to look for signs of agreement such as a quick nod of the head. Agreement means the person is participating in what happens in their lives instead of being dragged along by events.

> *I am working with Ben, whose sensory world is chaotic. With him, I might say, 'May I sit down?' accompanied by a gesture pointing to a chair. I look for acknowledgement by a flicker of the eyes. Ben knows where I am, what I am going to do and has agreed to my doing it. I know that he has processed and understood my request, and is not likely to find an unanticipated action so intimidating that he will attack me.*

If we are going to give choices, we need to be sure that the person understands them or we may add to their difficulties. There may be circumstances where the effect of choice is just too overwhelming and in spite of what we believe to be a beneficial and respectful approach, we may need to avoid it altogether. This possibility is explored in the next history.

> *Debbie is six and at school. She has autism and is unable to join class activities except when they involve food. She can tolerate sitting in a group when there is a biscuit or orange juice in sight. (If we are right about certain activities being 'hard-wired' into the brain, in her disordered world, when she is eating, she knows what she is doing. Otherwise there is chaos.) At other times, Debbie is extremely upset and disrupts the class trying to look for the biscuit tin or wanders round outside flicking her fingers or some string. Sometimes she stops and looks at her reflection in a dark window. She 'knows' a few Makaton signs but does not use them meaningfully.*
>
> *Debbie has a special worker who takes her to activities such as the gym or sensory room. In the gym, Debbie will sometimes bounce a ball or jump on the trampoline but she tends to do this in a rather mechanical way.*
>
> *Her key-worker is careful to offer Debbie choices. She says, 'Go and stand by the door if you want to go to the hall,' but Debbie does not respond to such options. She retreats to her finger movements. Repeated offers simply confuse her and she ends up attacking a nearby person. However, we find that she responds at once if we give her a ball to hold, point to the hall and say, 'Hall'. Every time she is given a clear objective in a way that she understands, she complies immediately.*

Debbie is not being difficult. She simply cannot handle the information she needs to process in order to make choices. If we look at it from her point of view, we can see that trying to process alternatives is more stressful than understanding a simple request made in such a way that she can grasp and respond to it.

Summary

- Making choices may be empowering but is not always so, particularly for some people with autism.

- We must present choices in a way that a particular person can understand.

- Sometimes people will need a second chance to see the consequences of their choice.

- We need to simplify our language and, where appropriate, confirm it by using gesture and /or objects of reference.

Chapter 12

'Copy and paste'
Transferring a positive emotional load

As we learn any new language, we become more fluent in its use. We learn which elements indicate pleasure, which signify security and when a person is unhappy or becoming disturbed. Whatever the language, we look not only for sounds but for all the facial and body language that expresses feelings. By learning to use the elements that are meaningful to a person, we can enhance our empathetic communication with each other. We let them know we have taken on board their feelings and understand them. We can let them know what our feelings are.

It is sometimes possible to start to bring security where there is fear by moving a sound that has positive associations for a person to situations where they feel insecure. This can be particularly helpful to people within the autistic spectrum who are experiencing overload or fragmentation.

In Chapter 3, we looked at Donna Williams' description of her battle to understand what was going on in her life. Many people with ASD take refuge from the chaos in repetitive or compulsive behaviours. In a slippery world, they set up markers where they know what is going on.

In connection with this I should like to look at the particular fixation which some people develop around 'drinks'.

First of all, we know that some medication makes people extremely thirsty. They really do want an awful lot to drink, much more than fits in with conventional tea-breaks. However, I want to suggest a secondary component to this behaviour. When a person is living in a totally disordered world, certain things are landmarks. As we have explored before, according to Barron, when they are involved in repetitive behaviours, they recognise what they are doing (Barron & Barron, 1992). Momentarily, the fragments in the kaleidoscope settle and they can see the pattern of what is going on – even if it is restricted to their inner world.

> *Mike, who has very severe autism, spends much of his time outside in the garden. He finds people very difficult and chooses to separate himself from them. At intervals he presents himself at the door and says 'Drinks', with particular emphasis on the 'KS' at the end. It does not seem to mean anything to him to say, 'Soon', or some such time indicator. After he has had two drinks, instead of replying, I try just repeating back to him his sound, 'KS', 'KS'. He is immediately interested and pays attention to me. We get a conversation going between us, alternating his sounds between us. He relaxes and stops asking for drinks. Instead of running away, he comes inside the house. We sit down on the sofa together. I whisper 'KS' in his ear and he likes it.*

What I suggest is that Mike **knew what was happening** when he was drinking. In between drinks, his anxiety rose. This could be allayed by tuning in to a contextual signal, one that he associated with drinks in a way that was also non-threatening. It was a sound he could attend to without fear of fragmentation – of the signals breaking up. Fascination with this new presentation of 'his' sound enabled him to attend to the world outside. Mike's support staff used this as a way of making contact with him on a regular basis, both the sounds on their own and as 'bilingual' clues to draw attention to 'information'; for example, 'KS, KS, Mike, bath'. In this sense, one is 'gift-wrapping' information in the language a person feels secure with.

If we refer back to Sian Barron's account of the security he obtained from his repetitive behaviour (see Chapter 2), we can see that **what we are doing is placing our demand – that Mike have a bath – within the safe haven of a communication system that is Mike's way of letting himself know where he is and what he is doing. This renders it non-stressful and easy for him to process.**

Mike's staff also standardised what they said to him. For example, one of the times in the day Mike found most difficult was when he woke up. (This early morning confusion seems to be characteristic of some people with autism.) All staff woke him in the same way and this helped him through this period.

Mike and his support staff got to know and trust each other. He began to come in and was able to sit with a group briefly. Sometimes he would invite staff to sit with him by patting the sofa. He smiled and laughed in appropriate contexts. Whereas he had always become upset when he had to get out of a car before, he could now do so without hitting out. He was generally much more friendly and staff felt more able to handle things on the rare occasions when he was disturbed.

Mike's home is an assessment centre for seriously disturbed service users, some of whose difficulties make great demands on its dedicated staff. For this reason, staff have had to shift their priorities for the time being. Mike is no longer able to receive the attention he was previously getting and at present his outbursts, which were greatly reduced, have returned. This regression emphasises that if one is able to put into place a structure which helps a person with autism to feel safe, it must be maintained. As I point out in Person to Person, the positive outcomes are not the result of 'curing' the autism but of modifying the environment.

Creating a buffer zone

Mike was anxious about having drinks because, although he knew what he was doing when he drank, reality slipped away in between times and he could not gauge when it would return as he had no grasp of interval. We took a roundabout way to reassure him, detaching an element of his speech – 'KS' – which related to the stability he associated with drinking, and moved it, together with its positive emotional load, to anchor him in a situation where he was vulnerable to his anxiety. Putting it in computer language, we are talking about 'copy and paste', where a section of text is copied and moved from one page to another.

Mike is not the only person with whom this 'copy and paste' technique has been used. Hannah, described in Person to Person (see page 41), made inadvertent jaw clicks when she was eating, an activity she enjoyed, and these were used to divert her when she was being lifted, a situation that frightened her.

This positive feedback offered her a way out of her inner world when she was locked into an unhappy state. We may be able to use this strategy to tap into the inner world of a person when they have become locked into escalating stress as in the history of Kev which follows. Here, we are using the rhythm of his self abuse which he recognises.

> Kev hits himself when upset and becomes increasingly self-abusive. Eventually, he starts to lash out at people near him. Echoing back to him the rhythm of his smacks by knocking the table surprises him and he moves from being absorbed in his internal stress to looking round to see where 'his' sound is coming from. His attention shifts from his locked-in personal world to the world outside. He stops hitting himself and begins to engage with staff.

When we use a person's personal code to release them from the cycle in which they are trapped, we act as a bridge to the world outside. As with all codes, the key is very specific and, in order for it to work, we may need to use exactly the words, sounds or rhythms the person is using – simply putting oneself alongside a person empathetically may not seem to be enough to spring the trap.

> Roger is autistic. He attends a large and, inevitably at times, noisy day centre, almost the last environment that one would think was a suitable background against which to effect improvement.
>
> Roger wanders the day centre in a world of his own. He is disturbed by other service users and hits out at them if they come too near. He has quite frequent serious outbursts and is unable to take part in activities or even to go out on the centre bus.
>
> As with Mike, staff reflected back to Roger his sounds and repetitive behaviours. He became more aware of them and interactive with them. A predictable mini-environment was provided for him by using a team to work with him – they were always people he knew and who worked with him in the same way. This stability was extended to respite care so that he always received the same responses, even when he woke.
>
> The team tried out a number of approaches. Initially, they found Roger so exhausting that they tried working in two-hour shifts. There was no improvement in his behaviour. Reflecting on this, they saw that the constant turnover of staff might be stressful to him (as working with him was for staff). Management used this insight to help staff understand the nature of stress that Roger was experiencing. With management support, the team switched to working with Roger all day and found that the consistency that this provided, combined with other strategies such as Intensive Interaction (not in sessions, but using his sounds with him all the time in combination with verbal language where appropriate) was beneficial. His outbursts started to reduce.
>
> The team studied Roger's behaviour carefully and learned to distinguish between outbursts which were triggered by pain – he had problems with his ears – and those which indicated he was upset and could not cope with the situation in which he found himself. They learned to alue and be encouraged by small improvements. They learned how to keep the right distance during outbursts and handle them in a manner that did not escalate his disturbed behaviour.

The use of these combined approaches has made it possible for Roger to begin to relate to people, not only his team but also other service users, in a more friendly way. He clearly does not feel so threatened by them and may smile if they call his name. With his team he can go on the centre bus with another service user. On a good day, he can go out to lunch in a pub.

His mother says that at home Roger's outbursts are greatly diminished and are now usually related to pain, or sometimes unanticipated changes. At the centre, serious recorded disturbances have dropped from fourteen per week to one in six weeks (averaged over six months).

During this period, staff have focused not so much on teaching Roger how to do things but on how to be with him and communicate with him. Roger has always had a few words but has begun to use a wider range in an appropriate way. His latest achievement is to say, 'Coke' to the barman, hand over his money and wait for his change. This is a major step forward for him.

In spite of progress in his ability to relate and make use of appropriate words, the team still use his sounds to keep in touch with Roger. In a world which he still perceives as chaotic, keeping that link open is vital.

For Roger, what was needed to effect positive alteration in his life (which has resulted in improved behaviour) was the introduction by staff of what might be termed a predictable protective shield. This acted as a buffer zone which insulated him from externally generated sensory overload and also internally generated emotional overload. The 'buffer zone' provided a recognisable secure haven in which he could interpret the sensory and emotional input he received, even in the difficult environment where he lived.

Because he was now held together within familiar structure – and language was used in a form which he could process – Roger knew what was going to happen. Staff could keep in touch through his sounds – sounds which were not inappropriate in a public context. All an outsider would witness was an occasional murmured conversation between friends. This progress, which was achieved through the work of committed staff and good leadership, was the outcome of looking deeply at the underlying difficulties Roger was experiencing.

This buffer zone is not the same as a 'womb' which would cut a person off from the external world and, in effect, infantilise them. Rather, the environment is rearranged so that the individual has improved access to the outer world and can enjoy it without fear. Reduction in the quantity of input that is interpreted as 'hostile' results in improved processing and ability to relate to the world. Interestingly, Williams (1996) observes that when her visual confusion is reduced through the use of tinted Irlen lenses, her auditory acuity improves – she can understand sound better. It is my experience that when one is working within the stereotype, and therefore in a way that presents reduced threat, people with autism can interpret more complex language than is normally possible for them. Further, working in this way allows people to express their feelings and they will frequently do so – through direct eye contact, smiling, laughter and, even if they cannot normally tolerate physical contact, with hugs. People with severe autism may begin to use names and ask for contact.

The objection may be raised that we, who do not have autism, have the real vision of the world, a world that is unpredictable. It is unrealistic to expect society to offer special protection for people with autism. It is our job to steer them towards being able to adapt to our world. But such a suggestion presupposes that a person with autism starts on a level playing field in sensory terms. It makes no allowance for the fragmented kaleidoscopic perceptions which may be painful and do not allow a person to make sense of the environment. Even laying aside humane considerations, the question we have to answer is: 'Which system works for this individual?'

Instead of expecting people to conform to our world, we need to enter theirs and understand their difficulties, simplify and structure their environment so that they are not constantly being overwhelmed by sensory and emotional overload. Then, within their terms, we may be able to move together into a wider variety of experience.

Summary

- We need to become fluent in all aspects of a person's language – the way they reassure themselves.

- We need to learn to use parts of a person's language in a different context – 'copy and paste' – so that it can 'hold and deliver' our communications.

- It is crucial that once we have set up a system which reassures a person, we do not remove it as they apparently improve. The autism is not 'cured'; rather, the environment has been made more sympathetic. We may need to maintain a buffer zone.

- We must continue to understand the problems the person is experiencing.

Chapter 13

'A safe box and a scary box'
Containment and holding

We often work with people who have great difficulties in communicating from their world of sensory and emotional instability. In some situations, we have no way of unravelling the complexities of their distress. We may lack the therapeutic skill or the damage may be too great. Furthermore, in order to protect themselves, families may develop delicate webs of interaction which are difficult to explore. If these webs are broken, it will not just be the individual who is exposed. There is a real danger that the whole support system will break down.

Occasionally we hear outbursts from the depths of extreme distress dragging their undertones of isolation: 'You don't know what it's like.'

We can only agree and feel the separation. There is a chasm between us and we shall never experience what they do, not as equals. But sometimes we can help people through a technique known as containment which seeks to encapsulate and disarm the bad things of which they are afraid (and which they feel may overwhelm them). We can also hold on to and keep safe the precious objects, objects that are so precious because they form the link between dependency and independence. These are the transitional objects that Winnicott describes (1971).

Holding anticipation and fear

When bad things happen in our lives, we are not only upset when they happen, we are also afraid that they may happen again. Our feelings are not just about danger but about fear – and this fearful anticipation can be as bad as an actual event. Jolliffe says that she is so conditioned by this fear that she lives in anticipation of some terrible event (Jolliffe *et al*, 1992).

Containment is a technique that uses **resonant images** to disarm the fear. While containment does not eliminate the actual cause of the danger, it may reduce stress by domesticating the co-existent fear.

In the history of Jeff below, he uses a box so that he can protect his belongings and feel that he is more in control of his life.

> Jeff is obsessed by blood, dentists, clinics and drills. He is extremely restless and will not settle down to any activity. I suggest that we have two boxes, a 'safe' box and a 'scary' box. We draw pictures of images, some of which he finds scary. We cut them out and together put them in the appropriate boxes. Jeff learns to distinguish between the safe box and the scary box. He is fascinated by our task and it holds his attention.

Similar work was done with a child who walked round the house holding her 'box of scary things', which she had helped to draw and cut out. When she rattled it she could hear them inside her box. This did not take away the things she was scared of, but gave her some control over them. It domesticated them.

There are many ways we can use to hold and contain situations. In *Person to Person*, I describe drawing road plans with George who has severe autism (see page 33). He is fixated on them to the exclusion of other activities. Once he has enough space in the form of a very large piece of paper, he is happy to share this activity but feels threatened when, attempting to broaden the interaction, I add cars. George's distress is contained when we add a car park and park the cars firmly in it. This is an image in his language and it neutralises the onset of disturbed behaviour. (It is not necessary to remove the cars.) In a world that is unpredictable, once the cars are parked, they are no longer unpredictable – they are no longer a threat. In other words, we are cutting down on George's stress by containing unpredictability.

Another way to hold things which pose a threat because of the demands they make is to put them on a computer. In an interview, Donna Williams [no date] tells us that although she can handle questions put to her through a computer, she cannot manage it when the interviewer asks her a direct question. Similarly, Lindsey Weekes (no date) expresses a preference for the computer: 'It's nothing personal. I just cannot handle the face-to-face communication.'

The computer can also be used as a box to hold the unspeakable. We tried this with Liza (see page 161) and she was at least able to write the word 'pull' that she found so intolerable, without becoming disturbed.

If we remember what Jolliffe says about the threat that reality poses to her – when she describes her escalating fear of 'objects, objects that move, and objects that move and make a noise' (Jolliffe *et al,* 1992) we realise that almost anything can be scary for a person with autism, particularly when they are children and have not yet been able to build up any defence mechanisms. This may make it extremely difficult for them to learn, since the list of frightening objects can include the most basic objects used as educational equipment, such as bricks, pencils and pens. However, we can sometimes make these objects safe by 'holding' them in the stereotype. In *Person to Person*, I describe the history of a child who is fixated on 'Mummy's blue car' – she cannot say anything else until I make her a large wooden car, two sides with a box between. Now she can use and name bricks and other objects, provided they are 'in the car'. The stereotype holds the objects and renders them safe. They are non-threatening and will not cause overload or fragmentation in the child's brain.

In Chapter 1, I described how it was possible to shift the verbally offensive language of a young man by accepting it cheerfully and 'holding' it for him, when ignoring it had not had a positive outcome. Trapped in an emotional tangle, he needed a way out and the surprise evoked by laughing and agreeing with him was enough to move him beyond his behavioural dysfunction in our relationship.

Holding precious objects

We can actually make boxes, not just to disarm the scary things but also to hold and protect a person's precious objects. This is also described in *Person to Person* but here I want to look in more detail at the motivation which leads people to carry round their possessions with them and sometimes become extremely disturbed if they are removed.

To begin with, this type of protection may be simply about providing a secure place to keep objects which are otherwise likely to be taken by others – a not uncommon situation where doors are unlocked and individuals may lack any sense of private property.

Fay lives in an assessment unit and, although she has her own bedroom, at times, depending on the shifting balance of men and women in the house, she is sometimes moved out. She cannot really call her room her own and feels sufficiently insecure to carry around with her all her toiletries in plastic bags. She cannot manage a key.

In the workshop, we make a box large enough to contain Fay's bottles and tins and design a specially adapted locking mechanism. To open it, all Fay has to do is to push a pencil through a small hole against a flap of stiff plastic which hooks over a peg inside. This releases the lid. She now has a container she can open but others cannot. She can keep her precious things safely.

In some cases, a person's choice of precious objects may seem bizarre to our eyes. In *Person to Person* I explore the history of Jim, who desperately desires pieces of plastic to the point of breaking up furniture and bringing endless trouble on himself in order to obtain them (see page 79). As the pieces are removed, he eats them in order to retain them. His need overrides all attempts to divert or control his behaviour. Everything Jim does is focused on this end.

In order to see why this is so, we need to look more closely at what is meant by 'transitional objects' and understand the power that is vested in them.

Transitional objects

Transitional objects are part of the normal process of the development that all of us share. When we are born, we are totally dependent on our mothers and we believe everything is part of ourselves – we do not distinguish anything from ourselves, there is no such thing as 'other'. To put it personally, growth of my sense of 'self' outwards involves my learning to distinguish what is my 'self' and what is not 'myself', between 'me' and 'not me'. By continuous testing, my brain works out what is part of me and what is not. I learn to separate myself from my mother and move towards independence. Transitional objects are special objects which are part of the complex process of separation. They stand halfway between dependence on the mother and her breast, and independence and the development of a sense of self (Stern, 1985).

When we see toddlers sucking their fingers or clutching teddy bears and putting disintegrating bits of blanket in their mouths, it is difficult for us to recall the urgency that attended such objects. We were, quite literally, lost without them. Groping our way into a world which was unpredictable and sometimes appeared hostile and rejected us, these objects were stepping stones from total dependency on our mothers to independence. They were objects of security to which we could withdraw before returning to the struggle to make sense of the world into which we had been thrown. They were oases where we could retreat to suck the comforting breast substitute, biding our time until we had strength to return to our onslaught on reality.

If all is well, the child becomes stronger. As the objects in which they have vested so much attention fall apart, they move on, passing to another developmental stage. Sometimes, however, when the battle is too hard, the child bears scars which send him running for security later in life. If the struggle to separate themselves is too great, children may give up the battle to move on. They retain the need for objects of security.

Many people with very severe learning impairment have great difficulty moving through the developmental stages which are common to all of us. The next history, as also described in *Getting in Touch* (Caldwell, 1996), illustrates the plight of a woman in her early twenties who clearly is caught up in the need for a breast substitute. She has not outgrown the need to be fed and protected by her mother, not so much in a physical but in a psychological sense.

> *Norah collects plastic sacks which she rolls into a ball, regurgitates on and sucks. She is deeply upset if they are removed and will break open cupboards to acquire another, fighting off anyone who tries to stop her. The intensity of her struggle is of the order of a 'life and death response'. She feels so threatened by the outside world that her existence is at stake – she needs the sacks in order to survive. She is so locked into this need that it excludes the possibility of all other ways of responding to external reality.*

Not all transitional objects are so obviously related to the breast and maternal security. With Norah, the relationship is easy to see; however, sometimes it is difficult for us to understand why an individual chooses a particular object to fixate on – we cannot see its fascination. The object has no power for us and may even be disagreeable. However, it is recognisable as more than just an entity by the attraction it holds for an individual and their response to it.

How can we help a person who is caught in this developmental stage to grow through it? Anyone who has witnessed the outcome of trying to remove a child's teddy will be aware that we cannot 'frogmarch' a person to independence by removing the object on which they are dependent. They simply become more desperate for it; their dependency increases rather than decreases. We have to look for creative ways of working with people in the stage they are in.

I was able to begin working with Norah using a large wooden ball which was smooth and comfortable to hold. It is a breast-shaped object and has weight. She enjoys holding it. Gradually, I encouraged her to place it in a bucket and then to post it through a bucket with a hole in its lid. Now, sometimes she has it and sometimes not – but at the same time as letting it go, she knows where it is and can anticipate finding it. To the pleasure of security, we have added the spice of excitement. When we take off the lid it is still there, but Norah's security is no longer dependent on holding the ball all the time. She can let it go and still be safe.

Before we exclude ourselves from what we see as childish behaviour related to transitional objects, we should remember our soft toys, our lucky charms and probably, in addition to its biochemical lure, the draw of cigarettes. A transitional object has power over and above its natural qualities.

Summary

We can:

- use holding techniques to preserve precious objects and disarm threatening objects

- acknowledge the power of transitional objects

- help people to move on through developmental stages.

Chapter 14

'Difficult' behaviour
Rewiring the brain

This section draws on *The Emotional Brain* by Le Doux (1998).

In the past, people considered the brain as the organ they thought with. Emotion was a matter for the heart. Now, neurobiologists are beginning to unravel our emotional responses as part of brain function. The idea of the emotional brain is new. Put simply, there is a hotline from the senses – the eyes, ears, touch, taste, smell and balance – to the amygdala. The amygdala is an organ about the size of an almond in the mid-lower brain. In emergencies, it takes responsibility for organising responses, turning on the adrenaline, raising our heartbeat and generally preparing us for the freeze, flight or fight options. Afterwards, we may reflect: 'We never had time to think about it.'

In a sense this is true: the thinking part of our brains was not invoked. The pathway from the eyes to the amygdala is faster than that from the eyes (if sight was the sense which perceived the danger) to the thinking brain. The thinking brain comes into play later. Like it or not, when the amygdala perceives danger, we find ourselves in the position of a learner driver in a dual control car. The instructor overrides any action we might have taken, setting up responses designed to get us out of trouble. The few milliseconds saved may have made the difference between life and death. The part of the brain which makes conscious decisions has not been involved.

Whether or not we have impairment, we all respond to situations we find stressful – but the level at which an emotional response is triggered in any particular individual varies over a wide range. I may be terrified by an event that leaves you unmoved or we may both be scared of the same situation; even so, I may be much more afraid than you are and so respond earlier or more violently. Whether or not I react is dependent on whether I have 'learned' to link a particular situation with danger – if I have, I will react to it (or to long-term memories of objects I associate with the danger). I will carry the anxiety, and anything that reminds me of the situation will trigger stress and responses, even if I am not consciously aware of the source of my fear. This makes the system unreliable in terms of what is happening now. Responses may be triggered by an event or an emotional memory that accompanied the original trauma so that I may be reacting to something that happened a long time ago. As far as an outsider can see, there may be no obvious connection between outburst and a cause. Le Doux (1998) says that these (to our mind) irrational triggers are extremely difficult to extinguish. We need to look at a person's life to reduce their incidence. It is no use saying that the person needs to get used to the triggers. This may not be possible.

We need to distinguish between our immediate responses to such outbursts, dealing with situations as they arise, and our long-term strategies to try to reduce the incidence of factors which are acting as the triggers to disturbed behaviour. For example, if we know a person is upset by the colour red, we shall avoid wearing it. When we are faced with an immediate escalation of disturbed behaviour, Bennett (1998) discusses techniques we can use which are based on our understanding of the biological processes which are going on during the onset and build-up of aggression – and also the effect that a particular response will have, in biological terms, on that deteriorating behaviour.

Bennett discusses the characteristic stages of the fight response (triggering, build-up, crisis, recovery and post-event depression), the corresponding levels of arousal and the signs by which we can recognise these, so that our responses can be appropriate and not escalate the situation further. For example, Bennett points out that one of the effects of adrenaline build-up is to impair the ability to hear, decode and interpret language and speech – so a person may physically be unable to respond. They simply cannot co-operate: by expecting them to do so we are increasing stress and the flow of adrenaline.

In this book we have looked at various creative techniques that are useful in working with people whose stress causes them to behave in ways that we find difficult to handle. Through increasing our understanding of the circumstances that trigger 'difficult behaviour', we have been able to examine alternative ways of working with causes, such as:

1. **Intensive Interaction** (becoming fluent in people's own language)

2. the creative use of **resonant images** (images that trigger understanding and evoke positive feelings such as increasing confidence and feelings of well-being)

3. the uses of **surprise in a non-threatening context**

4. **'copy and paste':** the ability to shift an element of a person's language which carries a positive load and use it where they are distressed (neutralising negative feelings)

5. **'gift wrapping':** surrounding information in our language with elements of a person's own language (neutralising information that might otherwise be perceived as threatening)

6. u**sing a person's language** to re-establish contact between the inner and outer world when they have become locked into escalating disturbed behaviours

7. **containment through holding** (making things less frightening or preserving precious things).

All these approaches require complete attention to the individual in a therapeutic way, trying to understand their life as they see it and not as we react to it. We must learn to respect all the anxieties gathered from a person's encounters during reality testing, the blueprints from experiences that happened in the past and how these interact with current encounters with the outside world. We must also pay regard to their hypersensitivities.

I want to try to look more deeply at what it is we are doing when we say we are working therapeutically to reduce stress. Le Doux says:

'Psychoanalytic theory and conditioning theories assume that anxiety is the result of traumatic learning experiences that foster the establishment of anxiety-producing long-term memories. In this sense, psychoanalytic and conditioning theory have drawn the similar conclusions about the origins of anxiety. Psychoanalysis seeks to help make the patient conscious of the origins of inner conflict [helping them to become conscious of what was theirs but they had not known before and therefore making it possible for them to take responsibility for it. See Chapter 7: 'The lady with the knife'] whereas behaviour therapy tries to rid the person of the symptoms of anxiety, often through various forms of extinction therapy – with the aim of unlearning the negative emotional reaction.' (Le Doux, 1998, p263)

That is, the aim of behaviour therapy is to raise the level at which an emotional response is triggered by neutralising the occasions that cause it: if I no longer feel threatened by something, I shall not need to react to it.

Again, Le Doux (1998) says:

'Therapy is just another way of synaptic potentiation in brain pathways that control the amygdala. The amygdala's emotional memories are indelibly burned into its circuits. The best we can do is to regulate their expression and the way we do this is by getting the cortex to control the amygdala.' (p265)

In other words, we need to find ways of rewiring the brain. To make it more difficult, we are trying to do this with people who have limited or no verbal skills. All we have to go on is our power of observation, our creative skills and the general rule that we are seeking to reduce anxiety and stress at the same time as improving self-confidence. However, we have some powerful tools: the techniques afforded by Intensive Interaction and by using images that resonate for an individual. While these techniques lie outside the normal scope of psychoanalysis and cognitive therapy, they can have parallel effects in areas that would normally be considered inaccessible due to the depth of impairment.

Summary

We need to consider:

- the hotline from the senses – the part played by the amygdala

- reducing triggers to anxiety wherever they come from

- creative ways of approaching stress

- whether we can rewire the brain.

Chapter 15

'Bit'
Transitional phenomena and reducing stress

How can we bring order and meaning to people whose sensory lives
are chaotic?

Reading accounts of childhood autism, one is struck by the use of such
expressions as 'terror' and 'agony' – extreme words used by people to try
to give us an idea of the painful ordeals and danger of extinction that they
perceive. It is small wonder that they may respond with violent behaviour
which we do not know how to contain – just as they cannot contain the
violence of these assaults on their senses. Existing in a world without
parameters, these people may have nothing to cling to but a few repetitive
behaviours or objects on which they are fixated, activities which bring
them some relief from the onslaught of their senses by raising the level
of endorphins (the body's natural painkillers) in the brain.

> *Mandy is six. She has severe autism and is very disturbed. At school, she has frequent
> outbursts in which she attacks staff or pupils. She has a toy rabbit that she calls 'Bit', which
> she does not bring to school. Her class has a number of other disturbed children and, because
> of this, in spite of the best efforts of the teacher, there is tension and noise in the classroom,
> with children moving about in ways that non-autistic children might find intimidating. Mandy
> draws well but her attention span is short and she has frequent tantrums.*

If we go back to what people with autism say about their sensory experiences,
in her disorientated world, Mandy's safety is invested in 'Bit'. When she
has hold of it, she knows what she is doing – she can physically feel herself
hanging on to an object she recognises through touch. At school, she does not
have that security.

I suggest to Mandy that we draw 'Bit'. She immediately focuses on this idea and produces a recognisable drawing which she colours in. We cut it out and paste it on card. The next time she is upset she says, 'Be good, have "Bit".'

Navigating the gap between self and other

When she is disturbed, Mandy needs the security offered by 'her object', that is, an unchanging object in a slippery world, the one thing she can physically hang on to and know where she is in relation to it: a life-belt in a stormy sea. 'Bit' offers comfort and security and fulfils an equivalent function to a transitional object. Although it may not have arisen directly during separation from the mother and establishment of the self as a separate entity, it does occupy the same niche. Winnicott (1971) extended the concept of the transitional object to transitional phenomena. This includes anything which enables us to negotiate and navigate the gap between self and other – giving purchase on the unknown. Under this heading then, we can also, for example, include Mike's '-KS, -KS' – a verbal aid to making sense of his surroundings. Perhaps this is one way of thinking of some stereotypic behaviour.

In addition to this, we can not only use Mandy's 'Bit' to provide stability when she is upset, but also use it to focus her attention when she is calm – for example, 'Bit' can point out letters for reading. We can use the stereotype or fixations to maintain the position of objects that might otherwise 'move about' and therefore be seen as threatening. There is no associated anxiety that objects of fixation will slither around or alter dimensions. Temple Grandin is quite clear that such objects of fixation can be used to help teach children (Grandin & Scariano, 1986). Provided that the teaching material is related to or incorporated into the stereotype, the stereotype will help to focus their attention and objects will remain unthreatening.

Grandin is less happy about the use of self-stimulatory behaviours in a similar way, while Gillingham (1995) urges that repetitive behaviours should be eliminated because, as well as protecting the individual from pain, the raised level of endorphins cuts the person off so that they are unable to respond to environment and people – they are lost in their own world. However, Gillingham focuses on the need to reduce the level of sensory stimulation rather than trying to eliminate behaviours directly, since the latter process, if it is successful (and more often than not one eliminated repetitive behaviour is replaced by another), may leave an individual vulnerable to the stress and pain of fragmentation since they are denied the protection afforded by endorphins.

While agreeing completely with the need to reduce stimuli which are causing hypersensitivity, there is the practical problem that, for a variety of reasons, it is often very difficult to effect the conditions which would help this reduction. For example, in many centres as they are currently designed, there is no possibility for the provision of a quiet room and also, at present, a lack of awareness that this may be crucial to a person's well-being. In an effort to construct an 'attractive and stimulating' environment, most rooms are cluttered with pictures and conflicting patterns and designs. Gillingham says we should aim for tranquillity. In this respect, we need to rethink the service provided for people with autism with all the implications for training that this brings, so that they can have somewhere in their lives to go when they are overloaded that will not make the problem worse. We also need to take active steps to ensure that their environment is modified so they are not subjected to stimuli that cause them pain.

At the time of writing, it is gradually becoming clear that the use of Irlen lenses may provide some people with ASD with the sensory tranquillity they require, not because they 'cut out' certain colours to which people are sensitive, but because they adjust the frequency of visual input so that it synchronises with the ability to process the input.

The other approach, which should be complementary to attention to hypersensitivities is, as we have discussed, the creative development and use of a person's language to attract their attention.

'Coming up with creative ways to use the obsessions of a student with autism is a challenge well worth facing. By using the interests of a child to motivate learning, we have the opportunity to build rather than destroy.' (Gillingham, 1995)

Personal experience in working with people who have severe learning impairment as well as disorders within the autistic spectrum, suggests that there is little difference between using a person's fixations – for example, a fixation on bits of paper which are flapped in front of the face, and using self-stimulatory repetitive behaviours such as flapping fingers in front of the face as a basis for interaction. As I have suggested, fixations are not necessarily related to the outside world but, rather, to that part of the world which has been hijacked and brought in to be used as part of the furniture of the inner world (in *Person to Person*). Reflected back to a person, both fixations and self-stimulatory repetitive behaviours can give access to the inner world and allow a person to respond, since they do not trigger overload. Also, they retain their function of acting as a buffer between dysfunctional brain processing and those elements of the environment which disturb a person – even when bringing people out of their inner world.

Summary

This section looked at:

- bringing meaning to disordered perception; the stereotype as a transitional phenomenon

- reducing stress through paying attention to hypersensitivity and using an individual's language – a complementary approach.

Chapter 16

How can we help?

How can we help people who have severe learning disabilities as well as autistic tendencies?

At present we cannot 'cure' autism, but we can improve the lives of those experiencing it by the use of techniques which have positive outcomes, remembering that each person with whom we work is different – we need to tease out individually-based strategies for each one. In effect, we need to make a complete inventory of each person's life, asking ourselves all the time how they experience it.

Take account of hypersensitivities

- Use a soft voice.

- Let people know what we are going to do before we do it.

- If there appears to be visual hypersensitivity, look at the possibility of using coloured Irlen lenses if this is a practical option. (Visual hypersensitivity is not about having bad eyesight.) Apart from the more obvious indications of hypersensitivity, such as screwing up the eyes or preference for dim light or a certain colour, there may be more subtle indications. Among those which are currently being explored are situations that suggest a person is having difficulties with visual processing, for example:

    - spitting on, and trying to erase, reflections on shining surfaces or dark knots in the wood of a table

- having difficulty making choices (holding two or more images simultaneously)

- having difficulties adapting to the unexpected or coping with change (trying to marry an anticipated image to an alternative one).

Reduce sensory input and particularly the personal threat posed by people

■ Respect the space a person requires.

Make a detailed and objective observation of the person's body/ facial language and behaviours

■ How do they 'talk' to themselves?

■ What are they 'really' getting out of an activity? This may not be the same as they superficially seem to be getting out of it; we may need to try a behaviour ourselves in order to see what it is they are seeing. (A person twiddling a toy car as they look through it may actually be watching their face in its little window.)

■ How does the person respond to situations?

■ How does the person 'talk' to us?

Remember that communication is not just about exchanging information but also about building relationships

■ Work with the person's language to build mutual confidence and relatedness, giving them a chance to express feeling.

Simplify and standardise communications so that a person can understand what we are trying to tell them

■ Avoid abstract signs and minimise questions and choices.

■ Even if a person has some speech, it is often helpful to back up our information and requests by pictures or gestures and objects of reference (objects which are a recognisable part of the communication).

■ If a person gets stuck when they are trying to do something, we need to remember that this may be because their motor system has become disconnected from the brain so that they cannot proceed. (There is a difference between knowing what we want to do and being able to do it.) The connection can often be re-established by the use of a relevant gesture or 'clue' through an alternative sense.

Remember the difficulties that people have in working out what is going to happen and their inflexible and literal interpretations once they have managed to understand

■ Try to avoid unanticipated changes which arise because a person cannot marry their picture of what was going to happen with what is happening.

■ If these situations do arise, use gesture and objects of reference, or pictures if they are understood, to help negotiate the unexpected.

Help the person to know what is going to happen by introducing structures and timetables which are individually designed so that they will be able to make sense of them

■ The distinction between what is happening and what is going to happen must be visually extremely clear. Kitchen timers can be used to help people to understand the difference between 'now' and 'not now'. The structured educational approach of the TEACCH method (see Resources) is also helpful to children.

■ Once a helpful structure has been established, greatest caution should be exercised in trying to reduce it. Sudden reduction in the structure that supports a person may be catastrophic.

■ Give people time to process information.

Managing a successful programme

Successful programmes are dependent on effective implementation. Listening to some of the managers of strategies which have had effective outcomes, the following are qualities that they felt made for positive outcomes.

■ A management style that takes a pragmatic approach, creating an environment where it is possible to try out a strategy to see whether or not it is successful. Managers need to say, 'If it works, we will continue' and 'If it fails, we will reflect on why it is failing in a manner that is non-judgmental of staff'.

■ Appointment of a change facilitator, a key-worker or primary nurse working within a team. This person is encouraged to come up with ideas and is supported by individual supervision.

■ Staff being confident that, if they run into difficulties, leaders will support them with hands-on involvement, helping them to sort out the problems they encounter. These problems will be looked at, not just in the context of the service user, but also in terms of the interactions between support staff and user.

■ While theoretical background is important, managers need to emphasise the value of practical objectives such as, 'What we are going to do this week?'

■ Key-workers being encouraged to spread effective ideas laterally through their team to ensure consistency.

Each step we take may seem a small one, but the effect can be cumulative and can transform the lives of people who are struggling to make sense of their environment.

Chapter 17

What do we mean by success?

Until recently, we have tended to measure success in terms of improvements in skill, but many of the positive outcomes we have been discussing, including the following examples, are subjective.

- A woman with cerebral palsy sits up, smiles and starts to look round at her surroundings. (There has been nothing in her life which has been powerful enough to motivate this before.)

- A man with severe autism and disturbed behaviour becomes calmer and interacts with staff. His challenging behaviour decreases.

- A man with severe challenging behaviour who eats plastic is able to grow through this developmental stage. He starts to interact with his peers, to the extent of organising them to play games with him.

For people with ASD, we can draw up a generalised table of potentially successful outcomes using the approaches suggested in preceding sections.

Potentially successful outcomes for people with ASD	
Working with the stereotype	**Working against the stereotype**
Simplifying demands and language used	Controlling behaviour
The person becomes calmer – relaxes	The person remains stressed
More friendly	Isolated – chooses solitude
Lively and engaged, more able to enjoy themselves	Withdrawn
Increase in eye-contact on own terms. Smiles and laughs	Avoids eye-contact
Initiates contact	Rejects contact
Sometimes becomes more fluent in our language. Uses more words	Continues minimal use of our language
Capacity to handle a wider range of situations improves	No flexibility
'Difficult' behaviour decreases. In addition, staff find person easier to handle when they are upset	Behaviour management remains a problem

The primary effect of the type of interventions we have looked at in this book has been emotional – a general loosening up as an individual becomes less stressed and more confident. This is noticeable for support staff who work with the individuals – they simply become warmer, easier and often more fun to work with.

However, it may be less easy to be objective about such improvements than simply deciding whether or not an individual can brush their hair or recognise colours. One of the questions we have to ask before we evaluate improvements is what human value we place on deepening the capacity for emotional interaction and awakening the capacity for joy. In case this should appear too ill-defined an objective, the ability to connect with people facilitates everything we do with each other.

Chapter 18

'Back where we started'
Reciprocal attempts to communicate

Failure to communicate is not the only factor underlying challenging behaviour. Hewett (1998) lists sixty-five in his book, *Challenging Behaviour*, and even this extensive list does not include the difficulties and consequent behavioural problems that some women experience as a consequence of being unable to nurture (*Person to Person*). Yet, in one way or another, failure to communicate does account for a large slice of challenging behaviour. How can we set up relationships if we cannot 'talk' to each other? It is easy to have low self-esteem if we live in a world from which we are excluded. We can fall into a pattern of fighting for our existence in a world where nothing makes sense so that we always feel threatened.

Because most of the work I am asked to do concerns ways of setting up communication, much of this book is about people with autism. However, in most cases, the attitudes and approaches which we have looked at apply within and outside the autistic spectrum.

We need to:

■ work 'from' an individual rather than with them, looking at the world from their point of view and learning to use in a non-threatening way the language they have developed to talk to themselves and communicate with us

■ simplify our language to a level at which a person is most easily able to understand it

■ set up structures which present information that people can grasp in a way which is non-threatening.

All these techniques are universal and can be generally applied.

To end, I want to return, through a simple behaviour, to the dominant theme of this book – the need to learn that an individual's sensory experience may be totally different from ours and to look at their world through their eyes and ears and touch – their sensory experience. To do this, I should like to look at the experience of a staff support member who asked about a woman who was autistic and fixated on a certain drawer.

> *Beryl is fascinated by a drawer. A member of support staff says that he finds this inexplicable as Beryl apparently does not want anything out of the drawer but she is so desperate that she will climb over all manner of obstacles so that she can point her finger to it. I ask the support worker if he has ever tried pointing to it with her and he replies that he had once done this. He shows me how she turned to him, smiling and rubbing her hands together with pleasure.*

It seems that Beryl is fixated on an object to the exclusion of everything else. It dominates her thoughts and activities. To us, who are outsiders, there is no rational reason for an attachment we cannot share, even at second-hand when Beryl points it out to us. It is an impediment to a relationship, as well as being irritating when she goes on and on about it. But suppose we try looking at the drawer from Beryl's viewpoint. In order to do this, we need to go back to Sian Barron and what he says about his fixation with light switches:

- 'I know what I'm doing'

- 'It's the same every time'

- 'I feel secure when I'm doing it' (Barron & Barron, 1992).

It is now clear that what Beryl is doing is showing us and sharing what is, for her, the lynchpin of her existence; in a world of sensory turmoil, it is the object that holds her life together. It is the most important thing she has and we need to show her that we have understood this and taken it on board. As soon as her key-worker shows her that he understands it is important to her, she is able to connect with him, and he with her. They share understanding. Hewett uses the word 'celebration' to underscore the process of valuing a person's responses and attempts to communicate (Nind & Hewett, 1994).

Value who the person is

We must value a person's precious objects and activities and be honoured by their sharing them with us because that is where they are centred. In valuing these, we value who the person is. Far from enhancing the behaviours we find unwelcome, the frequent outcome is that beyond impairment, in letting go, we reach each other in the deepest sense.

The theory of mind suggests that one of the characteristics of autism is that an individual is unable to put themselves in another's position and so lacks the ability to empathise with them. The person has no access to our complex world of social interaction and relationships. There is a gulf between their literal understanding and our more subtle grasp of motives. They do not understand how our world works. Ironically, if we are not careful, we fall into the same trap – we judge their world by ours.

Donna Williams is right – we need to let go of our presuppositions and ways of thinking, and all the blueprints we find so important, so that we can become travellers in the mind.

The liberation can be astonishing.

Chapter 19

A GP's viewpoint

By Dr Matt Hoghton

This chapter is dedicated to the memories of Alan Mundy, Hugh Davies and Tim Armstrong.

For several years, my work as a doctor has been with adults with severe and multiple profound learning disabilities. In common with many general practitioners, I have found myself meeting people with conditions such as autism with which I had very little experience. I first came across the work of Intensive Interaction by chance, when a series of carers, nurses and doctors who had asked for help with difficult problems, particularly with regard to communication and challenging behaviour, suggested I talk to Phoebe Caldwell. Having read her previous suggestions in the notes of my clients, and seen her work on video, I began to realise that not only should we be interested in improving our clients' living conditions but, more fundamentally, should begin to achieve a meaningful interpersonal two-way contact. I started to see that doctors share the prejudices and ignorance about autism that are often found among the general population.

As doctors, we expect to help other people, and other people expect us to help them. This may make it difficult for us to acknowledge when we find we have inadequate skills. Using Intensive Interaction has helped me to redefine my relationship with people with autism and think of myself as an assistant rather than a carer. As a carer, I am invested with personal power over an individual but, as an assistant, the relationship is more balanced. Working in partnership with someone with autism can be difficult; neither those intimately caring, nor the professionals, have a monopoly on the answers. The best results are only obtained when those involved work together and pool their experience.

When one starts to train as a healthcare worker, one has only a small amount of experience from which to work. Initially, most of my diagnoses and problem solving was based on trying to work things out from first principles. However, growing experience, coupled with pressure of time, resulted in diagnoses which relied on pattern recognition. (This is helpful as it speeds up the process of healthcare but gets in the way when you meet individuals who do not fit the norm.) People with autism and some people with challenging behaviour do not fit easily into patterns. This is particularly true of autism and most of us struggle to understand its complex manifestations.

Apart from the knowledge gap, we have considerable communication difficulties. If a person is unable to communicate in our language, we often try to impose other languages (such as sign) on them, rather than simply trying to use their language. Most people with autism are able to communicate in their own language but we fail to observe it, recognise its importance and use it to engage their attention. Intensive Interaction allows us to observe, watch and reflect back to people their own language. Using this interpersonal approach enables us to connect and engage with people. Simply taking time to watch someone move, listen to their sounds, and reflect these back to them will start the process (and this does not require years of training to do). Most people will stop and notice when I use their language.

In my experience of teaching medical students, they can learn the necessary skills to get in touch with people with autism without too much difficulty. They are often delighted with the reaction they get. I show them that they can continue to hold an individual's attention by building on their responses to set up a conversation without words and I emphasise to the students the importance of listening for responses. The empathy generated can change the relationship from an unknown stranger to a friend.

John is a 24-year-old man with learning difficulties who is unwell. I am anxious, as I have heard he is difficult to examine and is sometimes aggressive, especially if he is having blood taken. He is the first person I have tried to communicate with in his language. He is sitting by his bed on the floor cross-legged without any shoes on. I sit down opposite him and adopt the same position. He then starts rocking his upper body and snorting through his nostrils. I copy his behaviour and then he stops and watches me. I then stop and he restarts. We then take it in turns to 'speak' to each other. In ten minutes, he is letting me examine him. I do not push my luck with blood-taking on this occasion but return the following week to pick up where we have left off. John and I are now good friends and he educates me regularly in the latest pop music. Working together with his carers has helped me to deepen my relationship with John. We both trust each other. I trust John will not hurt me or break my spectacles and I think he trusts me to work with him as a practitioner.

Many of us are frightened of working with people with autism. Where there should be trust, we feel alienated. Our fears derive from misconceptions, a lack of familiarity and knowledge. Our fundamental skills of flexibility and intuition need to replace the pattern recognition previously mentioned. Lovett (1995) says we need to develop a new respect for the intuitive.

Who has autism?

Wing found in 1989 that one-third of the residents of an adult mental handicap hospital had autism, whilst previous research had shown that 78% of those with ASC also had severe learning disabilities (Wing & Gould, 1979). As Gould (1999) says:

'Some children are very disabled with low level of functioning. Others have superior intelligence with very high levels of skills in certain areas.'

One of the difficulties is that this first group are usually treated as 'people with learning disabilities', sometimes with challenging behaviour, rather than people who come within the umbrella of ASD. This means that their autistic features are often ignored. I agree with Gould (1999) when she says:

'It is essential that the autism is recognised since it has important implications for treatment and prognosis.'

Some of the people who come and see me have very severe learning disabilities as well as presenting the behaviours and special needs which are also characteristic of people who have autism or Asperger's syndrome as at present defined. Most of the work which has been done seems to have been focused on high-functioning people – little appears to have been published in relation to people who are low-functioning and whose autism is linked with such disabilities as:

■ Down's syndrome

■ cerebral palsy

■ general learning disabilities

■ Fragile X syndrome

■ Rett's syndrome.

When Kanner first described it in 1943, the incidence of autism was believed to be one in 5,000 live births. Since then, there appears to be a marked increase in the prevalence of autism and Baron-Cohen in 2009 has shown at least 1% of the general population have autism spectrum condition so it is relatively common (Baron-Cohen *et al,* 2009). There are problems interpreting the data as the definition of the diagnosis and awareness among clinicians has changed but there is an apparent dramatic rise in the number of people, especially boys, affected.

Causes and diagnosis

Whilst genetic factors are implicated in the cause of autism, they only account for a small number of people with autism. There is indirect evidence that early environmental exposures of the developing brain to neurotoxic chemicals may also contribute. There is no convincing proof that vaccines cause autism.

Autism has only relatively recently been included in psychiatric classifications (1980) and the diagnostic criteria was not established until 1995 so many general health care professionals have had little or no training in diagnosis of this condition. This is improving but recognition remains poor, particularly in black and ethnic minority groups.

Wing identified the classic triad of difficulties with:

■ social interaction

■ social communication

■ imagination (Wing & Gould, 1979).

In the *American Psychiatric Association Diagnostic and Statistical Manual of Mental Illness* – DSM-5 (due for publication 2013) – it is proposed that the triad becomes a dyad (pair) of social communication difficulties and strongly repetitive behaviour, as some people with autism clearly have good imagination and it is a difficult area to quantify.

The following excessive behaviours and symptoms often present early in childhood and these should be a cause for concern.

■ **Self-stimulatory behaviour**
This is often stereotyped and repetitive behaviour such as opening and shutting doors, flushing the toilet repeatedly, head banging, self-injury, rocking when standing from front to back foot, teeth grinding and repetitive noises.

■ **Aggression**
This can be difficult to manage as the child's physical size and strength increases. Parents often experience difficulties with boys over six years of age.

■ **Hyperactivity**
Children will lack awareness of personal safety and require considerable supervision to prevent injury, especially if they run away. The focus on the child may put other children in the family at risk with lack of attention.

■ **Hypersensitivity to stimuli (hyperacusis)**
Sound, colours and other visual stimuli have been reported as being overwhelming for some people. Similarly, light touch may cause disturbance but often firm pressure is well tolerated and can even be calming.

■ **Bowel disturbances**
Constipation and diarrhoea can both occur.

■ **Sleep disturbances**
These can upset and disturb family life.

■ **Excessive eating or drinking (polydipsia)**

■ **Clumsiness**

■ **Special skills**

About 10% of children with autism may have a skill disproportionate to their other abilities, such as in music, art, calculations or memory recall. Other parents report a pale complexion with dark rings around the eyes and burning feelings often affecting the tips of the ears. In the UK, it is essential to obtain a strict diagnosis in order to access the limited specialised psychiatric and educational supports. It is clear that early intervention is needed but in order to get the 'passport' to resources, you need a firm diagnosis. Access to getting this diagnosis is often restricted by resources, so parents have to maintain sustained pressure in order to achieve the best they can for their children.

The NICE guideline (2012) on *Recognition, Referral, Diagnosis and Management of Adults on the Autism Spectrum* identifies the AQ-10 (British) as an appropriate tool for use in primary care to support a referral for a specialist assessment in people of normal intellectual ability. However, there is no such tool for people with a learning disability. Bhaumik *et al* (2010) reported that the presence of two or more out of five autistic traits gave the highest sensitivity (63.2%) and specificity (78.5%) in people with a learning disabilities, including:

- minimal speech

- poor social interaction

- lack of empathy

- presence of elaborate routines

- presence of stereotypies.

If the person with learning disabilities shows persistent difficulties in two-way communication and has stereotypic (rigid and repetitive) behaviours, or is resistant to change, we need to consider autism. The repetitive behaviour may suggest obsessional compulsive disorder (OCD) but usually the behaviour in OCD causes social anxiety and it rarely starts in childhood. Personality disorders may be considered but these do not exhibit obsessive narrow interests or resistance to change. People with autism and those with antisocial personality disorder (psychopathy) both have empathy deficits; however, in people with autism the deficit is in recognising (cognitive) what others may be thinking or feeling, whilst the ability to have an appropriate emotional reaction to others' feelings (affective) is generally intact. This differs from psychopathy where the intact cognitive element of empathy allows people with the disorder to deceive and manipulate others, whilst they do not care about others' suffering (affective).

At present we rely on observations, particularly from carers, to help make the diagnosis of autism. There are no useful biochemical markers or laboratory tests to aid the diagnosis but recent brain imaging studies hold some hope for investigations.

Potential hopes

Autism can present as so difficult for parents to manage that it is very tempting to grasp any new hopeful possibilities. As this book goes to press, in addition to the interpersonal approaches we have looked at, there have been claims for a variety of treatments including:

- hormonal interventions with ACTH, secretin, oxytocin, testosterone and melatonin

- restrictive diets and vitamins

- chelation (detoxifying poisonous heavy metals)

- hyperbaric oxygen.

So far there is no evidence that any of these interventions or medications modify the disease of autism (NICE, 2012).

However, anxiety and depression commonly co-exist in people with autism and treating these conditions, particularly the social anxiety, can be helpful.

There are two important principles to bear in mind when considering any medication for people with autism:

- Side-effects are more common and poorly tolerated. It is important to introduce medication at a low dose and slowly build up. Recommended dose ranges are not available for children and adolescents. Medication should involve close co-operation between the individual, carers, and the prescriber, with regular review.

- Medication may divert attention and focus from more important therapies, such as a structured environment and behavioural interventions.

The most important realisation has been that early intervention is essential in the development of social skills. PEACH and the EarlyBird Project (see Resources) have developed good practice with particular regard to the pre-school and primary years but these services are patchy across the UK. The focus now is on assessment and treatment of skill deficits – particularly in communication and language, and minimising dangerous or disruptive behaviours. As a local doctor, I have found it important to try to link people as soon as possible to the available resources, especially other parents.

It is important to remember that many people with autism struggle with group-based activities and need individually delivered social learning programmes.

The future

Parents, other carers and people with autism have fought to get the medical and scientific communities interested in this condition. My hope is that increased research and training will raise awareness amongst healthcare professionals so that we can work in partnership with people with autism and their families or carers. We need to offer help and care whilst building up long lasting non-judgmental relationships. We need to provide information and signpost resources and appropriate services. At the same time we need to make reasonable adjustments in our care provision so that services remain accessible despite new technologies and budget cuts.

Exciting as new developments may be, I believe all progress starts with establishing communication and creating a caring relationship with people. We may take time to develop skills in interpreting behaviour, but we must not be afraid of trying simple reflection – copying the person's behaviour and reflecting it back to them in a modified form. Inhibitions and embarrassment may prevent us if we think we will look silly but, once we experience the bond that an interpersonal approach helps us to establish, we will never look back. This type of intervention works with people of any age and is so important in our multicultural society.

Until now, the focus has been on children with autism but without learning disabilities. We must champion communication and help for the silent ones, the non-verbal ones with learning disabilities and autism. We need to use these small bricks of knowledge to build the wall of progress. ASD is sometimes referred to as the invisible disability in people with learning disabilities. It is now time to make it visible.

Dr Matt Hoghton
MBChB MRCGP FRCP
General Practitioner
RCGP Learning Disability Champion

References

A is for Autism (1992) Film. Directed by Tim Webb. London: A Finetake production for Channel 4.

Baker S (1997) *PECS: The Picture Exchange Communication System.* West Sussex Educational Psychology and Portage Service.

Baron-Cohen S, Scott FJ, Allison C, Williams J, Bolton P, Matthews F & Brayne C (2009) Autism spectrum prevalence: a school-based UK population study. *British Journal of Psychiatry* **194** 500–509.

Barron J & Barron S (1992) *There's a Boy in Here.* New York: Simon and Schuster.

Bennett L (1998) *Making Sense of Violent Behaviour: SLD experience 22.* Kidderminster: BILD.

Bhaumik S, Tyrer F, Barrett M, Tin N, McGrother C & Kiani R (2010) The relationship between carers' report of autistic traits and clinical diagnoses of autism spectrum disorders in adults with intellectual disability. *Research in Developmental Disabilities* **31** (3) 705–712.

Caldwell P (1996) *Getting in Touch: Ways of working with people with severe learning disabilities and extensive support needs.* Brighton: Pavilion Publishing/Joseph Rowntree Foundation.

Culshaw T & Purvis P (1998) Developing practice in a residential team. In: D Hewett (Ed) *Challenging Behaviour: Principles and practices.* London: David Fulton.

Davis M & Wallbridge D (1990) *Boundary and Space: An introduction to the work of DW Winnicott.* London: Karnac Books Ltd.

DeBono E (1983) *Atlas of Management Thinking.* London: Penguin Books.

Dunbar R (1997) *Grooming, Gossip and the Origin of Language.* London: Faber and Faber.

Eardley J (1988) Private communication.

Emblem B, Leonard J, Dale K, Redmond J & Bowes R (1998) The challenge of class six. In: D Hewett (Ed) *Challenging Behaviour: Principles and practices.* London: David Fulton.

Ephraim G (1986) *A Brief Introduction to Augmented Mothering.* Playtrack pamphlet. Radlett, Hertfordshire: Harperbury Hospital.

Ephraim G (1994) Private communication.

Gillingham G (1995) *Autism: Handle with care.* Alberta, Canada: Tacit Publishing Inc.

Gould J (1999) Recognising autism. In: L Smeardon (Ed) *The Autistic Spectrum: A handbook.* London: The National Autistic Society.

Grandin T (1995) *Thinking in Pictures.* New York: Doubleday.

Grandin T & Scariano M (1986) *Emergence: Labelled autistic.* New York: Warner.

Grant L (1998) *Remind Me Who I Am Again.* Cambridge: Granta.

Guess D, Benon HS & Siegel-Causey E (1985) Concepts and issues related to choice making and autonomy among persons with severe disabilities. *Journal of Association of Persons with Severe Handicaps* **10** (2) 79–86.

Hewett D (1998) *Challenging Behaviour: Principles and practices.* London: David Fulton.

Hewett D & Nind M (1998) *Interaction in Action.* London: David Fulton.

Horvath K, Stefanatos G, Sokolski KN, Wachtel R, Nabors L & Tildon JT (1998) Improved social and language skills after secretin administration in patients with autistic spectrum disorders. *Journal of the Association for Academic Minority Physicians* **9** 9–15.

Jolliffe T, Lansdown R & Robinson C (1992) Autism: a personal account. *Communication* **26** (3) 12–19.

Kanner L (1943) Autistic disturbances of affective contact. *Nervous Child* **2** 217–500.

Le Doux J (1998) *The Emotional Brain.* London: Weidenfeld and Nicolson.

Lovett H (1985) *Cognitive Counselling and People with Special Needs.* Eastbourne: Prager.

Lovett H (1995) Video. Bolton Institute of Higher Education. Inclusive Education Conference.

NICE guideline (due in 2012) *Autism: Recognition, referral, diagnosis and management of adults on the autism spectrum.* London: NICE.

Nind M & Hewett D (1994) *Access to Communication.* London: David Fulton.

O'Brian A (1988) Private communication.

Peeters T (1997) *Autism: From theoretical understanding to educational intervention.* London: Whurr Publishers.

Stern D (1985) *The Interpersonal World of the Infant.* London: Basic Books/Harper Collins.

Swain J (1989) Learned helplessness theory and people with learning difficulties: the psychological price of powerlessness. In: A Brechin and J Walmsley (Eds) *Making Connections.* London: Hodder and Stoughton.

Ware J (1997) *Educating Children with Profound and Multiple Learning Difficulties.* London: David Fulton.

Weekes L (date unknown) *A Bridge of Voices.* Radio documentary. London: BBC Radio 4.

Williams D [no date] NBC film.

Williams D (1992) *Nobody Nowhere.* London: Doubleday.

Williams D (1995) *Jam Jar.* Film. London: Channel 4.

Williams D (1996) *Autism: An inside-out approach.* London: Jessica Kingsley Publishers.

Williams D (1996) *Like Colour to the Blind.* New York: Time Books/Random House.

Williams H & Jones RPS (1997) Teaching cognitive self-regulation of independence and emotion control skills. In: SE Kroese, D Dagnan and K Loumidis (Eds) *Cognitive Behaviour Therapy for People with Learning Disabilities.* London: Routledge.

Wing L (1989) *Hospital Closure and the Effects on Residents.* Aldershot: Avebury Press.

Wing L & Gould J (1979) Severe impairments of social interaction and associated abnormalities in children: epidemiology and classification. *Journal of Autism and Developmental Disorders* **9** (1) 11–29.

Winnicott DW (1971) *Playing and Reality.* London: Routledge.

Resources

EarlyBird

EarlyBird is a support programme for parents whose child has received a diagnosis of an autism spectrum disorder (ASD) and is of pre-school age (not yet of statutory school age). It is run by the National Autistic Society (see below). More information is available at: www.autism.org.uk/earlybird

The National Autistic Society

393 City Road London EC1V 1NG
Telephone: 020 7833 2299
Fax: 020 7833 9666
Email: nas@nas.org.uk
Web: www.autism.org.uk

Irlen centres

There are Irlen centres throughout the UK. To locate a centre visit: www.irlenuk.com/centres.htm

Peach – Parents for the Early Intervention of Autism in Children

Peach is a parent-led charity that promotes Early Intensive Behavioural Intervention (EIBI) for young children with autism.

Peach, The Brackens, London Road, Ascot, Berkshire SL5 8BE
Telephone: 01344 882248
Email: info@peach.org.uk

TEACCH Autism Program

TEACCH is an evidence-based service, training, and research program for individuals of all ages and skill levels with autism spectrum disorders. Find more information online at http://teacch.com/contact-us

Crossing the Minefield

Establishing safe passage through the sensory chaos of autistic spectrum disorder

Phoebe Caldwell

Originally published by Pavilion as a single volume in 2003

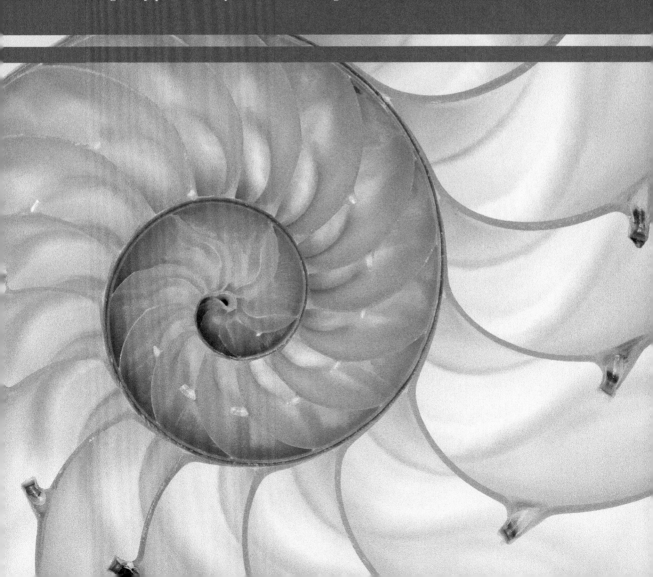

Introduction

'Perhaps the most indispensable thing we can do as human beings every day of our lives is to remind ourselves and others of our complexity, fragility, finiteness and uniqueness.' (Damasio, 1994)

I shall start with an analogy: one that many people will still recognise. Princess Diana is promoting her campaign against landmines. A photograph, published in the newspapers worldwide, shows a fragile looking Diana crossing a minefield, following a path marked out by ribbons indicating where it is safe for her to tread. She is able to walk through this hostile environment because she knows where she is going. Neither she nor any of us would venture into such a danger zone without those guiding lines. It would be easier not to try, to stay in safety rather than to hazard our life.

This is a book about autism, or rather autistic spectrum disorder (ASD), especially – although not exclusively – where it is linked to severe learning disabilities. Its main theme is an exploration of how we can find ways to mark out a safe and meaningful progression from the isolation and sensory chaos experienced by people with ASD to relationship, by putting into the person's life points of reference that the brain will recognise and latch on to. This technique gives them confidence to move through situations that would other- wise drive them further back into their inner worlds. Furthermore, it values an individual as they are, which helps to build their self-esteem.

I have also tried to consider the affective field, the feelings that arise during interaction, and how these feelings can be employed to help both partners involved in the co-creative process into a powerful relatedness, sometimes to the level of bonding.

One of the most difficult aspects of trying to make contact with individuals who have ASD is that by the time their sensory experience is processed, it tells them that the world outside is chaotic and threatening.

'Imagine your thoughts constantly interrupted by thoughts of terror, your own voice sounding like a thunder of garbled words being thrown back at you and folks screaming at you to finish your task. People are screaming at you to stop the aggression. You find your body and voice do unusual things and you aren't in control.' (Seybert, 2002)

Or as Ros Blackburn, another person with ASD, put it:

'For me the whole world is a totally baffling and incomprehensible mayhem which terrifies me. It is a meaningless mess of sights, sound and noise from nowhere going nowhere.' (Blackburn, 2002)

So they defend themselves by retreating to an inner world where they think they are safe. We need to find ways to help people who are stuck in their inner world to feel safe enough to start moving out of isolation towards relationship. Like the ribbons guiding Princess Diana across the minefield, we are looking to establish guidelines, markers that the brain recognises as safe and can focus on. When we do this, the individual no longer feels they are in peril and at the mercy of their environment.

To start with, we need to ask what it is we think we are trying to achieve when we work with people with severe learning disabilities, especially those whose disabilities are linked with severe ASD or behaviour that is difficult to manage. What do we mean by a relation- ship with someone who may not just reject us (that would imply that they had noticed our existence) but fail even to differentiate us from our surroundings, as though we were a piece of furniture? If we try to get any closer the person may present him or herself as hostile to our presence. Is it simply that we want to find ways to contain situations that may seem to us bizarre and sometimes unmanageable? Is it that, urged on by the feeling that there must be some way to ease what may present to us as very distressful, we are looking for something more? Or is it that we see real value in each person as he or she is, and want to share our self with them in mutual exploration?

Crossing the Minefield continues the exploration of themes discussed in *Person to Person* and *You Don't Know What It's Like*. Some of the paths may look familiar but they will take us round new corners, to see a bit further. Fresh territory is also explored. The main emphases is still on the search for what it is that has significance for this particular individual and how we can use it to bring about effective change and empower them.

Rather than starting with our own reality, it is necessary to accept that the sensory reality experienced by many people with learning disability (and/or a variety of behavioural disorders), or the interpretations that they make of their sensory intake, may present them with a completely different sensory scenario to the one that those of us without disability perceive. In particular, they may experience as scary a whole range of inputs that we see as benign. For example, a person who is deaf or who only has peripheral vision may have no warning of objects or people moving in from the side, so these present as potentially threatening because they happen suddenly and unexpectedly. The person may react in what we perceive as an aggressive manner, in order to protect themselves.

We all look at the world from our own point of view. We 'know' that 'our reality' is the true one and we respond to it in ways that correspond to our experience of it. Alternatives threaten our sense of order. Because the perception of others is different, they may react emotionally in ways that, based on our own experience, we do not expect. We find this unsettling, sometimes intimidating. It focuses our attention on the difficulties of managing their response, rather than the problems that the person is experiencing. Are we trying to cope with the effects of their behaviour rather than what is upsetting them?

Just how different the sensory reality experienced by another person may be was brought home to me by a mother who told me that her daughter, who has ASD, bites her when she tries to hug her to express her love. Naturally the mother is distressed. However we know that for some people with ASD touch is painful and that emotional expression can trigger a tidal wave of feeling. In the film *A is for Autism* (1992), Temple Grandin describes how, as a child, she longed to be hugged, but when someone tried to do so she was engulfed by her own sensory feedback to the sensation. Instead of feeling pleasantly affirmed, she was overwhelmed. On the video this situation is illustrated by graphics of a child being swallowed up into the experience. Under these circumstances it may be that to ignore difficult behaviour in a person with ASD is to reward them – and to praise them may be experienced as punishment. What is for some of us a warm, bonding experience may be really unpleasant or even painful for someone whose sense of reality is derived from a different sensory feedback. In order to demonstrate our care and love and respect their needs, we may need to temper our own desires to express emotional closeness.

It is very easy to fall into the trap of trying to frogmarch people whose sense of reality is different from our own into the reality we know to be true for us. We may quite unconsciously project our reality onto them; we genuinely believe that what we experience is what everyone else also sees, hears and feels. My reality is real; deviations are false. But expectations, behavioural judgments and strategies based on our own sensory experience can add to the levels of stress experienced by people whose world picture is different from our own, driving them further back into their inner world. If we are prepared to learn their language so that we can enter their world, we can begin to explore what has meaning for them in ways that do not threaten them. They become interested in this non-threatening relationship and turn towards the source of a new but safe extension of their own world. We can use this approach to mark out a path between our two worlds and establish communication through processes that are meaningful to them.

Our task is to put aside our own reality and logic and keep our minds open to what is important in their world for the people with whom we work. Even where their world touches ours, we need to understand that their interpretations of situations may differ.

In the inner world, the brain and body are engaged in an internal conversation. The brain tells the body what to do and the body tells the brain it has done it. The person's focus is directed at what is going on inside them rather than making connection with the world around them. This may be because they have severe learning disability, or it may be that for one reason or another they find the outside world threatening.

Chapter 1

The uses of surprise

- Intensive interaction: getting into the brain/body language

- The 'periscope' brain

- Feeding the inner world

- Surprise as a discontinuity in expectation

- The use of surprising combinations to shift attention from the inner to the outside world

Maureen is a young woman with severe learning disabilities. She does not join in with group activities, although sometimes she will sit in on them. She is restless, preferring to stay in the corridor, where she often sits on the floor. She twists a belt or string in her hands and is distressed if this is lost.

I have met Maureen twice: once to see if I could help find ways to get in touch with her and again, ten months later, when I revisited the centre to see how she and the staff were getting on.

Maureen has a number of physical difficulties. She is mobile but leans to one side when she walks. She has a slight squint, which can make it difficult to assess whether or not she is avoiding eye contact. She hesitates when she comes to a change in floor colour, kerbs or stairs. She does not like objects coming from the side and is more able to accept them if they come from behind her. It seems likely she has tunnel vision. She has diabetes and care needs to be taken with her diet. She can become upset when her blood sugar levels are low or she has PMT or her teeth are hurting. Her behaviour reflects how she is feeling. Sometimes the reasons for her upsets are not so clear. When she is agitated she will bite her wrist, bang her head or pull her hair.

Maureen is generally non-verbal. She makes sounds and has a few words she uses occasionally. She seems to seek out the company of one particular person, a fellow user of the centre, who 'talks back' to her using similar sounds to those that she makes – they are using the same language.

Maureen has a number of characteristics that seem to come under the umbrella of autistic spectrum disorder:

- she has a number of strong repetitive behaviours

- she has an inability to form relationships

- she is inflexible, finding it hard to adapt to new situations

- she needs routines and is deeply upset by deviations from these; for example, she is upset by the appearance of her mother at the centre when she is not used to seeing her there

- she is hypersensitive to some smells

- she likes her own space – this needs to be qualified as she is generally tolerant of other service users; nevertheless she does not enjoy crowded situations such as travelling on the bus; she can manage better if people sit behind her rather than in front and she does not like to be in a room with a closed door

- she does not give good eye contact and is unresponsive to interaction and attempts to relate with her

- she needs to know exactly what is happening.

Maureen responds to Intensive Interaction. This is a technique based on the primary infant/mother interaction. It uses a person's own behaviour to get in touch with them, building their movements or sounds into a 'language' that can be used to interact and hold conversations with them. The first lesson all of us learn as infants when starting to communicate is that if we do something – make a sound or movement, for example – someone will respond in a way that has meaning for us. The parent figure will confirm our utterances. Peeters (1997) says that unless we receive significant responses to our overtures we eventually give up trying. The approach known as Intensive Interaction seems to have arisen spontaneously in many countries and goes under different titles.

In the UK it was initiated by Ephraim (1986) as 'Augmented Mothering', and developed as Intensive Interaction by Nind and Hewett (1994) at Harpebury Hospital School and (particularly with adults) by Caldwell (1998), and many others. It is used with people whose attention is focused on their inner world and seeks to shift their focus from solitary self-stimulation to shared activity and interaction.

The term 'Co-created Communication' is used by Nafsted and Rodbroe (1999) to describe a similar approach with deaf/blind children: 'Fluency is co-created on the level of micro-exchanges, as moment to moment adjustments.' Similarly, Nadel and Canioni (1993) describe it as: 'An on-line process of adaptation to each other within which intentions and emotions are shared and negotiated.' Rodbroe and Souriau (2000) emphasise the emotional content of the exchanges:

'Typical ways to react in a communicative way to "utterances" (an initiative by the partner which is not necessarily perceived as auditory, for example movements, pointing) is to match them by making similar movements to attune to them, by doing something which expresses that the emotional state is shared, or to imitate the contours of an utterance using another modality.'

I want to look at how this works in practice, using Maureen's history as an example. The activities that interest and hold Maureen's attention are obvious, but to convert her transitory low-level attention into focused engagement I have to present my interventions in a way that, while partly familiar, is not quite what her brain is expecting.

My first task is to see how she is talking to herself. What feedback is she giving herself when she is self-stimulating? What is it that has significance for her in her world?

Looking at her repetitive behaviour, Maureen makes sounds and twists her belt. I find that by simply echoing these back to her I get some response. She looks up to see what I am doing.

Maureen's attention is attracted by something she recognises. As human beings we all live in a delicate balance with our environment, with everything that happens to us. From infancy we learn to respond in ways that are advantageous to us (as we see it). 'Deciding well is selecting a response that will ultimately be advantageous to the organism in terms of survival and the quality of that survival' (Damasio, 1994).

Whether or not we like it, we become biological periscopes. In the interests of survival we spend our life scanning the horizon to see if there is anything of interest. It may be an event we do not recognise and need to assess; it may be something we know is good or bad for us. In all cases our brain weighs up the situation and takes appropriate action. We are constantly on the alert. Spotting something unexpected may scare us. Our unconscious brain is notified before our conscious brain becomes aware of the danger. Two messages are sent: a fast one (the P300) to the amygdala, which prepares the body for defensive fight, freeze or flight response, and a slower one to the cortex, which weighs up the danger and if it judges there is no threat shuts down the amygdala (Greenfield, 1997).

(An example of this response occurred to me quite recently when a lorry backfired as it passed me in the road. To my surprise I found myself cowering in the hedge. I had reacted without thought to what my amygdala assessed to be a potentially threatening situation, and taken defensive action: in this case, flight. My cortex received the slower message; reassessment showed me I was in no danger and I straightened up, relaxed and laughed at myself.)

At whatever level we operate, our brain builds up a bank of images and sensations that experience has taught us require a response. As soon as we recognise one of these our brain swings into action, comparing it with previous experience and assessing its value to us. We are interested in its potential – adverse or advantageous – and this interest leads us to check up on its source. We shift our attention outwards towards events that surprise us and check them out in terms of possible benefit or threat.

> *Maureen recognises her sounds and looks up when she hears similar ones and when she observes me twisting a belt. However in both cases she is easily distracted by the bustle and goings-on in the busy passage.*

Although it is possible to attract her attention by echoing back her behaviour, this attraction is not sufficiently intriguing to hold it. She slips back into her inner world.

At this point I begin to look at other aspects of her behaviour. I have been told that she enjoys physical contact on her back, so decide to reinforce her sounds by tapping the same rhythm simultaneously on her back. This combined approach brings a very positive response. She begins to smile, laugh and watch my face to see what I will do next. She looks straight at me and repositions herself for more tapping. She becomes very relaxed and her face loses its tension. Whereas previously she had shown concern that her mother was in an adjacent room, she now walks past the room with barely a glance. After we have finished the session she spends the rest of the afternoon quietly with a member of the care staff. She does not show her usual restlessness.

When a person is locked into a repetitive loop of behaviour they are self-stimulating. In a scary or confusing world, the person knows what they are doing (Barron & Barron, 1992). The repetition soothes them and produces endorphins in the brain that feel good. Self-focus lulls them in their inner world. While they may recognise their behaviour if it is echoed back to them from an outside source, this recognition is not always enough to shift their attention from inward focus to the world outside. On occasion it may simply add feedback from the outward source to the feedback they are giving themselves. Under these circumstances the technique can reinforce the repetition. Intuitively the practitioner feels they are no longer involved in 'conversation' but are being 'used'. Far from enhancing interaction, they have become part of the furniture of the person's inner world.

The contrast between reinforcing the inner world and interacting with the world outside was particularly brought home to me during a session with Jimmy.

Jimmy is 15 and has Down's syndrome. He used to say more words but is now non-verbal apart from being able to say 'No'. He has a number of repetitive behaviours – touching his hair, ears and flipping a bundle of tickets, often so they touch his lip. He enjoys touch very much and likes to be stroked with a fibre optic strand and touched or rubbed on his back and shoulders. His moods swing and it can be difficult to predict how he will be. He can become disturbed and this behaviour makes it difficult to be with him. Recently he has started to self-harm by head banging and he can nip and pull hair. He makes sounds that change from barely audible to screaming, depending on his mood.

Jimmy likes to be in the sensory room and particularly enjoys the fibre optic lights. He will carefully choose one strand and hand it over to his care worker for them to stroke his forearm with it. He can easily use this to feed his inner world in a way that cuts out interaction. He retreats to his inner world and 'switches off'. It is as if he 'hi-jacks' objects and activities on which he is fixated and uses them to reinforce self-stimulation. This makes it difficult to communicate with him.

In this case it is not that the techniques of Intensive Interaction are at fault; rather, the approach has not been sufficiently thought through. When his arm is stroked Jimmy's brain knows what to expect and has decided that it is not worth bringing it to his conscious attention; his consciousness ignores what is familiar. We have to look for a more powerful way of attracting but also holding his attention in a sustained, focused and interactive way. We need to ask how we can make the stimulus that the person recognises more powerful and interesting than that offered by the shadows of their inner world. In practice the answer seems to be to change slightly the way in which the stimulus is presented, while retaining its general character. This can be done in a variety of ways.

Just echoing back Jimmy's sounds is not enough. To capture his attention I suggest that we echo back his sounds and simultaneously stroke his arm, using the rhythm of the sounds he makes. Whenever he makes a sound I make a movement on his arm that corresponds to the sound he has made: a short movement for a short sound, a longer one for a long sound and a wavy one for an undulating sound. We then go on to explore a number of permutations using his body language to develop interaction rather than just using the sensory equipment as relaxation. Jimmy's facial expression becomes attentive. After each movement and interaction we wait, giving him time to respond. Each time we alter the pace of the strokes to fit his sounds. He is no longer just experiencing a sensation passively but responding actively with eye contact and grinning, moving himself closer for more when asked if he wants it again. He watches my face to see what my reactions are and we maintain this mutual engagement for about an hour, until I have to end the session. His key-worker, who has known him for some years, says she has never seen him respond in this lively and engaged way before.

Working with Jimmy, there is a very strong contrast between the effect of simply joining in with his stroking and combining the stroking with his sounds: sounds that are meaningful to him, so the strokes complement them. If we return to the idea of the brain as periscope, we have introduced an additional factor: a stimulus that is sufficiently familiar because of its rhythm to be non-threatening but also different enough to be intriguing. This is interesting enough to persuade the brain to refocus on the source so that Jimmy begins to engage more deeply with the world outside.

This enhancement of the feedback a person gives himself can be done in a variety of ways.

Vicky is microcephalic. She makes a variety of sounds that can become very noisy, to the point that staff find it difficult to work in the room with her because her noises over-ride any activity they try to do. She is very cut off and they can get no eye contact. You can see she is literally talking to herself and she thinks very carefully about which of her sounds she will make next.

When I try echoing her sounds back to her through a kazoo she responds with great pleasure and makes good eye contact. She makes a sound and then turns towards me to see what I will do in response. I steer the interaction towards 'conversation'. Instead of echoing her sounds I 'answer' them. This session is filmed on video.

Watching the video later it is clear she is most intrigued when I repeat a high sound she has made and then extend it down, down, down beyond her initial utterance. As it moves beyond her initial squeal her attention becomes more acute. Her eyebrows lift, her pupils widen and darken. Her expression is almost one of disbelief: 'That's my sound but where's it going?' When I stop she turns to me and laughs. We share the joke.

Surprise is very often a discontinuity in expectation. I think I know what is going to happen within a given sequence of events, and then it doesn't, or something else does. My periscope immediately swings round to check; I start to pay more detailed attention to my surroundings in order to identify the source of the discontinuity. In practice it is 'surprise' in the context of a person's language that is critical and most often shifts their attention from their inward world to the world outside. It plays a vital role in the process of engagement. Working with deaf-blind children, Rodbroe and Souriau (2000) point out that regulating interactive play means you are always looking for ways to introduce variations to keep the interest of your partner. At the same time you have to be alert to variations suggested by your partner and respond to him or her: 'On the one hand you have to make use of repetition to create conditions that will help a deaf/blind person to have an overview and support cognitive development. On the other hand you have to add novelty to a well-known act in order not to make it dull and thereby lose the interest of your partner.'

Surprise does not always have to be in the form of an addition, something relevant added in an unexpected way. It can also arise when an anticipated event fails to happen.

> *Gilly has ASD and is very difficult to contact. She likes going for walks and bangs her feet on the pavement. Because there is no room to walk beside her, I follow her. Each time she treads she thumps her foot on the ground. I do the same. I have a feeling she is listening to what I am doing and this is confirmed when I deliberately miss out banging my foot. She immediately stops, turns her head and looks at me in a completely different way.*

In this case it is omission that draws Gilly's attention to the world outside her inner self, but it is still a discontinuity in expectation.

Chapter 2

Drawing back the curtains

- Needing to know what we are doing

- Moving on from 'games'

Ten months after I first visited Maureen, the manager of the centre tells me there has been a vast improvement in her behaviour. He describes it as though 'someone has drawn back the curtains for her'.

The set-up of the centre is a little unusual in that many of its service users are elderly, from a hospital next door and not necessarily tolerant of someone whose behaviour might be seen as (and occasionally was) threatening. I decide to go again to see if it is possible to observe the changes and to tease out what has been helpful.

Staff have clearly worked very hard and there is a noticeable change in Maureen's ability to relate. Although some of her autistic features remain, the overall impression of Maureen as someone with ASD is more difficult to sustain. Although she has good days and bad days, she now presents as lively and interactive and really enjoys being with people.

Maureen responds when her name is called by looking and sometimes smiling. She will now sometimes respond to a request for a kiss or a cuddle. Her posture has changed. Her head is more often up and she is more alert, watching what is going on. She still plays with her belt in the passage but is delighted when her key-worker joins in her games. She makes better and more frequent eye contact, laughs, initiates relatedness and watches to see what response she gets.

Although she still finds change difficult, she is more flexible and has been introduced to a number of new activities. She is not so rigid about activities always having to take place in the same location. She no longer gets upset if she has to travel on a different bus to the one she is used to. She does not have to be in the same room to eat her dinner and has learned to wait for her meal.

Her behaviour at meals is also greatly improved. Under guidance she can eat her meal with a spoon instead of shovelling food in with her hands. She no longer tears open sandwiches to eat the contents but eats the whole sandwich if it is offered in quarters. She attacks people less often. In response, other service users understand her better and are kind to her. The only user she is likely to grab is one elderly person, who is the most intolerant of her.

The major difference is that the staff now feel much happier about their interactions with Maureen. They use her sounds and body language to have fun with her. She has a particularly good key worker who enjoys 'talking' to her. She responds joyfully and her whole demeanour has changed. It is much easier to get her to come to the toilet and go for walks. They use her sounds with her, banging when she bangs, playing ball. Requests are accompanied by simple gestures to let her know what is going to happen. However Maureen is very literal. Simply pointing to the garden to indicate going out for a walk is not enough to allay her fear of the unknown. Staff first point outside and say: 'We are going for a walk …', then point to where she is standing and say, '… and we are coming back here again'. This seems to reassure her that she will be returning to a known safe place and there is now no difficulty in getting her to go outside. (These days I believe the staff don't always remember to do this but Maureen is so much more alert and relaxed that she picks up what is happening more easily.) Her key-worker says that introducing her to new things also takes less time and it only needs one person to take her out, instead of two. Also Maureen will now play a social game, responding to hiding and reappearing.

Maureen does still have off days, which may well relate to how she feels physically. There is still work to do. For example, she looks anxious when her key-worker has to leave her temporarily. She needs to know what is happening and (as with helping her understand that she is not only going for a walk but returning to a place she feels safe) it is better to show her by gesture that you are leaving her but you will be returning.

In the middle of a game with her I am called away. I tell her where I am going and point in that direction. I then say I am coming back and point to the ground beside her. She nods and her face clears at once. For Maureen it is absolutely imperative that she knows what is going on because she feels totally threatened and abandoned otherwise.

It is critical for us to realise how serious a matter this is. If a person is unsure about what is happening, when something unexpected occurs they may quite literally feel their life is threatened. Under these circumstances the brain calls into play all the defence mechanisms we have developed throughout our evolutionary history to protect us when we think we are in mortal danger. We have to understand the degree of fear that may be motivating the person and take steps accordingly to modify our behaviour so it doesn't appear to them to presage imminent catastrophe. Helping the person understand what is going to happen allows them time to prepare for the event, to take part in their life rather than it being a lurching sequence of unpredictable and therefore scary situations. With Maureen it pays to take it slowly, breaking down each activity into small steps and getting her agreement to each before proceeding to the next.

When a person starts to come out of their inner world they may respond joyfully to 'games' based on their own body language. The danger comes if a game begins to have its own 'rules', to define itself. The process and end become predictable; the brain knows what to expect and lapses into a repetitive process. There is nothing to renew the person's focus on interaction. Instead of being an open-ended arena of potential growth, the game becomes a fixed process with no outcome. For staff also, it becomes something they have learned to 'do' with the person. Feeling themselves trapped in a situation that no longer involves exchange and has become a ritual, they will frequently ask, 'What do we do next?'

The danger of 'games' is that both parties become locked into certain ways of responding to each other. Apart from anything else, it is such fun to be able to 'respond' and get responses from someone with whom you have never been able to make contact before that there may be little incentive to try to move on. This is particularly so if neither side offers 'new' material. We know what works, and it is less demanding and safer for both parties to stay with a familiar way of enjoying each other rather than attempt to move on to unfamiliar territory. Unfortunately, if the brain is not confronted with 'new' material it can lapse into incorporating the games into self-stimulation.

This is not to say that games do not have their place, because this is when we learn to trust each other. In new situations we are vulnerable and trust is vital. Any move to incorporate unknown material represents threat, in the sense that its potential dangers have not been assessed. If we do not trust each other the interaction closes down, leading away from communication.

With Maureen it is time to move on from playing games with her to a deeper form of engagement. When I am with her I start to respond to her in ways that, while they respect her language, also contain an element she is not expecting. When her noises are placed in conjunction with touch (which is related through rhythm), she is able to use a second sense (feeling) to double check on the sound.

I also increase the interval I leave before expecting a reply from her, to give her time to think about my response, which is a little different to the one she is anticipating as she has got used to copying games. I show her key-worker how to do this and we observe how Maureen becomes quieter and more thoughtful when engaged in this type of interaction, looking at us and really thinking before she replies. She begins to initiate. At one stage she nods her head and is really pleased when we nod back, doing it again and watching carefully to see if we will answer. Instead of feeding her inner world she has shifted her focus to what is happening in the world around her. She has learned that if she nods her head she can get a response from us. It is not just about control; it is also about sharing. She has found a way of sharing in our world and is beginning to let us into hers. We can begin to explore each other in an open-ended situation.

Human beings are sentient; we have feelings, and we feel closest to people who empathise with our feelings, who understand us – even if it is understanding that we feel bad and want to be left alone. We tread on each other's feelings at our peril; this is a quick route to a broken relationship. We also let others know what our feelings are not only by how we describe them but also through our body language, which may reflect how we feel even though we are trying to conceal it.

If a person is more able, it may be that what their brain recognises is not just a reflection of its dialogue with the body but also patterns of thought and persistent themes that have been part of the conversation that the brain has with itself. For our interventions to be meaningful to them, we have to get into their mind-set.

> *Bob has absolutely no idea where he is in relation to his surroundings. He is fascinated by football. His key-worker has the inspiration to describe to him where things are by locating them on a football pitch: 'Look in the penalty area.' Bob finds this direction perfectly intelligible.*

> *Lizzie's ability is overlaid by severe anxiety. She has an interest in television soaps. Her brain very easily links up the wrong messages so she 'gets the wrong end of the stick'. We need to try and explain to her that sometimes our brain tells us things that are not true. She is unable to grasp what we are saying until it is explained in terms of an episode of Eastenders she saw. She is able to understand a complicated idea through a second-hand scenario. She does not have to think about it in relation to herself, where it threatens to overwhelm her, but can visualise it as happening in a familiar programme she has watched. Once she has grasped the concept she can move on. Another step has been taken up the ladder of understanding.*

There is a footnote to the history of Maureen. Just before going to press I received an unexpected letter from her key-worker. She writes of the progress that has been made:

> *'Maureen seems more confident and is generally accepted with other service users now. Everybody speaks to her and passes the time of day with her. The barriers are down. She stands at the back door waiting for the clients to come in and all members greet her when they enter the building, which is nice. She seems more relaxed now and likes to be included in various activities.'*

The photograph that accompanies her letter shows Maureen seated in a group at a table, turning towards a friend. Her facial expression is lively, open, alert, even radiant as he leans slightly towards her. It is her birthday and they seem to be sharing a joke.

Chapter 3

Crossing the minefield

- Finding the way in

- Ribbons across the minefield – using a person's 'language' to let them know what they are doing

- Reducing the hypersensitivities

- Distressed behaviour

Speaking during the plenary session of a recent conference on Intensive Interaction, a young teacher said: 'We can change people's lives.' There was a groundswell of assent from the 160 delegates present, most of them practitioners, many of them teachers in schools. The confidence with which these words were spoken is a far cry from the situation even 15 years ago, particularly for those working with adults, when the deputy manager of a large hospital wrote: 'We do not want an interactive approach in this service.'

Clearly attitudes have changed. One of the reasons is the closure of the large, long-stay hospitals. With the setting up of small group homes it has become less easy simply to warehouse people whose behaviours present management problems or who are very withdrawn. In small houses we are physically and psychologically too close to each other to ignore difficult behaviours; the movement for normalisation and age appropriateness has in many ways improved the way people with learning disabilities are perceived. Yet there is still a core of people for whom neither an improved environment nor more compassionate care nor behavioural training has provided a solution to their isolation and behavioural distress.

It is only recently that we can begin to feel that, yes, we can work effectively with these people, so many of whom shelter under the umbrella term 'autistic spectrum disorder'. Apart from changing techniques there has been a revolution in the way we think about what people with disability are experiencing. Previously, where it has been considered at all, the assumption has been that we have a common experience, that in sensory terms it's a level playing field. On the contrary, this level playing field turns out to be a whole range of mountainous landscapes. We have had to learn to recognise the validity of alternative ways of seeing things: not 'just my way is right and yours is wrong' but developing understandings of worlds that may present totally different levels of threat, triggering defence mechanisms that result in the behaviours we find challenging.

The shift has also been one of empathy, from 'training' and 'control' to motivation.

My own understanding has deepened so I now see more clearly what I am trying to do. I started out working as a helper in a department of occupational therapy in a large hospital for people with learning disabilities. It was my job to look after a group of mainly non-verbal men whose behaviours ranged from throwing furniture at each other to more personal assault. They would sit at two rows of desks with a box of beads or a clothing catalogue each, which they thumbed through. They were clearly bored. My job was to keep them quiet. Self-preservation suggested I look for some way of motivating each one of them, something they might enjoy. This led to the construction of 'games' based on whatever I could find that interested them.

Roy liked trains so I sat beside him with a fretsaw and cut out the pieces of a jigsaw of a steam engine in a station. He took the pieces one by one as they were cut off and fitted them together. We made many such puzzles. He became progressively more gentle until one day this man, who previously had been hitting people and thrusting his arms through windows several times a week, came in clutching a red rose bush he had uprooted from a garden. Blood poured over thorns as he presented it to me. It was the most touching bouquet I have ever received. (The gardener from whose flowerbed the plant had been uprooted took a rather different view.)

Together the men and I painted the walls of the corridor that formed our day room with life-sized scenes that related to their lives.

Charlie had been brought up in a pub. The bar was so life-like that Charlie tried to pull himself a pint. He also placed his ear against the landlady's chest to listen to her heart.

Fred told me his Dad had been a greengrocer. By his desk we made a shop. We painted bricks and stuck them on. We made boxes of fruit and veg. He started to tell me about his day-to-day life in the shop – an achievement, since he had very slow and limited speech.

In retrospect some of the equipment was perhaps not age appropriate. For example Jack, who had movement in only one arm, used it to lob heavy objects down the corridor, with considerable accuracy. I diverted his attention by making him a windmill that ran very smoothly on a skateboard bearing. He loved it; with it he found a better use for his one hand and sat there rocking and twirling and making happy sounds. At the time it bought us some respite. However not only was this undoubtedly a toy; perhaps more importantly, I now realise that I was feeding his inner world rather than encouraging communication.

Later on his care team realised that he loved any form of transport so they took a series of photographs of him standing, getting onto or riding on different lorries, cars, motor bikes etc. This made it begin to be more possible to hold his interest in the outside world.

If we want to help people communicate and take an interest in the world outside the inner world in which they are locked we must not just use objects or activities they like to do by themselves – which may feed their inner sensations – but rather those that we can share in open-ended exploration. At the same time they must be objects or activities that the brain recognises as non-threatening so that their deployment does not drive the person back into themselves. In a reality system that is sensory chaos the activities we offer a person are going to have to act as waymarks across the minefield, so that the person feels safe doing them. Then we can begin to use them as vehicles for interaction and extend the range of their interests.

To make quite clear what I mean by this I shall refer back to the history of Roger (*You Don't Know What It's Like*, p176).

Roger is autistic. He attends a large and, inevitably at times, noisy day centre, almost the worst environment against which to effect improvement. He wanders round the day centre in a world of his own. He is disturbed by other service users and hits out at them if they come too near. He has quite frequent serious outbursts and is unable to take part in activities or even to go out on the centre bus. Roger makes a variety of small sounds and has a few words.

Roger's team tried out a number of approaches. Initially, they found him so exhausting that they tried working in two-hour shifts. There was no improvement in his behaviour. Reflecting on this, they saw that the constant turnover of staff might be stressful to him (just as working with him was for staff). Management used this insight to help staff understand the nature of the stress that Roger was experiencing. With management support the team switched to working with him all day and found the consistency this provided, combined with other strategies such as Intensive Interaction, using his sounds with him all the time in combination with verbal language where appropriate, was beneficial. His outbursts started to reduce.

> The use of these combined approaches has made it possible for Roger to begin to relate to people – not only to his team but also to other service users – in a more friendly way. He clearly does not feel so threatened by them and may smile if they call his name. With his team he can go on the centre bus with another service user. On a good day he can go out to lunch in a pub. At the centre, serious recorded disturbances have dropped from 14 a week to one every six weeks (averaged over six months).

During this period staff focused not so much on teaching him how to do things but on how to be with him and communicate with him. Roger always had a few words but began to use a wider range in an appropriate way. A major achievement was being able to say 'Coke' to the barman, hand over his money and wait for his change. However, in spite of progress in his ability to relate and make use of appropriate words, the team continued to use his sounds to keep in touch with him. In a world that he still perceives as chaotic, keeping the link open is vital.

For Roger what was needed to effect positive alteration in his life (which resulted in improved behaviour) was the introduction of what might be termed a predictable protective shield. This acted as a buffer zone, insulating him from externally generated sensory overload and internally generated emotional overload. The 'buffer zone' provided a recognisable secure haven in which he could interpret the sensory and emotional input he received, even in the difficult environment where he lived. Because he was now held together within familiar structure – and language was used in a form he could process – he knew what is going to happen. Staff could keep in touch by responding to his sounds – sounds that were not inappropriate in a public context. All the outsider would see was an occasional murmured conversation between friends. This progress, which was achieved through the work of committed staff and good leadership, was the outcome of looking deeply at the underlying difficulties Roger was experiencing.

At this stage there was a change of leadership and because Roger was showing little sign of disturbed behaviour the special interventions were reduced, including the daily use of his language. In effect, everything he recognised was withdrawn. The effect was immediate and disastrous. He returned to his previous chaotic behaviour. Retraining the team restored the situation to one where his language was used with him and his challenging behaviour disappeared once more.

People whose sensory world is in chaos need points of reference that are intelligible to them, onto which their brain can latch. Like ribbons marking a path across a minefield, these tell them where they can safely venture. If we remove these indicators, we plunge them back into a world that is inherently unstable and may be perceived as life-threatening.

To return to the hospital and the group with which I first worked, five of the 11 men who had previously been non-verbal started to use some words appropriately. There were fewer outbursts and a marked improvement in behaviour. I now understand the basis of this approach as working through things that have meaning for the particular individual.

There are some people whose lives are totally disordered. This is reflected in behavioural outbursts that make it difficult to find care staff willing or able to look after them. One such person is Sidney.

> *Sid has ASD. He is extremely disturbed. He attacks staff, head butting, hitting and pulling hair. After breakfast he returns to his room, bangs his head against the wall and screams. Sometimes this will last all day. As with a number of people with ASD, his sleep pattern is disturbed and he will scream in the night. A number of staff report that he responds badly to people and crowded, demanding places.*
>
> *Sid likes hot drinks frequently and some of his behaviour seems to centre around not being able to ask for them in an appropriate way.*

I tried using Intensive Interaction with Sid, using his own body language to engage his attention in way that had meaning for him. In Sid's case the way his brain and body talk to each other is through touch. He strokes his face with his hands and makes sounds. These escalate as he becomes more distressed.

When I first saw Sid he was in the dining area. I sat with him while he had a cup of tea and used my hands to stroke my face and chin in the way that he was using his. He noticed fairly quickly and watched, looking at me sideways to see what I would do. When he realised that if he made a movement I would respond, he smiled.

After breakfast Sid went upstairs, following his normal pattern of behaviour, which was to shut himself in his bedroom. He became very disturbed, shouting and banging himself. I stood outside in the passage and 'answered' each of his sounds with a softer call. At first he seemed a bit confused by this but then started to come out and check whether I was still there, particularly when he heard the door at the end of the passage slam. It sounded as though I had left and he shot out to check on me. I went on using his sounds – and, when he came out, his movements. Eventually he went downstairs and into the sitting room. I stood in the downstairs passage at right angles to the room, where he could hear but not see me, and continued with his sounds. (The house manager sat at the top of the stairs and could see his responses.) It took a little while but his noises gradually subsided. At one stage he banged his head on the door – but not violently – and each time referred back to me, to see what I made of it. Each time he did this I hit the wall, but not too loudly. I particularly used a kind of sh-shushing sound he made through his fingers. In the end he went into the front room and sat down, completely calmly, by himself. For at least half-an-hour he was calm and attentive to our interaction. This intimate attention was also felt by the team leader who was observing, to the point where she felt annoyed when she was interrupted.

At this point, I made the mistake of seeing if he would tolerate my going into the room with him to work in a closer proximity. (In fact I heard the intuitive voice warning me that it was too soon to try but allowed it to be over-ridden by the practical difficulty that my time was limited.) His sounds rose and he became disturbed. However, even when he attacked a member of staff she said he was easier to disengage than normal. After he had had a cup of tea he went up to his room and made no more sounds for another half hour while we were there. His house leader said this was unusual.

It was clear from Sid's response that Intensive Interaction offered the possibility of getting through to him in a way that staff had not found possible up until now. Guidelines given to the staff team reminded them that it was very important to get the spacing and timing right. Particularly, they should not hurry him but give him time to think and to respond. They should be careful not to 'hype him up', always aiming to calm him and paying careful attention to the emotional content of his sounds, letting empathy sound in their replies. While it was important at times to have fun with him, when he was distressed they needed to learn to 'stay with' his upset.

Two weeks later his team leader reported that Sid was getting better and responding to her team's use of his 'language'. He now touched her head to say, 'Goodbye': a personal gesture that he had not been able to make before.

If people with autism are upset it is because they cannot handle the amount of sensory input they are getting. When it is too much they get overloaded. The images, sounds and other sensory feedbacks, both from their inner and outer worlds, break up. This is a process known as fragmentation, which also involves confusion and sometimes severe physical pain. A small boy complains his head is going 'fuzzy', another that his head is 'going away'. Lindsey Weekes, interviewed in the Radio 4 programme *A Bridge of Voices* (undated), described how, when he became sensorily overloaded as a child, he would crash his head against the wall or run in front of a car – anything to stop the pain.

Not only do we need to use a person's language so that we can share their lives; we also need to look at what triggers what is, in many cases, a manifestation of extreme distress, which is how I interpreted Sid's disturbances. However, most people with ASD do seem to devise coping strategies that they learn to use as they grow up, to protect themselves from too much sensory overload. Such strategies fall roughly into two groups:

a) Repetitive behaviours that produce endorphins (the feel-good factor). Also, in a world of sensory chaos, they let a person know what they are doing and provide a point on which to focus so they do not have to listen to what is going on around them. More able people may focus on themes such as particular videos or interests, rather than bodily sensations. These become part of the furniture of their inner world and we call them fixations.

b) Exit strategies that remove the person from the source of their discomfiture in one way or another. (For example this might include physically removing him or herself from the source of discomfort, gaze avoidance, shutting eyes, or attacking people so they will go away.)

However, there are some people, and I think Sid is one of them, who seem to have been unable to develop effective defences to protect themselves, even when they are adult. When we looked at his environment with this in mind, it was clear that the dining area was extremely noisy at breakfast: a lot of people, some of whom were also disturbed, milling around in an unpredictable fashion in a small area to the extent that I also felt the pressure. I suggested the team should look for some way of offering him a more tranquil environment.

The team leader suggested he should be taken to MacDonald's for breakfast, to get him out of the house until the other residents had left for their daytime activities. You might think this would also be a potentially threatening environment but it is quiet at that time of day and there is another important difference: the local McDonald's is not personally invasive; no one trespasses on the privacy of his inner world in way that distresses him; it does not impinge on his private space in the same way as the hurly-burly of his home territory.

This combined approach of using Sid's language, plus reducing the environmental impact he finds so difficult, seems to be working very well. His team still have some problems but overall they describe his behavioural difficulties as very much improved.

We need to change the way we perceive people with severe behavioural disorders so that when we are considering strategies, what we have uppermost in our mind is the sensory difficulties with which they are struggling, rather than the outbursts we find so hard to manage. For this reason it may be better to think in terms of 'distressed behaviour' rather than challenging behaviour (a term that, while it was introduced originally to describe behaviours that challenge the system, is now widely used to describe behaviours that present a personal challenge to staff). This can lead to care staff feeling endangered before they even start, by a reputation that should more rightly direct us to the inability of an individual to handle the distress they are experiencing.

At the end of a visit to Mike, who has severe distressed behaviour, his house leader says to me:

'Always before people have come and tried to tell us how to change him. No one has suggested before that we need to change ourselves.'

Chapter 4

We didn't believe you

■ Using a person's language to reduce distressed behaviour

'When you said that if we learned to use Reg's language with him, learned to talk to him through his sounds and movements, his difficult behaviour would diminish, we went away and laughed. We didn't believe you. However, we did it because we were told to and that is precisely what happened.'

The speaker was a young care worker at a meeting to discuss how life had changed for Reg – and the people who looked after him, since an original intervention two years previously.

Reg is 22 and lives in a separate flat in a community home. His behaviour presents as falling within the autistic continuum. He avoids eye contact. He routinely 'touches' walls and surfaces, continuously checking on his space, probably trying, as Jolliffe puts it, to work out the pattern of what is happening and reassuring himself as to where things are.

When I was first asked to see him Reg's reputation for negative behaviours was such that I doubted very much whether I could help. He spent a lot of his time in his room, shouting and self-injuring violently, which would extend to attacking staff who tried to intervene. He would wander about naked. On occasions he would become agitated and strip off in public places without warning. Sometimes it was possible to assign causes to his outbursts – at others the reasons were untraceable. It had reached the stage where staff admitted they were scared to come to work, scared of him and particularly scared that they would not be able to cope with him in public. They said they rarely got through a day without incidents. Often these were prolonged and difficult to handle.

Remember, in sensorily chaotic surroundings a person who uses a repetitive behaviour knows what they are doing. People with ASD maintain their sense of coherence in a multitude of different ways. Donna Williams, in her book Somebody Somewhere (1994), describes how, as a child, 'she would search the eyes looking back in the mirror, looking for meaning, looking for something to connect with'. In the Radio 4 programme *A Bridge of Voices* Lindsey Weekes (undated) describes how people with ASD at a disco will focus on the strobe lights to cut out the sensory chaos. For a number of people, it seems that the sensation of 'feeling in the sense of touch/holding' may not break up when the other senses do. For example, another person with autism, Gunnilla Gerland describes how, when she heard the sound of a moped, all sense of a coherent environment broke down so that she was unable to distinguish up and down. In order to maintain some sense of coherence she would cling to iron railings. At least she could feel something stable (Gerland, 1996).

A man keeps a clothes peg on his finger; at least he can feel that. A child asks for his fluffy pig when he is becoming upset. Holding something their senses recognise lets these people know what they are doing at a time of sensory breakdown.

Each of these people is reaching for a sensation to which they can cling in order to maintain some sense of stability when everything else is falling apart.

> Reg's communication is limited although he has a few 'words' that are his private sounds for different objects. If he is happy to let you touch him and feels safe in his surroundings he will reach out his hand and say 'mop', but apart from this he is unable to communicate effectively. He is always fixated on something, particularly the colour of his shirts and sweaters, although the favoured colour changes from time to time.

To distract him his key worker used to 'draw' with him, but not in way that was interactive. Engagement was mechanical – Reg getting other people to do the drawings. If prompted he would hand over the pens he wanted his key worker to use, but showed little interest in the process, looking round in other directions. He would spend a considerable amount of time taking the 20 or so essence and coloration bottles from the shelf in the kitchen cupboard and lining them up on the work surface. When he had identified them all, he replaced them. Attempts at diversion did not work and distressed him. It was impossible to interrupt him. Observation suggested his activities were actually a way of keeping people at bay rather than engaging with them.

> *Reg also has a number of sounds and body and facial movements, such as hands to the mouth and clicking. These activities have real meaning for him and express how he is feeling. (Staff say of his sounds or gestures, 'That is a happy sound/gesture – that is stressed'. It is possible to tell how Reg is feeling by observing his body language.) When these are echoed back to him and used as a framework to 'talk' to him he will begin to give real and interested eye contact.*

Using a person's own language, it is often possible to work with their self-injurious behaviour. The one time Reg hit his chest when I was with him (which was when the hall in the centre was particularly noisy) I smacked mine and continued to do so at intervals. He stopped trying to hit himself and his interest focused on me. He held out his hand and said, 'mop'. I had the feeling we were in empathy with each other. (This technique was also tried successfully by Jim, his key-worker.)

Meeting two years later with the team leader and staff involved, we discussed the changes in Reg's life and what it had meant for the people working with him. Jim said that the introduction of an interactive approach, both in terms of using his sounds and touching Reg's hands as conversation – and also in using all his activities as opportunities for sharing – had led to them communicating with Reg on his terms in a relaxed, low-key way. (They are careful not to hype him up but rather make sure they keep the interaction quiet and centred.) Previously they had been trying to 'manage' and 'control' Reg's life; they were telling him what to do. In particular they felt they were trying to teach him skills in a way that was actually increasing his stress levels and hence the levels of disorientation he was experiencing, driving him back into his inner retreat. Now they were sharing activities, doing them together. They felt they had a different model for the relationship and were much more laid back and responsive. They started with his agenda rather than their own, making fewer demands on him.

Another member of staff who used to work with Reg but had not seen him for some time said she could not believe the difference – not only the reduction in his distressed behaviour but also the increase in his general responsiveness. When she returned for an occasional shift, she soon slipped into a 'conversation' with him. He began to test how far she could manage, eventually taking his sounds up to a high squeal. She reacted quite spontaneously, throwing up her hands and laughing: 'I can't manage that', and he burst out laughing with her.

This may sound a small incident but it marks the change from an isolated, unhappy life to one where initiating and sharing fun and jokes is possible. It highlights the change in his quality of life. Previously staff viewed his noises and body language as something that Reg should be distracted from, so the message he got was that the activities that had meaning for him were not important. Now people listen to his communications and take notice of what he wants to do. He is a valued and more self-confident person, with control of his situation.

Reg's care staff soon forgot to be self-conscious. (Some people do find this difficult initially, particularly if the person they are working with is banging himself or an object, as the instinct is to restrain him. In practice the brain is surprised to hear its rhythm coming from elsewhere and the person almost always stops and listens, which gives us a chance to break into the inner cycle in which they are locked when we respond to them in an empathetic way.) The staff soon found that using his language became a matter of course throughout the day; they did not wait until there was a crisis to deal with. In public they just use small sounds so that it does not draw attention to him as 'different'.

Outbursts are a rarity. If they do occur staff feel confident to go into his room and deal with them, which previously they were reluctant to do. Because Reg also feels more confident as an outcome of interaction, he has begun to initiate activities himself. One day he was with his key worker, Jim, who was using his language with him. He became very relaxed and happy. Later, when he needed to get dressed, Jim offered him his pants, which he threw back. Instead of pushing the issue, Jim continued in his language. In a little while Reg got up and dressed of his own accord. On another day he and Jim were watching a video. He suddenly got up and went and loaded the dishwasher without any prompting. If he comes down in the morning before dressing, he wears his pyjamas instead of coming down naked. Situations that would have triggered outbursts no longer do, even those that are stressful. At a football match the ball was accidentally kicked hard into his chest. After an initial surprise reaction, he settled back quite calmly to watch.

In spite of what we may instinctively feel, it is not disrespectful to engage with people through their own language; on the contrary. Donna Williams, in the Channel 4 film *Jam Jar* (1995), talks about the terrible strain of always having to talk and be in 'their world', in a world where alien sounds have to be interpreted into meaning. It is important that we do not judge what is meaningful for the people with whom we work by what is meaningful for us.

Chapter 5

Over and over again

- The use of repetitive behaviours

- How Intensive Interaction can keep the brain-body conversation open-ended

Infant initiates, parent confirms and the infant moves on. When we are little we are faced with experiencing everything and comprehending nothing. We are the experiences that happen to us. To survive, we wrestle to bring order out of chaos; finding worlds we cannot control, we struggle to create those we can. For example, our infant brains repeatedly tell us to wave our fingers or say a sound until we receive confirmation of our activity. We test our sensations on our senses – when we feel 'waving our fingers', they move, and vice versa. We double check on our external references – our parents, who copy back to us what we do, confirming our activities. We continually repeat the action until we are satisfied we know what will happen when we perform a particular action. We go on until we are sure the pattern is established – a benign form of perseverance. At this stage the brain moves on to give the body another set of instructions. The trigger for the 'switch-off' is very specific: the recognition that the particular message sent by the brain to the body produces a recognisable response in our body in terms of its activity. This is the way we have all learned what we are doing.

Ideally, a dyadic relationship is set up between mother or mother figure and infant. In this game, the infant initiates a sound or behaviour – for example, 'Boo' – and the mother or parent figure echoes it back until the infant's activity is sufficiently confirmed and it goes on to something else.

The mother suddenly realises the baby is no longer on 'Boo' but has moved on to 'Da'. This is the pattern of reality testing and one of the means by which communication is established and the baby learns. It is also a form of repetition that the baby switches out of once it has established a particular pattern. Either the brain turns off the message or, judging it to be of little importance, we stop listening to it. But what if for some reason, the switch-off mechanism fails?

Gunnilla Gerland tells us: 'I had no natural brake inside me' (Gerland, 1996).

I want to look at what happens when individuals are caught up in repetitive behaviours where for one reason or another the brain is failing to switch off. Such people have become stuck in a groove, with the brain continuously sending the same message over and over again. This may be because at the time they were born the brain was not ready to 'play' the exploration game. By the time the brain had matured enough to do so, the parent had given up trying, so the switch-off mechanism does not develop because the brain never gets a meaningful response. Alternatively, it may be that the switch-off mechanism does develop and then fails. Either way we are left with a brain that, instead of talking to the world outside, talks to itself.

Temple Grandin's description quoted earlier of the discomfort caused by her hyper-sensitivity to touch (*A is for Autism*, 1992) also illustrates the inability of her brain to terminate the feedback from her body. 'If you put on a pair of scratchy pants and then take them off, that is the end of your discomfort, but if I wear scratchy pants and take them off, a fortnight later I am still experiencing that discomfort.'

I had always considered this anecdote in terms of the experience of discomfort until one day I was thinking about perseverance and realised that what Grandin was actually talking about was the inability of her brain to switch off the feedback she was getting from her body. This led me into further speculation about the nature and origins of repetitive behaviour.

As pointed out previously in *You Don't Know What It's Like*, we all have repetitive behaviours: breathing, for example. I also paid tribute to the extraordinary account by Donna Williams in *Nobody Nowhere* (1992) of the evolution of a repetitive behaviour, moving from her early fascination with coloured flecks in the air through to a fixation with glass beads. The question is, whether or not we are focusing on these behaviours, are we conscious of what we are doing? During our childhood we explore particular objects or activities with all the tenacity of full-blown fixations. We become linked into a particular physical sensation or feeling or activity. We begin to investigate its possibilities, playing with it in our minds in ways that 'progress beyond simple investigation of the physical sensations it arouses, to a process which can allow us to explore our anxieties and understand the world around us' (Moyles, 1989).

Playing with feelings allows us to adjust as we make the transition from dependence on the mother to what Winnicott calls the 'insult of reality'. He points out that, if weaning is successful in psychological terms, as the mother withdraws her breast and reality impinges the child develops a third space, a transitional space that is a parallel world, neither 'me' nor 'not me', a sort of testing ground where they cut their new experiences down to manageable size. 'This third part of the life of a human being is an intermediate one of experiencing, to which to which inner reality and external life both contribute' (Winnicott, 1971).

It is here, in this free-floating pre-integrative space, before everything has been fully taken on board and ordered, that the child learns to cope by dealing creatively with anxiety through games and simulated scenarios, modifying and improving its understanding. For all of us, this is a journey that helps us bring meaning to our circumstances. We call it play: through it we learn to make sense of our senses and the feedback our senses initiate.

If we are lucky, that is; it does not always happen like this.

'Of every individual who has reached the stage of being a unit with a limiting membrane and an inside and an outside, it can be said there is an inner reality to that individual, an inner world that can be rich or poor, at peace or in a state of war.' (Winnicott, 1971)

If we encounter an outside world that we perceive as totally hostile or chaotic, the only way that we can build a world we can control is through and in our inner world. Instead of focusing on the world about us we give up and retreat to a world that is unassailable. We start to take refuge in the sensation for itself and can become trapped, revisiting it again and again. The object or feeling becomes an end in itself. In the film *Jam Jar* Donna Williams (1995) describes her disastrous childhood – the demands she could not meet and the failure of those around her to understand her world: 'All that created a war in me and I went back into my world.'

Either we learn to range freely in our world through creative exploration or we retreat. Sometimes both possibilities can co-exist. This is illustrated in the following history of one small boy, as told to me by his mother. In particular, his story explores a movement out of a potentially closed behavioural pattern to an open-ended resolution through the medium of his mother's intuitive assessment of the child's motivation. Confirming the meaning of his play she allows him to move on. I quote it with her permission.

> Doug has ASD. At the age of three he was holding on to his bowel movements until he was in bed. He then smeared himself – a messy business that left him and his plastic animal toys and bedclothes covered with faeces. This happened repeatedly until the community nurse suggested regulating his movements with senna, so that he would have to release them during daytime. One evening before the new regime of medication was started, his mother was late bringing the washed animals to him in bed. As soon as she brought them, Doug passed his motion and proceeded to dip their faces in the stool, making mouthing sounds. His mother realised that Doug was feeding them. When she gave Doug Coco Pops as a substitute, the smearing ceased and did not recur.

If we use the criteria of our world, how easy it is to mis-assign motivation. However, there is another important point to this story. One of the features looked for in diagnosis of ASD, along with the level of communication and ability to relate, is the question of whether the child is capable of imaginative play. Doug deals with anxiety through an activity that is clearly rudimentary play, no different from any other child feeding his or her dolls with pretend food. He knows about feeding so he feeds his animals in the only way he has at his disposal, however inappropriate it may be deemed to be. In a world that he must have been finding chaotic in sensory terms this 'play with intent' became a way of coming to terms with an impossible situation, learning how to cope with what was happening in a way he could control. His anxiety became extremely pronounced if he was not able to follow his routine when he needed to. (This 'play' was so striking that I checked on the nature of his assessment. Was he really autistic or was there some other disability? Doug had been assessed at the age of 26 months as having ASD by a psychologist, followed by an assessment centre.)

Doug is now four. He continues to feed his animals Coco Pops out of a cereal bowl. However, although he has other repetitive behaviours this is not one of them as it is no longer compulsive. What started as a game and looked as if it was going to become a fixation was opened out through his mother's accurate assessment of its importance and meaning for him. He still plays it sometimes, but for fun rather than under compulsion.

We know that repetitive behaviour is present in infants and is in an infant an essential part of learning. Is it possible that what we call stereotypical and fixated behaviour can, at least sometimes, start as a game but, because of a general tendency to be unable to switch off once a pattern is established in the brain (perseveration), end up as a fixation? This would imply that the capacity for imaginative play may be present initially but that perseverance takes over. What is evident is that Doug, age three with ASD, was capable of playing a 'game' that was in danger of becoming part of a repetitive cycle. Thanks to his mother's observation, the action taken by her both confirmed his behaviour and introduced a creative resolution and Doug was able to move on.

What I am suggesting is that, at least in some children with ASD, the instinct to play is present but because of adverse circumstances, which may be either internal or external, this instinct is swallowed up in perseverance: that fixations and repetitive behaviours start in the same way as games but become closed off. Intensive Interaction helps to keep games open-ended by confirming the activity and so encouraging the brain to move on in ways that are safe for that person.

Chapter 6

Finding each other

- Knowing where we are; getting lost in sensation

- Projection

- Where am I? Being present; finding ourselves so that we can be present to others

- An excursion into 'feeling'

- The transitional playground: what does it feel like? Affect

- Moving beyond disability

- Relatedness

- Where shall we meet? Being simultaneously empty and present

- The doorway of sensation

This section draws on Damasio's Descartes' *Error* (1994) and *Autism and Sensing* by Donna Williams (1998).

Where are you?

We are all engaged in three conversations running simultaneously. The 'thinker' is involved in internal messaging. Simultaneously the brain, the 'works manager', is talking to and receiving feedback from the body, while the 'negotiator' talks to the world outside. To do this we need to be able to shift our focus from our inner world and engage with the world outside. We have to change gear.

To which of these conversations am I listening? Which is uppermost in my mind? Each of us will have a different balance of attention. For example, if I am hurt I am going to pay most attention to the works manager. If I am trying to write, my brain is listening to myself; I am thinking. When I am relating to someone else my mind is on interaction, so the negotiator is uppermost, but the thinker is also present to monitor our conversation. The balance is constantly shifting according to need.

When a person finds the outside world too hostile they cease to relate to the world outside. For many of them, the works manager comes to dominate the brain's activity. They listen to and engage with the feedback they are receiving from their own bodies. For example they may listen to their own breathing rhythm, something we might only do if we were practising certain forms of yoga or meditation.

But communication is a two-way business. When a person is locked into their inner world our first task is to understand how that person is talking to herself, so we can ease into the conversation using her brain-body language. This sounds straightforward but in this section I want to consider the complexities that may arise when a person is so totally identifying with a sensation she is giving herself that, in effect, she 'becomes' that sensation. Where, for example, do I address a person whose sense of self appears to emanate from her foot, from her shoulder or even from outside herself, from a toy?

How do I speak to someone who in a psychological sense seems to have moved house?

If you ask someone how they know that they are, how they know they exist, they will probably say that they 'feel' they are. Sitting on this chair I feel my feet on the floor and the seat against my legs and backside. The hardness of the wood is experienced in my flesh. I get feedback to my brain from an external source that tells me my position. Balance is called into play to keep me in an upright position so I do not fall off. At any one time I know that I am because of the feedback I get from the objects that surround me and from the secondary feedback from my own body.

It is interesting that when we receive a signal that gives us information about the world outside, our brain actually receives two signals. The first is information about the object and the second is from the sense organ that senses it, simultaneously telling the brain which sense (smell, touch, taste etc) processed the information. Learning something about an object that is outside us is accompanied by learning about our own body state.

'A special sense, such as vision, is processed at a special place in the body boundary, in this case the eyes. Signals from the world outside are thus double. Something you see (or hear) excites the special sense of sight as a "non-body signal" but it also excites a "body signal" hailing from the place in the skin where the special signal entered. When you see, you do not just see, you feel you are seeing something with your eyes.' (Damasio, 1994)

Most of us who do not have ASD have a good idea of our body boundary. Although we do not often think about it, we know where 'I' stops and where 'the other', 'not me', begins. Information about our body state normally remains in the background unless we deliberately turn our attention to it. It is a question of where our interest is focused. Previously (in *Person to Person*) I have described how some people with severe or profound disabilities or ASD will focus on simple repetitive behaviours such as breathing rhythms, which it would be normal for us to ignore unless we were practising some such exercise as yoga. What I am trying to bring out is that when people who do not have ASD focus on a particular activity or object, in addition to the sensory information we receive about that external object or activity, we also get information about the interface: which bit of the body is receiving the signal. So if an object is outside us and we are paying attention to it, because of the double signal (one from the object to the brain about the object and one from whichever sense organ perceives it to the brain, telling the brain that the eye or ear or skin has received the information, depending on the mode), we are also getting information about our boundaries – where in the body the signals are arriving – that is, through our eyes, ears or skin. We learn about our boundaries at the same time as we receive information about the world outside. Lack of this may be critical for a person who has very little sense of who and what they are unless they are focusing on a behaviour that is familiar. Sean Barron (1992) tells us how secure it made him feel to switch the lights on and off – 'he knew what he was doing'. It seems possible that his enhanced sense of security derived not only from being able to control at least something in a chaotic world but also from becoming conscious of his body state, knowing his boundary, being able to differentiate between himself and other, knowing who he was.

> *A child who bangs her head responds to her doctor who asks why she does it by saying that she does it to know she is there.*

In a confusing world she needs a violent sensory stimulus that she can recognise to help her know her body state.

> *Janice is totally absorbed in rubbing her thumb on her fingers. This is where she 'feels herself', where she experiences her self, to the extent that when she is invited to come for a meal she fails to respond, even when prompted through an object of reference in the form of her plate and a spoonful of dinner. However when it is suggested that her thumbs might like some dinner she comes without hesitation. It is clear she has identified with the place she feels herself to be.*

Janice has identified with an affect. This is where her attention is. It is only here, through the doorway of this sensation, that we will be able to make contact with her. This is where we must look.

Therapists will talk about a person being 'centred' or 'off-centre'. These are states that are difficult to describe except in intuitive terms. They relate to whether the person is truly herself as she is, or whether she is somehow misaligned. In some cases the person may actually relocate her sense of self to the object or sensation with which she is engaged. In extreme cases she may have identified with some other activity or person, or projected on to someone else a part of herself that she cannot handle.

> *Marie's only spoken language is a repetitive phrase, 'Rupert the Bear, Rupert the Bear'. It is not just that she is fond of her toy bear but more that she identifies herself with it. Like Janice, just inviting her to a meal does not get through to her. She only responds, gets out of her chair and walks to the door, when asked if Rupert the Bear would like lunch. She becomes stressed by demands she does not understand when the question is addressed to her directly. This is not where she is. It is as if the postman has delivered a letter to the wrong address.*

In Marie's situation, it would be proper to understand 'Rupert' as a 'transitional object', a link object that stands between dependence on the mother and independence (Winnicott, 1971). Such adopted objects have great significance in developmental terms. To try to remove or ignore them is to cause great distress and damage, setting the person back in developmental terms. They cling to them for security. For Marie, Rupert is so important that she identifies herself with it. The way forward is through acknowledgement and attention, and through using the object as material for open-ended games.

Sometimes I am asked if it is not retrograde to 'pander' to this form of communication, whether it is not more appropriate to insist that a person responds to 'our language'. To do so would be to prioritise our reality over and above the person's ability to understand. What this really shows is a lack of understanding of the processes in which people can become trapped. The downside of this route is that, while they may understand from body language that a demand is being made of them, if the demand has no meaning for them the level of stress is increased. They may learn to conform by making signs or sounds but still not attach meaning to them, leading to disappointment and frustration when they do not get what they hoped for.

For a person with autism, very severe learning disabilities and distressed behaviour, the primary consideration should be the need for contact. Above everything else we need to establish communication; the need for this should override our worries about the way in which it is done. This is more important for them than that we are able to feel we have taught them something. The outcome of trying to frog-march people into understanding what is for them a threatening input may display itself in outbursts of distressed behaviour, however desirable the end may seem to us.

In these situations it is not just enough to know how a person is talking to herself; we also have to know where it is she feels she is, in the sense that she feels in sensory contact with herself. A good place to start looking is where or how that person is giving herself sensory stimulus. Unless we understand this, we may find we are addressing empty space.

As well as knowing where the other person is in psychological terms, it is also helpful to know where we are, so that we do not impose on and attribute to others feelings that properly belong to us. Because I know where my boundaries are and who is related to whom, I must not assume that you do.

Where am I?

Autism (and much learning disability) happens when the brain is 'not wired up properly' as Lindsey Weekes puts it in *A Bridge of Voices* (undated). The aim of this section is to move beyond disability to relationship. It is trying to grapple with the essence of what it is to be me and you together – us. If this means an excursion into some rather shadowy speculation I am unrepentant, because the deeper we look into what it is that we are doing, the more we become aware of our common humanity, what it is that binds us together and what we can give to and learn from each other. I am aware that I am trying to present sometimes subtle psychological states in simple language. If the attempt opens our eyes or even helps us to look, it will be successful.

I know where I am – we all do. We have a very strong presence of self, derived from our sensory feedback that tells us where we are and what we are doing.

Or where we think we are – because, like some of the people we work with, we also may be displaced. At the simplest level, we may be physically present but not mentally alert to the situation we are in. Our attention may wander.

> A key-worker is observing a session of Intensive Interaction. He turns to speak to another member of staff as they pass. While his aside is relevant, as he turns his head away he misses the moment at which Robbie starts to attend and respond – the left corner of his mouth starts to twitch at the beginning of a smile. By the time the key worker has turned back it is no longer clear which was the critical sensory stimulus that captured Robbie's attention.

We cannot afford to withdraw our attention or let it wander for a second or we may miss the one signal that tells us the key is starting to turn in the lock, when the person first begins to relate to the world outside them. We must be present for the person we are working with.

I can only speak for myself, so much of this section will be deliberately written in the first person. This is because self-scrutiny involves working with feelings – and mine is the only inner world of perception I can locate. I may surmise or presume about yours, or be inclusive by writing 'we', but with all the possible weaknesses and blind alleys that beset self-examination I cannot know what you feel in the sense of experiencing it. To talk about 'you' or 'one', to depersonalise the journey into 'it', is to move into second-hand territory. The point of this journey is to reach the centre, not only that of the person with whom I am engaged, but also my own. Without this we may miss out on each other.

The word 'feeling' is a linguistic quagmire because we use the word in so many different ways. 'I feel the chair' is simple. It is a direct sensory experience – in this case touch, a response to an external stimulus. This is immediately complicated by the fact that, although I feel the chair if I turn my attention to it, most of the time I have learned to cut out this type of sensation even while it is happening, in order not to clutter myself with unnecessary stimuli. So attention is also a factor in the equation of feeling. In addition, such an experience may also be that of internal sensation: for example, balance or proprioception. 'I feel angry' describes my emotional state. It is a response, sometimes to a real external trigger, or it may be that anger has been so long the pattern of my life it has become a state and I will respond with anger to situations that would not normally demand it. 'I feel that you are angry', moves into the shadowy and subliminal world of perception where I pick up on your emotion and it triggers feeling in me. This is a danger zone because on the one hand I may be picking up your anger and on the other it may be that I cannot bear my own anger so I transfer it to you. Rather than being able to own my anger, I see it as yours: 'I feel that you are angry with me.'

Even this very brief analysis of how we use the word 'feeling' demonstrates how easy it is, in terms of language, to confuse triggers with reactions to triggers, the causes with our internal responses, the emotions with the footprints of sensation (what we are left with).

I use the term 'affect' here to describe my emotional response to a sensory experience. Thus, I feel the chair is hard: the affect is my irritation at being made uncomfortable. According to Damasio, in this sense – the sense of affect – our feelings are: '… the direct perception of a specific landscape – that of the body…they are the result of a most curious physiological arrangement that has turned the brain into the body's captive audience' (Damasio, 1994).

We learn to draw from its context the sense in which the word feeling is used. However, whichever way we choose to express it, all imply attention as well as proximity, either in the physical or the psychological sense. (I may reject a feeling but that is a matter of choice, even though the reasons for my decision may not be deemed important enough by my brain to be brought to my conscious attention. For example, my brain is aware through sensory feedback that I am sitting on a chair but has decided it is not important enough to bother my conscious mind with, unless the chair is unexpectedly tilted, in which case I am in a situation that is potentially threatening and my balance organs immediately inform me. Until the chair was tipped, my brain had made a decision based on previous experience without bothering to inform me.)

However, as best I can, I have learned that I am – and I also know that you, out there, are different from me. I have a strong feeling of my 'self', the 'me' and the 'not self', 'not me'. Although they are to some extent flexible, I know my boundaries. (If I am writing, my sense of me may include the pen that I write with. This is partly because of where the sensation is: not only the feeling on my fingers of the pen but also, beyond that, I am feeling the pressure of the pen on the paper. To take it further, when I am driving I may enlarge my sense of self to cover my car, the boundary then being my wheels and the tarmac.

I may include my possessions in the feeling of self and react as if I myself am threatened if my possessions are threatened. (Under certain circumstances I may even feel threatened enough to ask what people are doing on 'my road', trying to take possession of something that is clearly not mine.)

It was not always like this. As an infant I was unable to distinguish between myself and other. I thought, or rather experienced, all the world as 'me'; I did not know there was anything else. Differentiation came slowly as I learned through exploration of the senses to distinguish myself (in this body) from other things and bodies, from the reality of out there. Certain things always responded to me – if I waved my fingers I could see the movement. I learned to test reality by double-checking through an alternative sense: in this case feeling and vision. Other things responded to me if I cried. My mother came – but not always; her attention was intermittent. Presence and absence must have been helpful in showing my self what was me.

'From the beginning the baby has maximally intense experiences in the potential space between the subjective object and the object objectively perceived, between me-extensions and the not-me. This potential space is at the interplay between there being nothing but me and there being objects and phenomena outside (my) objective control.' (Winnicott, 1971)

I learned by exploring the boundaries of my control through physical sensations. Gradually I became aware not only of others but also that others experienced a different reality from mine. I learned to negotiate and compromise. Through relationships with others I came to know not just that I am but also who I am.

Donna Williams, who is high functioning, brings us remarkable insight through her books, video and film, which help us compare our experiences of differentiation with that of a person with ASD. In her book *Autism and Sensing* (1998) she describes how, in her earliest years, she accumulated experience of things outside herself in an unsorted jumble of indiscriminate sensory experiences. She talks about 'merging' and 'resonance' to describe her early relationships with objects outside herself, and continues:

'One could ask what is the experience of merging, of resonance, worth if there is none of the reflection or consciousness which comes with bringing a conscious sense of self to the experience. Perhaps only in death will I ever know again what it is to lose myself so wholly in the experience of "other" without sense of time or space, with no past or future and no here. There is

no deeper experience than the total encapsulation of self within an experience until one is indistinguishable from that experience.' (Williams, 1998)

This suggests a retreat to the undifferentiated perfection of the womb. Progress in differentiating herself from objects outside appears to have been uneven and difficult, progressing through a stage she calls 'mono' where she was either able to sense an object or herself but not herself in relationship to the object: 'I could not process information from the outside and inside at the same time. I was either in a state of jolting perceptual shifts, or remained in one sensory channel or the other.'

In fact, she explored physical sensations without processing her bodily response to those sensations: 'Either I existed or other existed and I did not.'

She goes on to distinguish between merging, or resonating, which involve no intent, and acts where consciousness is involved:

'Trying is an act of mind and mind is consciousness and this is to have a conscious "sense of self". To merge with an object is to become it and one cannot do that with an intact sense of separate simultaneous existence… Once there is a conscious sense of self there is always separateness from other and always separability… one filters information and interprets sensory experience. This…begins to limit how we perceive something external to us. We no longer take it in exactly as it is.' (Williams, 1998)

Exactly how we perceive our boundaries may also be cultural, and I recognise that my feeling of individual 'self' is personal and a part of the western experience. There are parts of the world where what I experience as 'self' is perceived as 'we'; the sense of the collective is stronger than that of the personal. I also understand that this other way of 'knowing' is just as valid as my experience, but I have to stick to my own baseline. It is worth noting, however, that the closer I am to my feeling of myself, the more available I am for others, the more I can enter the collective experience of 'we'. In Winnicott's terms, the boundary that I have perceived as a gulf between 'me' and 'other' becomes an intermediate playground, the place where my world and the world of other can overlap in a creative way and I can truly experience what is 'not me'. Put very simply, I need to be myself in order to know others and, as developmental psychologist Suzanne Zeedyke (2002) has pointed out to me, paradoxically I need to know others before I can come fully to know myself. 'We' is the path to 'I'.

Hobson puts it in terms of language:

'Consciousness is a matter not just of thinking but also of feeling. Self-consciousness (as awareness of self) involves adopting a perspective on oneself through identifying with the attitudes of others. We cannot understand the concept of "I" and "You" until we grasp the possibility of reciprocal roles in speech. It is the person who speaks who anchors meaning to the word, I. We have to grasp relation- ship before we can identify and think about self.' (Hobson, 2002)

Winnicott (1971) lays great emphases on the creative aspect of this overlapping transitional playground as the root of our creativity, but it is difficult to describe this amorphous area of human experience in terms of affect, what being in it and sharing with other feels like. When you are trying to evoke elusive experience you need to avoid foundering on the twin rocks of sentimentality and nebulous subjectivity. Just because we are giving our minds free rein does not mean we cannot observe what is happening. We may have suspended our boundaries but we are not drifting helplessly.

What does the experience of sharing a creative playground actually feel like? The more we try to pin it down in words, the more it has a tendency to slither away. It is resistant to crystallisation. So I am going to approach it obliquely by borrowing from a different discipline, from the description of an exhibition of abstract paintings of luminous beauty by an artist called Hugonin. The art critic Lubbock writes (2002):

'... though it asks nothing but looking ... and is made with perfect ocular pitch and is so light sensitive...I'm not even sure that it is inherently a visual art. Its means are visual ... [but] what it offers is a structure of experience, a form of intense though calm attention, which involves change and continuousness, without repetition and without conclusion – and this is something the mind can find in looking, or equally in some kinds of reading or thinking. But however it happens, it takes as long as you've got'.

The review continues by comparing the paintings with those in another exhibition: 'Both bodies of work have a penumbra of spirituality which may be another word for dedicated attention.'

In other words, through what I have referred to previously as 'intimate attention' (Caldwell 2000), it is possible to move beyond the particularities of an immediate shared sensory experience (in the example above, a visual experience shared with the painter) to a place where the mind wanders, reciprocally moved and moved on by what we discover in those we share with – and what they and we uncover in ourselves. What I experience in terms of feeling is awareness without interpretation, a deep stillness combined with wonder.

Referring back to Donna Williams in *Autism and Sensing* (1998), this is more than merging. The mind does not actually identify with 'other': on the borderlines of consciousness it is aware of self and what self is doing. One might call it a state of reciprocal induction, 'as it is' but also 'in the presence of', non-judgmental, active in the sense of awareness and response, passive in the sense of floating rather than swimming. As the reviewer says, it takes as long as you've got.

To return to earth, attention is on the particularities of what we are doing but is also on, or 'in,' the partner with whom we are sharing the sensory experience, whatever it is. What is evident when you enter this wandering state of mutual response is how much pleasure it gives both parties involved. While I do not wish to project my feeling onto the person with whom I am working, this sense of tranquillity and wonderment is characteristically present and can be observed and recorded (Caldwell, 2002).

What relevance does this rather philosophical approach have? Does it matter if we know what we are doing and who we are?

It is important not because we need to endlessly dwell on ourselves but so that we can be as present as possible to the people whose attention we are trying to engage, and also so that we avoid if possible projecting our own feelings on to them. If we know ourselves better, next time we are at the sharp end of a tantrum we will be more aware of all the issues involved. We will be able to distinguish between our feelings and those of the person who is upset, between our fear and their despair, pain, frustration or anger. We will understand a little more that the person's outburst is not personally directed but arises from her inability to handle the situation in which she finds herself. Under the circumstances she is in, she is overwhelmed by her defensive reactions to a situation she finds intolerable.

Even more important, it moves beyond disability and is something we both give and receive. It values the other person and the feeling that he or she is valued empowers them. They are able to give as well as receive. This is the equality that we talk about so much.

When they respond to our overtures we need to welcome them, drawing them into all the possibilities of creative relationship in a way that is safe for them. At the same time, we need to trust them and allow ourselves to be drawn into their creative sphere. If all this sounds complicated it is only because it is helpful to reflect sometimes on an ideal state. But we are none of us perfect. What we can do is to be aware of pitfalls. We can relax, lay aside our own preoccupations and suppositions, look and listen with intent and, to borrow a phrase from Winnicott, be 'good enough' (1971).

The next question I want to address is not so much a developmental one, how this consciousness of self arose, but what happens if this goes wrong: if I have failed to develop a sense of my singularity or if, having developed it, the sense of self is displaced. How can this happen?

I am informed by the feedback from my external and internal senses. If all is going well there is constant free trade between my brain, body and the world out there, telling me what I am doing and adjusting my responses. Problems arise if my sensory experience is so erratic that the boundary that helps me to define myself fails to develop, is amorphous, or if it has become a barrier. In one case I am not able to properly separate myself from the world out there so I do not recognise 'other'. Alternatively, the boundary is present but because of its solidity I am not able to reach out from 'my world' to 'the world'.

This may be the outcome of physical limitation. If one or more of my senses is deficient I shall have an additional struggle and must rely on extra sensitivity and training of the remaining senses to reach and be reached by the world outside. But it can also be that, having approached the world outside, my experience of it is just too scary to handle. I retreat back into my inner world where I feel less threatened. Then, since I am cut off from the world outside, my overwhelming sensory experience is derived from my internal feedback. I focus all my attention on a particular sensation, to the exclusion of everything else. I scrape the grain of the wood or scratch the fabric of my chair with my fingernail and listen to the sound it makes. I am completely absorbed and may even identify my sense of self with this activity.

Under these circumstances my retreat back into my inner world may be total. In the Channel 4 film *Jam Jar,* Donna Williams (1995) describes how, when she found the demands of the world too frightening, she withdrew from relationships. She explains that all the relationships she should have had with the people out there she made with the shadowy world inside. She illustrates this by using glass beads as people. She sorts them into related pairs and groups according to their properties and says:

'Everybody knows who they are in relatedness to everybody else. But what if the knowing really scares you? What if the knowing doesn't give you a good knowing? What if the knowing doesn't tell you, you have a brother or cousin? What if the knowing tells you that you are not at all related to anybody and the best you can do is be an impostor in that other solar system?' (Williams, 1995)

Gunnilla Gerland describes her isolated world:

'I spent a great deal of time inside myself, as if in my own world screened off from everything else. But there was no world there inside me, nothing more than a nothing layer, a neither-nor, a state of being hollow without being empty or filled without being full. It just was, in there, inside myself. I was inside the emptiness and the emptiness was inside me – no more than that. It was nothing but a kind of extension of time. I was in that state and it just went on.' (Gerland, 1996)

Where can we meet someone who feels herself to be alone, 'living in an alien world', as an unidentified child with ASD put it in the Radio 4 broadcast *A Bridge of Voices* (Weekes, undated); someone who simply does not recognise the body language and interactive systems that bind us into friendships and relationships, with all their possibilities? If you want to meet me you are going to have to come to the front door of my sensory experiences. This is where I am.

Where shall we meet?

But before we try to meet we need to look at the psychological preconditions for such an encounter. One of the questions put to me at one of my workshops is: 'Do you empty yourself when you work?'

The answer to this question has to be 'yes and no': 'yes' in the sense that I try to lay aside my preoccupations, expectations, theories and projections, and 'no' in the sense that I have to be present to react and respond to the person with whom I am working. They will not be interested in empty air. I have to offer them myself, because this is the most valuable thing I have.

To say 'I am here for you' is to be completely open, to shed our defensive shells. To be 'I', present in the place of 'me' and simultaneously in the presence of other, is not only to be vulnerable, it is also opportunity. Here we can meet 'not-me' (other) in ways that are not possible while we are dug in behind our protective ramparts.

Another questioner says: 'Do you go in with a welcoming face and open body language?' Looking at video of myself, I wonder why I do not and realise that what is uppermost is intense concentration. Apart from the fact that to assume the person I am working with would perceive, for example, a smile as welcoming and not threatening, that their sensory perception occupies the same territory as mine, I need to put aside what I want to do with them and focus with all my attention on what they are doing so that I notice the tiniest movement and the smallest sound and, particularly, changes in these. What I am doing is looking for what has meaning to them, so I can respond to that rather than make assumptions about how we will relate. It is through sharing our selves and exploring each other in mutually creative ways that we are empowered.

When I am asked why we don't just leave people where they are, I have to reply it is not just that those accounts we have of living in the inner world paint it not only as a refuge but also as a prison. This can be lonely and scary. It also misses out on the positive enrichment offered by social interaction. Human beings are not programmed to be solitary animals. Even those who feel they wish to live on their own are totally dependent on the infrastructure of the society in which they exist. We cannot assume that the aloneness of those with disability is voluntary. 'People with ASD do have feelings. I do feel lonely' (Jolliffe *et al*, 1992).

We cannot, and would not wish to, force social contact on those who choose not to engage. What we can do is offer a means of enrichment in terms that are acceptable, and usually welcomed because they are non-threatening, to people whose world is scary and who do not have the intellectual resources of those who are high functioning. Those who are low functioning cannot find their way out of the maze on their own so they retreat into an interior life. They do not have the freedom to choose. When a high-functioning autistic person says 'I like myself as I am', this implies a considerable degree of self-knowledge and self-esteem.

Relationship is not a possibility for those whose disability is more severe. However the capacity for enjoying warm and loving interaction is not a function of intellectual ability; anyone can be enriched by it. What is very noticeable is that when a person starts to shift their attention from solitary self-stimulation to sharing their world, their whole demeanour and body language alters. They relax and begin to smile; they are able to give eye contact, interact by holding out their hands and may offer a hug – this even from people who normally find physical contact distressing and avoid touch. Stress is reduced to the extent that some will, of their own accord, start to use relevant words. It is clear that they want to communicate. The world is no longer seen as a hostile place but one that they so often choose to be in. This change can be dramatic.

> Vera has no sight. She was 16 when staff were first shown how to use her sounds to talk to her. At the time she was banging her head so badly that she had to wear a helmet for self-protection and the home was also considering padding the walls with foam. Two years later her mother, who had described the increasing difficulties of containing Vera's wild behaviour both at school and at home and was present at the first session, says: 'You could see the change in her from the day people started using Intensive Interaction. After about five minutes she relaxed and became a different person and that is how she has stayed since then.' Vera no longer wears a helmet. Staff use her sounds as a way of talking to her and letting her know they are around all the time. She won best pupil award at school last year.

When I start to work with someone new, particularly if they have ASD, I may often wonder how on earth I am ever going to get close to them. It is not so much that I feel rejected; I feel simply ignored. I am not part of their world. But in order to learn to trust each other we have to meet in the sense that we need not only to observe their affective space – how they feel – but also to allow the other person to come into our space, where we are feeling and responsive. The prerequisite is proximity, getting it right in both the physical and psychological sense. We have to get close to each other in a way that feels right for both of us. We need to learn how to come and go in ways that are both respectful and fun.

Unfortunately there is no agreement that we should meet. When we start to try to engage the people with whom we are working they have not consented to the encounter. We have to go camouflaged, to slip in under cover of their language so they begin to enjoy the encounter before being alerted to possible danger. We need to get in under their defences without triggering alarm. We have to look for the feedback they are giving themselves because it is through this doorway of sensation that we shall be able to make contact. This is where they are. We will meet when their brain recognises something familiar. This will obtain low level attention from them. As explained in Chapter one, in order to move on to engagement we may have to add an element of surprise.

The ways in which we can do this are endless. It may simply be an infiltration of the way the person is talking to himself through feedback and sensations, but if the person is deeply withdrawn or afraid our overtures may also have to be sufficiently interesting to draw their attention away from their distress. We may need to climb over the fence while they are not looking.

> *A speech therapist is working with Richard, who is very afraid. If people come near him he makes noises of distress. As he becomes more threatened these rise almost to a bellow. She returns his sounds. This is not very effective until she starts ending them with a smacking sound made with taut lips. There is a look of amazement on his face as he turns to her with a radiant smile.*

When we are working with people who have some speech we can be misled into thinking they are trying to comm unicate with us when sometimes they may be using words as a barrier behind which to hide. Very often it is not so much what they say as how it sounds. We need to listen to the tone of the voice. Is it free-running and flexible or tense with anxiety? Does it sound unattached? Characteristically, an individual who is using speech to protect himself will speak in the third person, often in a high-pitched, rather monotonous way. Their speech will sound flat, lacking in colour, modulation or change in tempo.

Sometimes the phrases people use reflect what has been said to them. You can almost hear the condemnatory tones of the original speaker in the words: 'Silly noises, stupid faces!'

The more able the person is, the more sophisticated the avoidance systems may be. In *Nobody Nowhere* (1992) Donna Williams describes how she adopted a variety of characters, each with their own voice, to survive particular situations that were otherwise intolerable. Recordings of her voice in each situation sound completely different; the change in quality of voice is very noticeable. Her most extraordinary achievement is that, even though she has severe ASD, she has also been able to learn to speak at least sometimes with her true voice, from her innermost self, without defence systems. This is something all of us need to learn.

The ability to relate to each other moves us from solitude to the possibilities of sharing, having friends and allies and being able to love.

Chapter 7

More to seeing than meets the eye

- The quality of attention

- Tuning in

- The byways of capturing attention

- Pattern recognition

- Pointing the way – opening out

This section turns again to what we mean by the quality of 'attention', looking at a range of different ways of gathering it. This is not simply to create a longer list but to help explore some of the byways it leads us into. It is both about the focus of the person with whom I work on whatever it is that is the centre of their interest and what it means to them – and the essential focus that I must have on them.

Tuning in

If there is a tune on the radio we particularly want to listen to, we either turn up the volume or pay closer attention. We cut out extraneous noises and fine-tune our attention until we don't just hear, we listen with intent. If we really care about it we search and research the airwaves, moving closer to and becoming more and more involved in the source.

Attention is at the centre of our ability to engage: not just passing awareness but through sustained focus. We move from low-level attention to consciousness so that we begin not just to do something but to know what we are doing.

We are all capable of carrying on with behaviours of which we are not aware. A student swings his leg throughout a morning workshop. Near the end he says: 'I don't really know what you mean by repetitive behaviours.' He is quite unconscious of the low-level conversation going on between his brain telling the appropriate muscles in his leg to contract and relax and the feedback his brain is receiving in the form of what is presumably positive sensation, telling his brain that his leg has moved.

As our brains and bodies talk to each other we can listen either with low-level or focused attention. Moving into consciousness, we become the observers of ourselves – and also of our activities with objects (or people) that (or whom) we can modify, or be changed by. These objects with which we interact and the feelings that we draw from our interactions tell us both that we are and what we are doing. In Damasio's words: 'With consciousness there is the presence of "you" in a particular relationship to some object. The simplest form of such presence is the kind of image that constitutes a feeling – the feeling of what happens when your being is modified by the acts of apprehending something. The presence must be there or there is no you. Consciousness is the unified mental pattern that brings together the object and self ' (Damasio, 1999).

So when I attend to continually using my forefinger to scrape the fabric of my chair, I engender a sense of self. Those of us who live in an ordered and reasonably predictable environment can only begin to guess how critical this is for a person whose world is constantly falling apart. Both the films *A is for Autism* (1992) and *Jam Jar* (1995) try to show us what are the actual physical effects experienced by people with ASD. In the first, a small boy shows us squiggly lines, constantly on the move, retreating particularly when he tries to focus on them. He tells us that the more he tries to concentrate on them the more they run away. Under these circumstances we cannot overestimate the importance of recognisable pattern, some theme, anything familiar to grab hold of in a chaotic world, anything to which the brain can relate.

Andy touches the skirting with his foot as he walks. This is seen as kicking. Another interpretation is that, in a world where he cannot rely on the visual sensory information regarding dimension and direction, he needs to reassure himself with the sense he does have, that of touch, as to the constancy of the line between the wall and the floor. Because it wriggles, he needs to know where it is and where he is in relation to it.

Thirty years ago when I was beginning to understand the need to find out what is important for a person in order to gain their attention, I was asked by a teacher if I could think of any way of helping a child with ASD and considerable behavioural problems that endangered other children.

Jennie is five. She attends school but cannot be engaged at all, except that she appears to be interested in reflected light flashing across the walls or ceiling: for example, the reflection from a piece of shiny metal. She becomes alert and follows it with interest. Otherwise she is cut off and occasionally hits other children. After some experimentation I make her a box with flanges that can be rotated horizontally on a frame. The surfaces are covered with styrene mirror in the hope that, as she turns the box to obtain the visual stimulus she enjoys, she may also start to look at herself. Her teacher works with Jennie every day. At first she just turns the box in order to see the light that bounces off it flit round the room. Gradually she spots and becomes more interested in her own image. In parallel, her aggression towards others decreases. Her attention has been drawn and engaged through the very specific stimulus that she recognises and enjoys.

However we need to be incredibly careful over presentation, since the stimulus that attracts one child may be dangerous for another. (In the case of the mirror box this is particularly important since it became a popular piece of equipment in special schools, where it is still sometimes used just as a general way of persuading a child to engage in anything and without thought for particular intention.) An occupational therapist reports the history of a child with epilepsy who puzzled care staff because every time they gave her a bath she had a seizure. They could not understand why until the therapist suggested that the origin of the problem might be reflected white light coming off the surface of the water.

Sandra refuses to have a bath because there is a snake in it. It is suspected that she is hallucinating until her carer bends down and looks at the water from the level at which Sandra sees it. The reflection of an overhead strip-light wriggles like a serpent on the surface of the water. The same stimulus of reflected light that was a doorway for one child proves to be a quite different type of trigger for others.

It is not always essential to present the particular stimulus that catches a person's attention in the same way as they are giving it to themselves. Very often they will recognise a familiar rhythm or pattern that underlies their self-stimulus.

Such pattern recognition can be visual or auditory or tactile, and can be represented in a different mode to that in which the themes were originally expressed.

> *Micky sits in a chair turning the dial on a toy telephone. He is unresponsive to approaches until I move my finger in a circle on the back of his hand, following the movements of his dial back and forwards as he does it. He smiles and pays attention.*

> *Sue demonstrates a similar recognition of related pattern. She is in a class of more able children with ASD and disrupts their work with noises and generally chaotic behaviour, which it is difficult to get past. Among a number of repetitive behaviours it emerges that she likes to spend time twirling a windmill. She is immediately interested and focuses on my forefinger when I rotate it in the air in a similar fashion.*

> *Rod is very difficult to make contact with and has very disturbed behaviour. He has no sight but he licks his lips in a circular manner. When I move my thumb round on the top of his foot in time to echo the movements of his tongue he becomes very attentive and laughs so loudly that it can be heard all over the house. Staff come running in. They have not heard him laugh before.*

> *On the other hand, Betty recognises the rhythm of her action when the wall is banged in time to her head banging.*

Each time it was the pattern that was recognisable: an underlying pattern or theme that related to the sensory feedback the people were giving themselves. I was confirming for the individual swhat they were doing and at the same time affirming them to themselves. But I had also broken into the stereotypic sensory loop and was opening out what had been a closed situation. From now on there were other possibilities because her attention was able to move through territory that was familiar (and therefore safe) but also held the potential for new exploration. A behaviour that had been unconscious or semi-conscious was now fully conscious and, because we trusted each other, we could do things together without the risk that had kept the stereotypic behaviour going up until then. She could safely look out of the door; our attention now overlapped in the transitional playground. Our activity was joint-funded; we could explore together, sharing our delight and pleasure at each new innovation.

Through attention we move from seeing to looking, from looking to careful watching and from touching to feeling and conscious exploration. From passive participation we move into trust and from here into the endless creative possibilities of 'What if ...?'

Pointing the way

There are times when the people with whom we are working take very specific steps to point us towards ways of helping them to escape their repetitive loop. This is particularly true of people who are verbal, and it is absolutely critical that we listen very carefully to what they have to say.

> Cassie, who has ASD, has occasional violent outbursts that start with her asking if you know about the number seven. This is a warning shot across the bows. From there on she builds into a tantrum over which she has no control and which presents dangers to those around her. During the build-up she actually says: 'The number seven is important!,' drawing our attention to the centre of her storm. When I use this to refocus her attention back into our world by asking if she is going to make seven sandwiches for her supper (an activity at which she was engaged at the time), she turns away laughing: 'No, I'm going to have three,' and goes back to getting her supper ready.

Even at the height of her storm, when the adrenalin was flowing freely, Cassie's brain took the lure. She was able to switch off and return to this world – but it was she who had already told me where she was in terms of where the 'core' was that was fuelling her frightening outburst.

There is a difference between this scenario and that of diverting attention. In diversion the person's attention is directed away from the subject to another, whereas in refocusing it is the subject itself that is removed from the inner to the outer world by changing its context.

In terms of letting us know how to help him, Jeff is even more explicit.

> Jeff does not like to have a bath. He can be difficult when asked to do so for reasons of hygiene. However, in his mind he has a girlfriend, a different one each week, and it is important that we know her name and keep up with his current favourite. One day his care worker was trying very hard to get him into the bathroom and eventually said, out of pure desperation: 'Maybe your girlfriend would like you to have a bath so that you are nice and clean.' Jeff repeated it back to him: 'Yes, maybe my girlfriend Mary would like me to have a bath so that

> *I am nice and clean.' Thereafter whenever his care worker wanted him to have a bath they would go through this routine dialogue, but it only worked if the care worker inserted the name of the particular girlfriend of the week. If he got it wrong or failed to say a name, Jeff would correct him and say: 'Yes maybe my girlfriend Janice (or whoever it was that day) ...' He would then wait for his key-worker to accept the prompt and repeat the sentence with the right name included. Then he would go off and have a bath. From being totally hostile to the idea of a bath he had become ambivalent: the idea of being clean for his girlfriend outweighed his distaste for washing. But he would make absolutely sure he obtained the release to let him out of his quandary by directing his care worker to use the proper word.*

In this case it was if Jeff selected the right key from a bunch and thrust it under his care worker's nose, saying: 'Here's the right one. Use this to let me out.'

> *Tom, who has ASD, asks his mother when it is suppertime and she replies, 'Soon'. He bursts out: 'You know I can't manage soon!' but calms down at once when she says 'Six minutes'. In this case the distress is not about the repetitive loop. Tom is telling his mother that he cannot understand an abstract concept such as 'soon'. Although he can say it, the word has no meaning attached to it and throws his brain into confusion.*

All the above situations underline the importance of really taking on board the reality experienced by the person with whom we work.

Chapter 8

Who's afraid of whom?

- Fear as an ingredient of relationship

- Fear as part of a defence mechanism

- Fear of inadequacy

- Fear of not knowing what will happen

Working with people with severe learning disabilities – and particularly those with ASD – we sometimes come across people whose behaviour is such that we are at a loss how to relate to them. They may have outbursts, during which they may harm themselves and those who live with them and threaten us, sometimes to the point of injury. We are afraid. We feel we cannot cope. We do not like to talk about it in case others think we are inadequate. We feel they may laugh at us and we may be excluded from a team who appear to be managing. We exclude ourselves in order not to have to face the possibility of rejection by others.

What about the people we work with? The probability is that behaviours we see as challenging are the outcome of their also feeling afraid – part of their defence system against circumstances with which they cannot cope.

When this happens, fear becomes an ingredient of the relationship and this is a bad basis for interaction. We have to try to tease out what is really happening, who is afraid of whom and what are the roots.

'I spend my whole life being afraid, not just of what is happening now but also that something terrible may happen in the future.' (Jolliffe, 1992)

'It got to the point where I was afraid of coming into work, not just because I might get hurt but also because I was afraid of being put in situations that I couldn't cope with.'

The first quotation is from a woman with ASD, describing the sensory distortions she experiences and what it feels like to exist in a reality where you are constantly afraid of the chaos and pain caused by various hypersensitivities. The second was said by a key-worker, a young man, reflecting on a situation two years previously when the behaviour of the man he was looking after was extremely threatening, endangering both himself and those who cared for him. These quotations highlight the complex and diverse nature of fear, and in particular the part played by anticipation and the stress that this can cause. Fear is not just about what is happening now but what may happen in the future.

Roots run deep

'Irrespective of the fact that our ability to feel scared probably developed independently from our capacity to deal with danger, being afraid is the emotionally visible part of a defence mechanism which ensures our survival. Interactions between the defence system and consciousness underlie feelings of fear – but the defence system's function in life is survival in the face of danger.' (Le Doux, 1998)

We are dealing with primal stuff. It is normal to feel afraid when we feel we are entering a dangerous situation – and the people we work with sometimes come with the label 'DANGER' clearly tied to them. Quite often this refers to the outcome of inappropriate treatment they have received. As soon as you start to use the language that their brain recognises as non-threatening and therefore respectful, this distressed behaviour usually melts away. We have caused so much of what we perceive as challenging.

The difficulty is that we are not always very good at assessing the degree of danger. We may exaggerate it, particularly if we are in situations we find difficult to read or when we misread the extent of the threat because of blueprints we are carrying round that derive from previous experiences and are only superficially related to the current circumstances. Sometimes the danger is in our minds.

Drawing on my own experience to illustrate how easy it is to misread a situation, the first time I visited a hospital for people with severe learning disability I was scared, almost entirely because I had never met people with disability before and was unable to read the facial and bodily language of a man because of his particular disability. He turned out to be the most gentle person.

(For me, one childhood blueprint still evokes an irrational but recognisable fear of walking through woods, which relates to the terrible fate of Red Riding Hood, Babes in the Wood etc. It always seemed to happen in the forest. Despite the fact that my rational brain is not deceived, wolves and ogres live on. They colour my current emotional responses.)

Our instinctive reactions to danger are those of avoidance, immobility, aggression or submission, responses with which we are all probably familiar in our daily lives. We need to be aware of what our own feelings are, because an aggressive response to a threatening situation will almost certainly make it worse.

People sometimes come with labels tied to them spelling 'DANGER' and reputations that frequently stem from previous inappropriate care. It is easy to allow this to dominate our feelings about them. But the astonishing thing is that as soon as you start to engage with them respectfully and use the language their brain recognises, their aggression begins to melt away.

Damasio (1994) points out that if we are conscious of our emotional responses, feeling our affective states offers flexibility. We can make choices about how we respond to a given situation. We do not have to respond instinctively. Instead we can look at ourselves, how we dealt with the fear that was triggered as part of our defence mechanism. As well as asking how we deal with the circumstances when we are attacked, we need to enquire what triggered the outburst. For example, it is very tempting to try to adopt the position of total control, putting the lid on and sitting on it. When I was trying to work with someone who had what was called 'difficult behaviour', a young man said to me: 'I don't know why you bother. He sits down if I shout at him.'

What he did not understand was that it was precisely his extreme attitude that was causing the stress that triggered the outburst in the first place. The same danger lurks in some behavioural practices if they are applied in ways that increase stress rather than promote tranquillity. We need to look not just at immediate containment but at why people are distressed.

Turning to our own fear, the key worker whom I quoted at the beginning of this section was quite rightly afraid of being hurt but he also said that he was afraid of not being able to cope. This is quite a common sensation if we are working with someone who is very difficult. (In this case the man he was working with had a tendency to strip off in public places, a situation that is very difficult to handle. What do you do about it? Sitting down in the middle of the road to persuade them may not be an option on a busy highway and a stand-up struggle is an equally unsuitable strategy.) The feeling of being inadequate to the situation is accompanied by the suspicion that others could have managed better and that you will be laughed at by colleagues. This leads directly into the life-threatening situation of feeling 'excluded'. We feed off primitive feelings. For our ancestors rejection from the pack could be a life sentence; no wonder we are afraid. But it is taboo to admit that you are afraid; which is why leadership and team working are so vitally important. We must always be positive in our support of each other, for the most basic reason that we can help to stop each other from sliding down the emotional slippery slope occasioned by fear.

At the same time we have to address the reasons why the person we are working with feels the need to attack us or to behave in an anti-social manner. What are they trying to tell us?

To illustrate this I am going to tell at length Jessie's story.

Jessie is 29. While there are many positive sides to her character she also used to have frequent and severe behavioural outbursts, causing injury to staff. It got to the point where people were extremely reluctant to work with her. Jessie lives in her own flat supported by a one-to-one service. I visit her both at her flat and at the resource centre and afterwards have a discussion with her support team, during which the following points arise. In spite of her behaviour, which is sometimes extremely difficult to manage, Jessie is an affectionate lady who loves to be told she looks good. She really thrives on positive personal input. She has a terrific sense of humour and likes people to be polite to her and say 'Please' and 'Thank you'. Although there are some features of her behaviour that could be seen as autistic, such as her desperate need for control and when she gets stuck in the middle of tasks, her sense of fun and ability to size people up suggest that her autism, if it is such, is not entirely typical.

When I first saw her, it was clear that Jessie had very poor self-esteem. In common with people who have this problem, her threshold for feeling threatened was extremely low and she reacted accordingly. The way staff had worked with her, giving her very close attention, had resulted in a marked improvement in her difficult behaviour during the last four years. There were fewer outbursts, although when these occurred they were serious. Outbursts were more likely to occur at the centre than at home. Staff could not tell what was going to trigger her off. They felt it was usually unpredictable. During her outbursts she was liable to kick, thump, rip and also hit walls. (When we label an outburst unpredictable it means that we have not been able to link it to a cause yet. We need to go on looking: outcome may be separated from cause, as in emotional overload. When this happens the response is delayed and separated by time from the cause (Williams, 1996).)

We held a large group meeting with all the people involved in Jessie's care to try to tease out what was really going on. It emerged through discussion that most of her distressed behaviour occurred if she felt she was losing control, particularly when she was working on a one-to-one basis and a third person came and interrupted. The actual point at which she became distressed was when her one-to-one worker turned away to address the needs of the incomer. It seemed to me that up until that time she knew what she was doing but as soon as she lost contact with what was going on she was projected into what was, for her, chaos. Considering this, we came up with the following guidelines.

- Jessie needs to feel herself to be in control.

- Jessie needs to know what is going to happen before it happens so she has time to think about it. (When we discussed this, staff said that they thought they had been doing this by giving her choices. What they had not realised was the need to break down everything they did with Jessie into small stages that she could grasp and get her assent to each stage.) If she says 'No' we need to accept it, so that she can run her own life in a way that she understands.

- She does not like it if other people come between her and the person with whom she is engaged. She finds it very difficult to wait.

- She cannot cope with change.

With people like Jessie you cannot over-emphasise the need for a negotiating attitude, as opposed to a control attitude. It has been pointed out to me by clinical psychologist Pete Coia that negotiation is successful when both parties are happy with the conclusion. In Jessie's situation the agreement must be heavily weighted towards her being in charge of what happens. Above all, Jessie needs to know what is going to happen before it happens, so she has time to take it on board. You can see her thinking about it when you tell her something. Explain and wait until she indicates by a nod that she has understood. You may have to tell her more than once. She responds well to negotiation, which gives her control. At the centre, if people come up and talk to the person with whom she is working, it is suggested that they turn to her before engaging the other person and say, 'Jessie, I need to sort this out. I'll be back with you in a minute. All right?' If they can get her permission before turning away, giving her time to agree, this gives her the control she so badly needs. She knows they will come back. As a result of using this technique, her outbursts have declined dramatically.

Another strategy staff have adopted is to telephone Jessie before she leaves her flat to let her know what she is going to do when she arrives at the centre. This works very well. She will now pick up the phone and answer it herself.

If it turns out that staff cannot comply with Jessie's wishes for reasons beyond their control, the way they lay down the boundary is critical; she must have time to process the change so that she is not faced with a sudden event which will activate her life-threatened response. To avoid this situation, if there is a change in plan while she is on her way to the centre, they use her escort's mobile to warn her. She never arrives at the centre without knowing what is going to happen.

To keep a person's attention they need to be highly motivated. For this reason it was suggested that on-site activities with Jessie in the centre should be based on things she most enjoyed doing, which would win reinforcing praise from others and make it easier to engage her. This would particularly include make-up sessions and attention to her hair, using a mirror to get her to look at herself. While Jessie finds a large mirror difficult, she will look at herself in a hand mirror.

Jessie's sense of humour, coupled with her love of being addressed politely, can be used to help her when she gets stuck. We cannot assume this is voluntary; sometimes the brain just will not issue the necessary instructions. In order to start her off again we may need to give clues in another mode. Elaborate over-politeness makes her laugh and she can then resume whatever she was doing.

Jessie would sometimes become distressed and have to be taken home from the centre. I suggested saying to her in the car, before she got home: 'I'm going to leave you in the flat so you can cool off. When you feel better, come and give me a knock in the office. OK?' This strategy gives her time to think about it before she gets home and also gives back to her some control by letting her decide how long the break should be.

Jessie is apt to tap people and they can find this irritating. In the past, no distinction had been made between this sometimes slightly inappropriate way of getting attention or exercising her sense of humour and when she hit someone. The staff needed to make sure they all reacted in the same way as some staff were still telling her it was bad to hit. Observation suggested that Jessie got quite a kick out of being told it was bad to hit; her tapping was having the effect she wanted and so she usually persisted. A better strategy seemed to be to make it into fun, to tap her very gently on the arm. This made her laugh and she might do it once more but quickly stopped. The same strategy proved helpful when she banged things.

Jessie has certain distinctive body movements, such as an upward and outward movement of her hands. While I did not feel specifically that Intensive Interaction would improve her ability to communicate, which was already extremely good, I found it helpful to incorporate her gestures into my own speech as a way of expressing solidarity with her and possibly increasing her attention.

While Blackburn (2002), quoted in the Introduction, describes how her anxiety stems from the unpredictability of behaviour, some people may feel that we have gone over the top by letting Jessie know exactly what is happening all the time. However, giving her control, accepting it if she says 'No', works. Her agenda is more important than ours. Her outbursts have more or less ceased. From staff feeling unable to work with her, they now feel confident and clearly enjoy working with her.

Jessie was afraid and because they were getting hurt and unable to figure out what was wrong, so were the people who worked with her. We were able to help her and move her on by isolating the root causes of her distress. She is no longer afraid and nor are the people who work with her.

One of the main problems is that, when we are afraid, techniques to control behaviour are liable to add to the stress that a person is experiencing and increase rather than decrease the 'challenges' the person presents, even if they are channelled into another route. Control is not enough. We must address the fears and needs that underlie the person's outbursts.

When we are afraid we need to look at whether our fears are real and relate to actual situations or if they are the trailers of trauma in our earlier life. If they are real we need to search and research the possible causes of a person's distressed behaviour because the most probable one is that they are afraid. We always need to support each other.

Conclusion

- Building a relationship through shared exploration

- Learning to listen

- The relationship – what does it mean for both of us?

It is very easy to fall into the trap of thinking when we work with people with learning disabilities that we are the teachers. Although we talk about 'valuing people' we tend to assume that we are the ones who give, they receive. We talk about equality but do not behave as if we have anything to learn from them. We do not 'listen', in the sense of paying attention to what they are saying to us.

The successful infant needs to learn the skill of making friends. This is a biological imperative that helped us to survive when we lived in groups in what was basically a hostile environment. We still use it to improve the quality of our lives. Friendless, we are vulnerable and lonely. We need allies to support us and we make these by sharing the things we enjoy, in the hope that our prospective friend will also enjoy them. We are trying to engage their attention with the things we value. The process by which we make friends is by offering and accepting shared interests. To do this involves making ourselves vulnerable to the savage pain of rejection (which may have life threatening implications in the biological sense).

However, there is a difficulty when trying to get in touch with people with ASD. We very often make the mistake of thinking that, because they do not show emotion, they do not feel it. Jolliffe (1992) tells us this is not so, that she is able to love and feel lonely. The problem for the person with ASD is that they cannot always handle the emotional feedback they get from their own nervous system, which may be painful for them. So they learn to avoid emotional contact. However, my experience is that if you use 'their language' and present it in a way that respects their hypersensitivities so that they do not find it painful, they frequently respond with warmth and a desire for contact. They will hug you, look you in the face, smile and show all the warmth one does for a friend.

We need to look at how it is they read the world – what is it that has meaning for them.

> Gabriel has very severe autistic spectrum disorder and learning disabilities, with the additional complication of epilepsy. He is non-verbal and is locked into a world of repetitive self-stimulation such as flicking bundles of string or leaves or the close scrutiny of beads and gloves, especially rubber gloves. Staff say they feel cut off from him, cannot reach him, do not know what they should be trying to do since he responds to very little outside his own intimate world and pays little or no attention to activities he is offered. Sometimes he is extremely disturbed, crashing round the room and banging himself, particularly if he wants something he cannot have, although what this is may not be evident. Eventually he will calm down. At other times he is very sleepy – which may be partly caused by his anti-convulsants or, possibly, a disturbed sleep rhythm, which is not uncommon in people with ASD.

When Gabriel flicks a bead on a string (or pursues any of his repetitive behaviours) 'he knows what he is doing.' Here is a sensation with which his brain is familiar, that is recognisable and non-threatening. It is, so to speak, 'hard-wired' in. By focusing on this specific activity he can lock out chaos. Repetition produces calming endorphins, the 'feel-good' factors of the brain. But the intensity of his inward concentration cuts out his capacity to exchange with the world outside. It excludes interaction. He holds us at bay by pursuing activities that feed his inner world and protect him from what he perceives as harmful.

For us, a bead is just a bead – but if we look at it through the eyes of someone with ASD, we learn to explore a world of enhanced sensory perception. The bead has colour that changes in the light. It also has shape, weight density, texture and movement as it flicks, and sound on impact. We begin to explore another way of understanding the world through what Donna Williams in *Jam Jar* (1995) calls 'the world of sensing uncomplicated by the need for interpretation'. Through attention and joint exploration we start to learn to explore our sensory world in a way we may never have been able to before: a world of touch and feel, the world of here and now unclouded by recollection of the past or anticipation of the future. If we will let them, the person with ASD will lead us further through the mysterious world of 'qualia', exploring the greenness of green, the tone of a sound and the muskiness of a rose, a sensory exploration in the transitional playground as yet unexplained in neurobiological terms.

For us, this adds an important dimension because we live in closed worlds. As infants we learned to cut out so much of our sensory world. We learned to choose what was good for us and exclude that which our brains decided was irrelevant. For example, if we stop what we are doing and listen we begin to hear what the world around us is doing: the business of traffic, clocks, bird song, electronic hums, the creaks of our house and the whispers of wind and rain; we hear sounds that may have no immediate relevance for us but which nevertheless exist in their own right.

Much of this sensory selectivity is necessary so that, in our complex world, we can concentrate on processing those events that do have meaning for us. The downside is that we learn to focus on ourselves; we live from our own needs, cutting our worlds down to the size of our own sensory reality. We call this 'our point of view' and base our judgments on our own realities, the scenarios that have worked for us. For example, when I walk into a room I may unconsciously make assessments based on that elusive quality known as 'taste', which comes down to whether or not I could share interests with the house's owner and therefore enjoy being friends with them. Would they make good allies? Whether I like it or not, I look at the world through the tinted lenses of my own perspective. How does this experience relate to me?

Through exploration of the enhanced sensory perception of the person with ASD we begin to move out of ourselves towards seeing the world as it is, uncluttered by our expectations. We begin to share in a world that is not based on our own needs. And, particularly, we start to be able to share fun, thereby completing the circle because it is through sharing fun that we most quickly make friends. By seeing the world through their eyes we are liberated, if only for a short time, from the burden of ourselves. We become for each other as we are.

What does our partner get out of it? In *Jam Jar* Donna Williams (1995) speaks of the war raging inside her that was set off by the difficulty of living in and conforming to a world that always insisted on her using a system based on attaching meaning and interpretation to sounds. Her brain worked directly from sensation. She describes a table as 'the flat brown lined thing' that 'impacted' with a certain thud when hit. She did not necessarily need to go on to call it 'table' or think, 'That's what you put the plates on'. While we may point out that it is difficult to generalise from this system, this was how she saw it and it worked for her. She was deeply stressed by people shouting at her that she was stupid and felt even more alienated from others.

In the same film, Williams speaks of the discovering the delight of discovering relationships, and illustrates it with video of herself and her friend Paul, who is also autistic. On the beach together they explore the sensation of the squelching sound their feet make in wet muddy sand. She comments: 'Now I can be, not just me in my world but me in my world and him in my world.'

The vast emptiness of a world lived in separateness is breached. She is no longer on her own; there is someone else with whom she can be a child and share fun.

When we work with someone with ASD they are allowing us to share something they value, and in the intensity of our mutual exploration there is nothing put on or phoney about the value we place on their gift and, by extension, on them. When we work with them in this way, both they and we cross the bridge out of ourselves and in our mutual absorption become 'WE'. This is what valuing a person really is: not some theoretical appreciation but being 'with' and 'in' and 'for' each other. Next time it will be easier. We will know that mutual attention to sensation can lead both of us to the art and joy of being together.

References

A is for Autism (1992) Film. Directed by Tim Webb. London: Finetake for Channel 4.

Barron J & Barron S (1992) *There's a Boy in Here.* New York: Simon and Schuster.

Blackburn R (2002) Flint NAS Seminar. 15 July.

Caldwell P (2002) *Learning the Language.* DVD. Brighton: Pavilion Publishing.

Damasio AR (1994) *Descartes' Error: Emotion, reason and the human brain.* New York: Grosset/Putnam.

Damasio AR (1999) *The Feeling of What Happens.* London: Heinemann.

Ephraim G (1986) *A Brief Introduction to Augmented Mothering.* Playtrack pamphlet. Radlett, Hertfordshire: Harperbury Hospital.

Gerland G (1996) *A Real Person: Life on the outside.* London: Souvenir Press.

Greenfield SA (1997) *The Private Life of the Brain.* London: Allen Lane.

Hobson P (2002) *The Cradle of Thought.* Basingstoke: Macmillan.

Jolliffe T, Lansdown R & Robinson C (1992) Autism: a personal account. *Communication* **26** (3) 12–19.

Le Doux J (1998) *The Emotional Brain.* London: Weidenfield and Nicholson.

Lubbock T (2002) Rich creations of patience. *The Independent* **2 July**.

Moyles JR (1989) *Just Playing.* Buckingham: Open University Press.

Nadel J & Canioni L (1993) *New Perspectives in Early Communicative Development.* London: Routledge.

Nafstad A & Rodbroe I (1999) *Co-Creating Communication with Persons with Congenital Deaf-Blindness.* Dronninglund, Denmark: Forlaget-Nord Press.

Nind M & Hewett D (1994) *Access to Communication.* London: David Fulton.

Peeters T (1997) *Autism: From theoretical understanding to educational intervention.* London: Whurr Publishers.

Rankin K (2000) *Growing Up Severely Autistic: They call me Gabriel.* London: Jessica Kingsley Publishers.

Rodbroe I & Souriau J (2000) Communication. In: JM McInnes (Ed) *A Guide to Planning and Support for Individuals who are Deaf/Blind.* Toronto: University of Toronto Press.

Seybert J (2002) Keynote speech. Maryland Coalition for Inclusive Education. 3 October. Maryland, Baltimore.

Weekes L (date unknown) *A Bridge of Voices.* Radio programme. London: BBC Radio 4.

Williams D (1992) *Nobody Nowhere*. London: Doubleday.

Williams D (1994) *Somebody Somewhere*. London: Doubleday.

Williams D (1995) *Jam Jar*. Film. London: Channel 4.

Williams D (1996) *Autism: An inside-out approach*. London: Jessica Kingsley Publishers.

Williams D (1998) *Autism and Sensing*. London: Jessica Kingsley Publishers.

Winnicott DW (1971) *Playing and Reality*. London: Routledge.

Zeedyke S (2002) Personal communication.

Also available from Pavilion Publishing and Media

Creative Conversations

Communicating with people with profound learning disabilities

Phoebe Caldwell with Pene Stevens

Intensive Interaction is probably the most positive and accessible way of getting in touch with and empowering people who may appear to be locked in their 'inner world'. This DVD training resource seeks to bridge the gap in the range of currently available materials by showing carers learning how to use Intensive Interaction with four adults who have profound learning disabilities, under the guidance of Phoebe Caldwell. The film includes discussion with Phoebe and co-author, Pene Stevens, and feedback from the carers.

Format: DVD (35 minutes) and A5 booklet (14pp) in plastic case
Price: £30 +VAT
Order code: BA3
ISBN: 978-1-84196-222-1

Learning the Language

Building relationships with people with severe learning disability, autistic spectrum disorder and other challenging behaviours

Phoebe Caldwell

A training DVD showing how carers can use Intensive Interaction to communicate with people whose severe learning disabilities or autism is allied to behaviour that presents significant management problems. Phoebe

Caldwell's work in this area is nationally known and has had unparalleled success in getting in touch with 'hard to reach' individuals by using an approach called Intensive Interaction. This provides the means to relate to individuals in a new way and to make a real difference to the quality of their lives. This unique DVD shows staff exactly how the techniques of Intensive Interaction work and the reason for their success.

Format: DVD in plastic case with A5 booklet (16pp)
Price: £30 +VAT
Order code: BA4
ISBN: 978-1-84196-221-4

Understanding and Supporting Children and Adults on the Autism Spectrum

A multimedia training and learning resource

Julie Beadle-Brown and Richard Mills

This unique resource, informed by both research and practice, is designed not only to help people understand autism spectrum conditions, but to give them a person-centred framework of intervention and support for children or adults on the autism spectrum.

Research shows that with good support, people with autism can lead fulfilled lives and make a real contribution to their communities. However, staff, carers and services can struggle to understand the true nature of these often complex conditions and consequently, people with autism may be consigned to live difficult and unhappy lives. At the heart of the resource is the SPELL framework, which uses cognitive learning theory to instil five key pillars of good practice:

■ Structure

■ Positive approaches and expectations

■ Empathy

■ Low arousal

■ Links

The SPELL framework is not the only element of good support for people with autism but it does lay the foundations for autism-friendly practices on which to build other behavioural and educational approaches. The resource is supported with experiences from people with autism and their families to demonstrate how it is necessary to understand the individual and how autism affects the person.

Format: Ringbound resource (173pp) with colour, laminated dividers and CD-rom with PowerPoint presentations, script for trainer, colour photos, worksheets, handouts, exercises and video clips. The text is printed on low contrast paper for direct use with people on the autistic spectrum.
Price: £199
Order code: E013
ISBN: 978-1-84196-271-9

Learning Disability Today (third edition)

The essential handbook for carers, service providers, support staff and families

Edited by Steven Carnaby

This fully revised and updated edition of *Learning Disability Today* provides an introduction to some of the key issues in the lives of people with learning disabilities and those who support them. Accessible and thought-provoking, this handbook offers practical strategies for offering person-centred, inclusive support to people with learning disabilities.

The book is divided into three sections: 'Setting the scene', 'Developing people' and 'Shaping lives together', with chapters dedicated to person-centred thinking, sexuality, communication, supporting people with autistic spectrum conditions and working with people with profound or profound and multiple learning disabilities.

Format: Handbook (237pp)
Price: £23
Order code: E104
ISBN: 978-1-908066-58-9

BV - #0007 - 201120 - C0 - 246/186/16 - PB - 9781908993007 - Gloss Lamination